The Origins of Feasts, Fasts and Seasons in Early Christianity

Founded in 1897, the Alcuin Club seeks to promote the study of Christian liturgy and worship in general with special reference to worship in the Anglican Communion. The Club has published a series of annual Collections, including *A Companion to Common Worship*, volumes 1 and 2, edited by Paul F. Bradshaw, a new edition of the classic text *Christian Prayer through the Centuries*, by Joseph Jungmann (SPCK 2007) and most recently *The Worship Mall: Contemporary responses to contemporary culture*, by Bryan D. Spinks (SPCK 2010). The Alcuin Liturgy Guide series aims to address the theology and practice of worship, and includes *The Use of Symbols in Worship*, edited by Christopher Irvine, and two volumes covering the celebration of the Christian Year: *Celebrating Christ's Appearing: Advent to Christmas*, and *Celebrating Christ's Victory: Ash Wednesday to Trinity*, both by Benjamin Gordon-Taylor and Simon Jones. The Club works in partnership with GROW in the publication of the Joint Liturgical Study series, with two studies being published each year.

Members of the Club receive publications of the current year free and others at a reduced rate. The President of the Club is the Rt Revd Michael Perham, its Chairman is the Revd Canon Dr Donald Gray CBE, and the Secretary is the Revd Dr Gordon Jeanes. For details of membership and the annual subscription, contact The Alcuin Club, 5 Saffron Street, Royston, SG8 9TR, or email: alcuinclub@gmail.com

Visit the Alcuin Club website at: **www.alcuinclub.org.uk**

The Origins of Feasts, Fasts and Seasons in Early Christianity

Paul F. Bradshaw and
Maxwell E. Johnson

Alcuin Club Collections 86

A PUEBLO BOOK
Liturgical Press
Collegeville, Minnesota
www.litpress.org

Published in Great Britain in 2011 by
Society for Promoting Christian Knowledge
36 Causton Street
London SW1P 4ST
www.spckpublishing.co.uk

and in the United States of America and Canada in 2011 by
Liturgical Press
Collegeville, MN 56321
www.litpress.org

British Library Cataloguing-in-Publication Data
A catalogue record for this book is available from the British Library

SPCK ISBN 978–0–281–06054–2

United States Library of Congress Cataloging-in-Publication Data is on file at the Library of Congress, Washington, DC

Liturgical Press ISBN 978–0–8146–6244–1

10 9 8 7 6 5 4 3 2

Typeset by Kenneth Burnley, Wirral, Cheshire

In memoriam

Thomas Julian Talley, 1924–2005

Contents

Acknowledgements

The authors gratefully acknowledge the permission granted by the following copyright holders to reproduce extracts from translations of ancient sources contained in the works listed. Where not otherwise attributed in the notes, translations of other primary sources are by the authors.

Every effort has been made to seek permission to use copyright material reproduced in this book. The publisher apologizes for those cases where permission might not have been sought and, if notified, will formally seek permission at the earliest opportunity.

Thomas J. Talley, *The Origins of the Liturgical Year*. Copyright © 1991 by The Order of Saint Benedict, Inc. Published by Liturgical Press, Collegeville, Minnesota. Reprinted with permission.

Raniero Cantalamessa, *Easter in the Early Church* (Collegeville: The Liturgical Press 1993). Reprinted with permission of the author.

Martin Connell, 'The Origins and Evolution of Advent in the West', Kilian McDonnell, 'The Marian Liturgical Tradition' and Gabriele Winkler, 'The Appearance of Light at the Baptism of Jesus and the Origins of the Feast of the Epiphany' in Maxwell E. Johnson (ed.), *Between Memory and Hope: Readings on the Liturgical Year*. Copyright © 2000 by The Order of Saint Benedict, Inc. Published by Liturgical Press, Collegeville, Minnesota. Used with permission.

Ephrem the Syrian: Hymns, translated and introduced by Kathleen E. McVey. Copyright © 1989 by Kathleen E. McVey. Paulist Press, Inc.,

Mahwah, NJ. Reprinted with permission of Paulist Press, Inc. <www.paulistpress.com>

Sebastian Brock, 'Mary in Syriac Tradition' in A. Stacpoole (ed.), *Mary's Place in Christian Dialogue* (Wilton: Morehouse-Barlow 1982). Reprinted with permission of the author.

Abbreviations

ACC	Alcuin Club Collections
ALW	*Archiv für Liturgiewissenschaft*
ANF	A. Cleveland Coxe (ed.), *The Ante-Nicene Fathers* (New York: Christian Literature Company 1885–96)
BCE	Before the Common Era
Cantalamessa	Raniero Cantalamessa, *Easter in the Early Church* (Collegeville: The Liturgical Press 1993)
CE	Common Era
DBL	E. C. Whitaker, *Documents of the Baptismal Liturgy*, revised and expanded by Maxwell E. Johnson, ACC 79 (London: SPCK 2003)
Ep.	*Epistula/Epistulae*
ET	English translation
JECS	*Journal of Early Christian Studies*
NPNF	Philip Schaff and Henry Wace (eds), *A Select Library of Nicene and Post-Nicene Fathers of the Christian Church* (Edinburgh: T. & T. Clark 1886–1900)
OCA	Orientalia Christiana Analecta
OCP	*Orientalia Christiana Periodica*
PG	J.-P. Migne (ed.), *Patrologia Graeca* (Paris 1857–66)
PL	J.-P. Migne (ed.), *Patrologia Latina* (Paris 1878–90)
QL	*Questions liturgiques*
SL	*Studia Liturgica*
SP	*Studia Patristica*
VC	*Vigiliae Christianae*

Introduction

The reader might well have expected this book to be titled *The Origins of the Liturgical Year* or something similar, just as was Thomas Talley's work,[1] to which ours is intended to be a successor. But it was not until relatively modern times that the concept of a 'liturgical year' began to be recognized, and the term itself only came into use from the late sixteenth century onwards.[2] Christians in antiquity did not view the various festivals, fasts and seasons that they experienced through each year as forming a unity, a single entity, and indeed those events themselves did not emerge in any planned or co-ordinated fashion but instead as a number of entirely unrelated cycles, with the result that they tended to overlap or conflict with one another.

The fundamental cycle was that of the seven-day week, which was taken over from Judaism by the first Christians but came to be centred on 'the Lord's day' rather than the Sabbath and with different days of the week designated for fasting from those customary among Jews, as the early Church sought to establish its own independent identity. As we shall show, however, the transition from Sabbath keeping to Sunday worship may have been slower than most scholars have previously supposed and to have left some remnants of Sabbath observance in later Christianity, even if the notion of resting on the Sabbath was firmly repudiated.

Alongside this weekly pattern, the oldest annual cycle was that related to Easter, or Pascha as it was called – both the name and the feast being

---

1 Thomas J. Talley, *The Origins of the Liturgical Year* (New York: Pueblo 1986; 2nd edn, Collegeville: The Liturgical Press 1991).
2 See Willy Evenepoel, 'La délimitation de "l'année liturgique" dans les premiers siècles de la chrétienté occidentale. *Caput anni liturgici*', *Revue d'histoire ecclésiastique* 83 (1988), pp. 601–16; Ambroos Verheul, 'L'année liturgique: de l'histoire à la théologie', *QL* 74 (1993), pp. 5–16, esp. pp. 5–6.

adopted from the Jewish Passover. As we shall see, while some early Christians also retained the Jewish date for the observance, although increasingly trying to distinguish it from its Jewish antecedent, others who began to celebrate it later in the second century chose to locate it on a Sunday, a practice that later became normative as part of a continuing desire to separate Christianity from its Jewish roots. In the course of time this single occasion was extended both backwards and forwards – forwards with a week or a whole 50 days of continued rejoicing, and backwards with first a day or two, and then a whole week, and finally a 40-day season of preparation. However, whether that 40-day period emerged simply as the final extension of the preparation for Easter or had an older and originally independent existence as a season in its own right has become the subject of some debate, which we shall explore in this book and, drawing upon the latest research, will argue for the latter as the true source of Lent.

From the fourth century onwards the final week of preparation for Easter, known as Holy Week in the West and Great Week in the East, attracted to itself services and ceremonies recalling significant occasions in the final days leading up to the death of Christ. While in certain respects this evolution enriched the paschal season for Christians, it also resulted in a diminution of the sense of Easter as the heart and centre of the liturgical year, as the unitive celebration of the totality of the paschal mystery – the Incarnation, Passion, resurrection and glorification of Christ, and the sending of his Spirit. Instead it became just one feast, though an important one, among others; and as a result of later Western Christianity's narrow focus on the death of Christ as that which brought salvation, it ceased to occupy such a central position in popular piety. The Easter vigil rite, the original core of the liturgical year, declined in importance until it became virtually unknown to ordinary churchgoers in the West, although maintaining a greater hold among Eastern Christians. In the popular mind, Christmas replaced Easter as the central festival of the year, and it was only in the movements of liturgical renewal in the second half of the twentieth century that attempts began to be made to redress the balance.

Christmas and Epiphany, and various feasts that emerge in connection with those celebrations, formed a quite separate cycle in early Christianity, and one that appeared on the scene somewhat later than Easter. This resulted in both the overlapping of the two cycles and also a constantly shifting relationship between the two, because this later cycle was rooted in fixed dates in the Julian calendar while the date of

Passover/Easter changed annually through its dependence on the date of the emergence of the first full moon after the spring equinox each year. There has long been a scholarly debate as to why Christmas and Epiphany came to be celebrated and why 25 December and 6 January were chosen for their observance. In particular, did they emerge as attempts to supplant pagan festivals previously observed on those dates – the so-called 'History of Religions' hypothesis – or were they the results of attempts to calculate the exact date on which Jesus must have been born – known as the Computation or Calculation hypothesis – or perhaps a combination of the two? We shall examine this question in some detail and attempt to bring some clarity to the debate. Perhaps more importantly still, we shall show that the celebration of 6 January appears to be considerably older than that of 25 December and to have been practised widely in the ancient Church, whereas Christmas began later as merely a local Roman equivalent and only relatively slowly gained acceptance in other churches to become in the end the almost universal feature of the Christian year that we experience today.

The last cycle, again independent of the other two and so potentially liable to conflict with particular observances in them, was that of martyrs and saints. Its roots were as ancient as the celebration of Easter in most communities and the celebration of their local heroes generally appealed much more strongly to Christian congregations than some of the newer feasts that ecclesiastical authorities later attempted to intro-duce, so that in a very real sense saints' days rather than festivals of Christ tended to form the heart of the annual calendar for most ordinary worshippers and to excite their devotion and attendance at church. Recent scholarship, in fact, has argued that it is the martyrs and saints, especially the cult of the martyrs, which not only shaped the piety and practice of Christian believers in the first three centuries, but even contributed to their overall understanding of the person and work of Christ. In other words, we simply cannot understand early Christianity without paying significant attention to the cult of the saints, which was, undoubtedly, much more formative of Christian identity than has often been acknowledged. Of 'other saints' in early Christianity certainly the Virgin Mary begins to play a significant role both in regard to piety and liturgical celebration. While this comes to the fore primarily from the fourth century on, and especially after the *Theotokos* decree of the Council of Ephesus (431), there is evidence that attention was being paid to her both liturgically and devotionally rather early in the Church's history, especially in places like Syria and Egypt. With regard both to the saints and Mary, then, what we see developing later is clearly as much evolution as it is revolution or contrast with what went before.

Diverse though their roots were, these various cycles together made up the kaleidoscope of changing feasts, fasts and seasons that marked the worship life of the fourth-century Church and formed the foundation of the liturgical year that evolved in later generations.

We are grateful to those who have assisted us in the work that led up to the production of this book, and especially to past and present doctoral students in liturgical studies at the University of Notre Dame, not least Katharine Harmon, Nathaniel Marx, Nicholas Russo and Cody Unterscher.

Paul F. Bradshaw and Maxwell E. Johnson

Sabbath and Sunday

Chapter 1

The Lord's day in the Apostolic age?

In a recent study of the reception of the Sabbath in early Christianity, Gerard Rouwhorst has pointed out that the conclusions reached in three major dissertations on the subject of the Sabbath and the early Christian Sunday strikingly match the practices of the particular denomination to which each of the authors belongs.[1] The Swiss Reformed church historian Willy Rordorf had argued that Sunday was a very early Christian creation unrelated to the Sabbath and was not a day of rest but the weekly occasion for celebrating the Eucharist in the evening, rooted in the resurrection meals of Jesus with his disciples;[2] the Roman Catholic Corrada Mosna, in his dissertation at the Pontifical Gregorian University in Rome, had argued that almost from the very start Christians celebrated the Eucharist on Sunday mornings;[3] and Samuele Bacchiocchi, a Seventh-Day Adventist, had argued in his doctoral dissertation, also at the Gregorian University, that it was only in Rome under Bishop Sixtus (*c.* 115–25) that the Christian observance of Sunday first began and that prior to that time Christians had observed the Sabbath.[4] These examples could be supplemented. The English Evangelicals Roger Beckwith and Wilfrid Stott, for instance,

---

1 Gerard Rouwhorst, 'The Reception of the Jewish Sabbath in Early Christianity' in P. Post, G. Rouwhorst, L. van Tongeren and A. Scheer (eds), *Christian Feast and Festival* (Louvain: Peeters 2001), pp. 223–66, here at pp. 226–36.
2 Willy Rordorf, *Der Sonntag* (Zurich: Zwingli Verlag 1962); ET: *Sunday* (London: SCM Press/Philadelphia: Westminster Press 1968).
3 Corrada S. Mosna, *Storia della domenica dalle origini fino agli inizi del V seculo* (Rome: Pontifical Gregorian University 1969).
4 Samuele Bacchiocchi, *From Sabbath to Sunday* (Rome: Pontifical Gregorian University 1977). For a refutation of his thesis, see Richard Bauckham, 'Sabbath and Sunday in the Post-Apostolic Church' in D. A. Carson (ed.), *From Sabbath to Lord's Day* (Grand Rapids: Zondervan 1982), pp. 251–98, here at pp. 270–3.

argued for the observance of Sunday as the equivalent of the Sabbath day of rest from the earliest period of Christianity.[5]

All this stands as a warning of the great danger of reading one's own preconceptions into this particular subject, and of the relative lack of very firm evidence for what the earliest Christian practices might have been. In the New Testament there are in fact only three passages that could perhaps imply that there were regular Christian gatherings on the first day of the week, and in every case alternative explanations of the passage are possible:

- 1 Corinthians 16.2: 'On the first day of every week, each of you is to put something aside and store it up, as he may prosper, so that contributions need not be made when I come.' Because this direction about making regular savings for the needs of the church in Jerusalem specifies that particular day, rather than just 'every week', it seems to imply both that this predominantly Gentile congregation was accustomed to the use of the Jewish seven-day week and also that the first day of the week had particular significance for them, as there is no evidence for it having any special importance in the surrounding culture, for example, that it was the day on which workers were commonly paid. While some have gone on to draw the conclusion that this must mean that the day was the one on which the community regularly came together for worship, others have noted that the passage stops short of stating that, and indeed could be held to indicate the opposite, as it appears to speak of individuals storing up the money for themselves rather than handing it over to church officials each week.[6]
- Acts 20.7–12: 'On the first day of the week, when we were gathered together to break bread, Paul talked with them, intending to depart on the morrow; and he prolonged his speech until midnight . . .' Some argue that this passage implies that Sunday was the regular

---

5 Roger T. Beckwith and Wilfrid Stott, *This is the Day* (London: Marshall, Morgan & Scott 1978) = *The Christian Sunday* (Grand Rapids: Zondervan 1980).

6 See Bacchiocchi, *From Sabbath to Sunday*, pp. 90–5; Rordorf, *Sunday*, pp. 193–5; and the works referred to in both these discussions. For the meaning of the Greek phrase translated above as 'aside', see the debate between S. R. Llewelyn, 'The Use of Sunday for Meetings of Believers in the New Testament', *Novum Testamentum* 43 (2001), pp. 205–23, here at p. 209, and Norman Young, '"The Use of Sunday for Meetings of Believers in the New Testament", A Response', *Novum Testamentum* 45 (2003), pp. 111–22, here at pp. 112–14.

day of the week on which the Christian community in Troas met to celebrate the Eucharist, and the only unusual feature was that Paul preached at great length, with disastrous consequences for Eutychus, who fell asleep and tumbled out of the window. Others claim that community had gathered on the first day of the week only because Paul intended to leave them the next day, and so the passage gives no information about their customary practice.[7] There is also the further question as to what is meant here by 'the first day of the week' – is it Saturday evening or Sunday evening? – because, it has been argued, a celebration of the Eucharist after midnight on Sunday would not have been 'on the first day of the week', and this factor would support the view that the breaking of the bread here was simply a social meal rather than a regular liturgical event. We shall return to this question later.

• Revelation 1.10: 'I was in the Spirit on the Lord's day . . .' While some interpret the unusual expression 'the Lord's day' (κυριακὴ ἡμέρα) as referring to Sunday, and thus implying that the first day of the week was being observed regularly as a day of worship in the Christian community of the author, others have understood it instead to mean the eschatological Day of the Lord, and still others Easter Day.[8]

Those who contend that 'the Lord's day' in this passage from the book of Revelation (conventionally dated in the last decade of the first century) does mean Sunday claim support from the occurrence of a very similar expression in what was probably a roughly contemporary text, the *Didache*.[9] This instructs: 'On the Lord's [day] of the Lord (κατὰ κυριακὴν δὲ κυρίου) having assembled together, break bread and give thanks, having first confessed your faults, so that your sacrifice may be

---

7 See Bacchiocchi, *From Sabbath to Sunday*, pp. 101–11; Rordorf, *Sunday*, pp. 196–202; and the works referred to in both these discussions.

8 See Bacchiocchi, *From Sabbath to Sunday*, pp. 111–31; Rordorf, *Sunday*, pp. 207–9; and the works referred to in both these discussions. For an account of the other usages of the adjective κυριακή, see Richard Bauckham, 'The Lord's Day' in Carson, *From Sabbath to Lord's Day*, pp. 221–50, here at pp. 222–7.

9 This work has been variously dated from the middle of the first century to the middle of the second, but the current consensus seems to be that it is no later than the end of the first century: see Kurt Niederwimmer, *The Didache: A Commentary* (Minneapolis: Fortress Press 1998), p. 53, n. 71.

pure' (14.1). While most scholars treat this as meaning Sunday,[10] there are some who have tried to argue that even here the reference is to an annual Easter[11] or to a Day of Atonement celebration by Jewish Christians.[12] Bacchiocchi, not surprisingly, believed that it referred not to a day at all but to the manner of celebrating the Eucharist, 'according to the Lord's doctrine or command'. He adopted a similar attitude towards the occurrence of the same adjective in Ignatius of Antioch's *Letter to the Magnesians* 9.1, 'not keeping the Sabbath but living according to the Lord's [day/life?]', although he admitted that when the word was used in the *Gospel of Peter* 35 and 50, it did refer to Sunday, but he dated that work later than many other scholars, in the second half of the second century, a time when he was willing to acknowledge that Sunday worship had become generally established.[13] Bacchiocchi's interpretation of *Magnesians* 9.1 has recently been supported by Clemens Leonhard.[14]

A letter written by Pliny the Younger when serving as Roman governor of Bithynia to the Emperor Trajan *c.* 112 has also often been cited as providing support for the early existence of Christian worship on Sundays, since it refers to the Christians he had interrogated as meeting regularly 'on a fixed day' (*stato die*) before daylight and again later in the same day to eat together.[15] However, this 'fixed day' might equally well refer to Saturday rather than to Sunday,[16] and indeed more probably so, because we have no other evidence that Christians anywhere met twice on a Sunday at this early period, morning and evening, whereas a Saturday morning gathering for the study of the

---

10 See, for example, Rordorf, *Sunday*, pp. 209–10; Niederwimmer, *The Didache*, pp. 194–6.

11 Most notably C. W. Dugmore, 'Lord's Day and Easter' in *Neotestamentica et Patristica*, Supplements to Novum Testamentum 6 (Leiden: Brill 1962), pp. 272–81.

12 Neville L. A. Tidwell, 'Didache XIV:1 Revisited', *VC* 53 (1999), pp. 197–207. His thesis has been refuted by Daniel Stökl Ben Ezra, *The Impact of Yom Kippur on Early Christianity* (Tübingen: Mohr Siebeck 2003), pp. 217f.

13 Bacchiocchi, *From Sabbath to Sunday*, pp. 113–15, 214–16. For a very cautious assessment of all these references, see Bauckham, 'The Lord's Day', pp. 227–32.

14 Clemens Leonhard, *The Jewish Pesach and the Origins of the Christian Easter* (Berlin/New York: de Gruyter 2006), pp. 124–9.

15 Pliny, *Ep.* 10.96; Latin text and ET in Pliny, *Letters*, ed. Betty Radice, Loeb Classical Library 59 (Cambridge, MA: Harvard University Press 1969), pp. 284–91. Rordorf, *Sunday*, pp. 202–3, supported its meaning Sunday, as more recently has Stephen G. Wilson, *Related Strangers: Jews and Christians, 70–170 C. E.* (Minneapolis: Fortress Press 1995), p. 231. Bacchiocchi, *From Sabbath to Sunday*, pp. 98–9, claimed improbably that the 'fixed day' might not have been on the same day every week.

16 This possibility is acknowledged by Dugmore, 'Lord's Day and Easter', p. 270.

Scriptures based on synagogue practice followed by a gathering to eat in the evening does seem a plausible explanation. Nevertheless, as this Saturday evening gathering would no doubt have occurred after sunset, when the Sabbath was over, it would still – according to Jewish reckoning – have been on the first day of the week, the Lord's day. Pliny reports that the Christians said that they had subsequently abandoned the evening meal as a consequence of his edict forbidding such assemblies. What they may have done was to transfer it to Sunday morning and reduce it in scale – which, if true, would make it our earliest known instance of such a celebration.[17]

In years gone by the *Epistle of Barnabas* was generally not adduced into the debate about the beginnings of Sunday observance, because it was conventionally thought to have been written around the end of the first quarter of the second century, but recently the weight of opinion has begun to shift towards a somewhat earlier date. Stephen Wilson proposes somewhere around 96–8, which could make it the first fairly sure reference to the regular Christian observance of Sunday, as *Barnabas* 15.9 states that 'we keep the eighth day with rejoicing, on which also Jesus rose from the dead . . .'.[18] There is widespread, though not universal, agreement that this expression refers to the weekly recurrence of the day and not to an annual celebration of Easter.

Thus, while the cumulative evidence for the early observance of Sunday by Christians remains somewhat flimsy, it is probably sufficient for us to conclude that by the end of the first century the custom had become established in some places, but not yet in all. Unless the fact that nearly all of the most likely early extant references to it come from the regions of Asia Minor and Syria is merely coincidental, that area seems the probable point of origin.[19]

In spite of the weakness of the evidence, a number of scholars have nonetheless presumed that the practice must have originated in Palestine, and at a much earlier date. Rordorf, for example, argued not simply for its existence in Pauline communities but for a pre-Pauline origin. Developing a view originally put forward by his mentor Oscar

17 This interpretation of the evidence has been made by Alistair Stewart-Sykes, *The Life of Polycarp* (Sydney: St Pauls Publications 2002), p. 67.
18 Wilson, *Related Strangers*, pp. 231–2. See also James Carleton Paget, *The Epistle of Barnabas: Outlook and Background* (Tübingen: Mohr 1994), pp. 9–30, who inclines towards the same date. For the use of 'the eighth day' to designate Sunday, see below, p. 13.
19 So Wilson, *Related Strangers*, p. 233.

Cullmann, he believed it had its historical roots in the post-resurrection meal-appearances by Jesus to his disciples, several of which are said to have taken place on the first day of the week.[20] Other scholars, however, have rejected this particular argument on the ground that it is more likely to have been the other way around – that it was the existence of regular Christian meal gatherings on the first day of the week that gave rise to stories about Jesus having appeared to his disciples at meals on those days.[21] Yet both these views discount the possibility that the New Testament references to the empty tomb having been discovered on the first day of the week and Jesus having appeared to his disciples on the same day may be no more than simple historical recollection, and neither the immediate cause nor the effect of the Christian transition to worship on that day. As Harald Riesenfeld observed, 'In the accounts of the resurrection in the Gospels, there are no sayings which direct that the great event of Christ's resurrection should be commemorated on the particular day of the week on which it occurred.'[22] It is important also to note that when the resurrection is mentioned by early Christian writers in connection with the observance of Sunday, it is not presented as being the primary reason for the choice of that day: *Barnabas* speaks of Sunday as the day 'on which *also* Jesus rose from the dead'; Ignatius has a similar expression, '. . . living according to the Lord's [day], on which *also* our life sprang up through him and his death'; and even Justin Martyr in the middle of the second century recalls Sunday as having been the first day of creation before he mentions it as the day of Christ's resurrection.[23]

Although recognizing the weakness of the arguments attempting to trace the origin of Sunday observance back to the resurrection appearances or even to the time of the writing of the Gospel accounts of the resurrection, Richard Bauckham still considered it likely that the practice went back to the Palestinian Jewish-Christian churches. He believed that the absence of any controversy over the matter among

---

20 Rordorf, *Sunday*, pp. 215ff.; Oscar Cullmann, *Early Christian Worship* (London: SCM Press/Naperville, IL: Allenson 1953), pp. 15f.

21 See, for example, Xavier Léon-Dufour, *Sharing the Eucharistic Bread* (New York: Paulist Press 1982), pp. 39–40.

22 Harald Riesenfeld, 'The Sabbath and the Lord's Day in Judaism, the Preaching of Jesus and Early Christianity' in Harald Riesenfeld, *The Gospel Tradition* (Oxford: Blackwell 1970), pp. 111–37, here at p. 124.

23 *Barnabas* 15.9; Ignatius, *Magnesians* 9.1; Justin Martyr, *First Apology* 67.8 (emphasis added).

second-century Christians could best be explained if Sunday worship was already established prior to the Gentile mission.[24] Wilson, however, dismisses such claims for an early date as 'pure speculation'.[25] In any case, was Bauckham right in saying that there was no dispute over the observance of the Lord's day? He assumed that Jewish Christians, who he admits were continuing to observe the Sabbath,[26] were doing so in addition to keeping the Lord's day and not instead of it. But was that true? He refers to the testimony of the fourth-century historian Eusebius, who described two types of a deviant Jewish-Christian sect known as the Ebionites still existing in his own time: one group observed the Sabbath and the Jewish law, the other added to this the celebration of the Lord's day 'as a memorial of the resurrection of the Saviour'.[27] Bauckham cites the second of these groups as possibly retaining 'the original practice of Palestinian Jewish Christianity', but the other he regards as having discontinued their original Sunday worship, perhaps as the result of pressure from their Jewish brethren.[28] Wilson, however, more plausibly suggests that it was the first group who may have retained the earlier practice, while the second reflected a later accommodation to the emergence of Lord's day observance among other Christians.[29]

Somewhat surprisingly, in another essay Bauckham acknowledges that the opponents criticized by Ignatius of Antioch in his letters in the early second century for holding separate Eucharists (see especially *Philadelphians* 4.1; *Smyrnaeans* 7.1; 8.2; cf. *Magnesians* 9.1), whom Bauckham identifies as probably mixed communities of Jewish and Gentile Christians, were likely to have done so 'on the Sabbath in distinction from the bishop's eucharist on Sunday'.[30] While Bauckham views this as an instance of 'Judaizing', that is, of slipping back into something that they had long given up or that had never been part of their tradition, the more likely explanation would seem to be that they were conservative communities which were resistant to making the

24 Bauckham, 'The Lord's Day', pp. 232–8.
25 Wilson, *Related Strangers*, p. 233.
26 Bauckham, 'Sabbath and Sunday in the Post-Apostolic Church', p. 257: 'Certainly the Jewish-Christian communities of Syria and Palestine continued to keep the Sabbath.'
27 Eusebius, *Historia ecclesiastica* 3.27.5. On the Ebionites, see further Gerd Lüdemann, *Heretics: The Other Side of Early Christianity* (London: SCM Press/Louisville: Westminster John Knox Press 1996), pp. 52–6.
28 Bauckham, 'The Lord's Day', pp. 237, 270.
29 Wilson, *Related Strangers*, p. 233.
30 Bauckham, 'Sabbath and Sunday in the Post-Apostolic Church', p. 260.

transition from Sabbath observance to worship on the Lord's day and thus came into conflict with the more progressive Ignatius. If this is so, then it suggests that the transition is more likely to have been of relatively recent origin than something reaching back to the earliest days of Christianity, and the motivation behind it seems to have been the desire to make a clearer distinction between Christianity and Judaism that we see emerging around the end of the first century.[31]

However, we still need to ask the fundamental question as to what 'keeping the Sabbath' or 'observing the Lord's day' might have meant in practical terms at this time, and especially when it was that Jewish Christians would have gathered to eat their regular Christian meal together. For Jews in the first century, as William Horbury has cogently argued,[32] the most significant meal in connection with the Sabbath was that held actually on Friday evening, before sunset and the onset of the Sabbath when the lighting of fires and cooking would be prohibited, resulting in little food, often cold, being eaten during the day itself. It seems all but certain therefore that it would have been this meal that became the weekly 'eucharistic' occasion for the first generation of Jewish Christians, and at least in some cases for succeeding generations. Some Gentile Christian communities, and mixed gatherings of Jewish and Gentile believers, might well initially have adopted the same occasion,[33] but others might have assembled instead when the Sabbath was over, after sunset on Saturday, which would technically have been the beginning of the first day of the week according to Jewish reckoning. It is possible that the gathering described in Acts 20.7–12 and referred to earlier in this chapter was an instance of this practice, as was the one reported to Pliny in Bithynia in the early second century.

The exhortations by early Christian leaders for certain congregations to abandon the keeping of the Sabbath, therefore, would have meant not simply ceasing to rest on the Sabbath but also transferring their weekly meal to Saturday evening, viewed now as the beginning of the first day of the week. Indeed, for some Gentiles it is likely to have been

---

31 Wilson, *Related Strangers*, p. 235, agrees that the motivation was probably anti-Jewish.

32 William Horbury, '*Cena Pura* and Lord's Supper' in Jack Pastor and Menachem Mor (eds), *The Beginnings of Christianity* (Jerusalem: Yad Ben-Zvi Press 2005), pp. 219–65.

33 Young, '"The Use of Sunday for Meetings of Believers in the New Testament", A Response', p. 117, went so far as to claim that 'it is inconceivable that Jewish Christians in the Apostolic era were meeting on any other day than the Sabbath; and if they were to meet unitedly with the Gentile Christians, the latter had to join the former on the Sabbath and not Sunday'.

the Sabbath-eve meal and the assembly for Bible study the next morning that would have constituted the main feature of their Sabbath observance, if they were unable to pass themselves off as Jews and take advantage of the general recognition accorded to Jews within the Roman Empire of their religious duty to refrain from working on that day. On the other hand, for any communities that were already accustomed to meeting for their eucharistic meal on Saturday evenings, what was required in order to distance themselves from the Jewish roots of their faith was not initially a change in their practice as it was starting to view the occasion as the beginning of the Lord's day rather than as something that ended the Sabbath. For we have no evidence at all of Christians transferring their meal to Sunday evenings. Rordorf's thesis that the first Christians must have adopted the custom of assembling on Sunday evenings for the Eucharist as a result of the resurrection appearances of Jesus having taken place on Sunday evenings lacks any firm support, and has been strongly refuted by Bauckham in particular. Bauckham points out that while some resurrection appearances of Jesus do take place on a Sunday evening, others do not, and only one of them is explicitly said to involve a meal (Luke 24.30–31, 35), while other meals in the Gospels with apparent eucharistic significance are not said to have taken place on that day.[34]

Thus, the transfer to Sunday morning can only have happened when a congregation finally abandoned an evening eucharistic meal and resorted to a token feeding instead. Some scholars have argued that this transition, too, took place at quite an early date, but apart from what may be inferred for Bithynia from Pliny's letter, any direct evidence for it is lacking until very much later, in the third century.[35] Even Justin Martyr's description of Christian assemblies as taking place 'on the day called "of the Sun"' is not necessarily inconsistent with their actually

---

34 Bauckham, 'The Lord's Day', pp. 234–5.

35 Tertullian's reference to Christians taking 'in gatherings before daybreak and from the hand of none but the presidents the sacrament of the eucharist' (*De corona* 3) has commonly been understood as the first explicit reference to a morning eucharistic celebration, but see Andrew B. McGowan, 'Rethinking Agape and Eucharist in Early North African Christianity', *SL* 34 (2004), pp. 165–76, here at pp. 169–70, who suggests that it may instead be to the reception of pre-consecrated bread on the station days of Wednesday and Friday (for which see below, pp. 29–35). If so, Cyprian, in the middle of the third century, would constitute our earliest sure witness (*Ep.* 63.16.4), though McGowan detects signs in what Cyprian says that others in North Africa were still holding their eucharistic suppers in the evening. See also Paul F. Bradshaw, *Eucharistic Origins* (London: SPCK/New York: Oxford University Press 2004), pp. 97–101, 108–10.

taking place on Saturday evenings and still involving a meal.[36] That is not to say that the transfer might not have happened earlier than this in some places, especially where congregations were growing larger and catering was proving difficult, but there is nothing to compel us to think that it did. Linked with this matter is the question of the manner in which early Christians would have calculated when a day began and ended. Some have thought that they might have abandoned the Jewish view that a day was to be counted from sunset to sunset at quite an early date and substituted either the Roman reckoning from midnight to midnight or alternatively the common Hellenistic reckoning from dawn to dawn.[37] As we saw earlier, this question is not unrelated to Acts 20.7–12. For Rordorf to be able to argue that the gathering described there took place on Sunday evening, he had to assume that such a change in calculating the day had already happened. However, because Christians continued to use the Jewish names for the days of the week for several centuries, except when addressing pagans,[38] it seems unlikely that they abandoned the Jewish reckoning of the day very quickly.

In order to undergird the adoption of Saturday evening as the proper occasion for the Christian weekly gathering, it was necessary for those early Christians advocating the change to do two things: to undermine the observance of the Sabbath and to give some positive justification for meeting on the day after the Sabbath. Bestowing on this day the desig-nation 'the Lord's day' – the day when true believers acknowledged the lordship of Christ and looked forward to the eschatological Day of the Lord – was one such step. But Christian apologists in the second century went further. They generally interpreted the commandment to observe the literal Sabbath as having been only a temporary measure, which had now been abrogated by Christ, that Christians should instead fulfil in a spiritual manner by living in holiness every day rather than by what they described as living in idleness on just one day, and that the true Sabbath was the rest that believers would enjoy in the age to come.[39] *Barnabas*, apparently originating in Alexandria as a concerted

---

36 Justin Martyr, *First Apology* 67.3. See further Bradshaw, *Eucharistic Origins*, pp. 61–75.

37 See Thomas J. Talley, *The Origins of the Liturgical Year* (New York: Pueblo 1986; 2nd edn, Collegeville: The Liturgical Press 1991), pp. 14–16. For a more detailed exposition of the variety of ways of reckoning the day in the ancient world, see Llewelyn, 'The Use of Sunday for Meetings of Believers in the New Testament', pp. 213–19.

38 See Rordorf, *Sunday*, pp. 39–41, and esp. n. 6.

39 For examples, see Bauckham, 'Sabbath and Sunday in the Post-Apostolic Church', pp. 252–69.

attack upon Jewish Christians, gives this a novel twist by claiming that the seventh-day commandment in the Old Testament was actually referring to an eschatological event and not a day of the week at all, and that therefore God rejects the present Sabbaths in favour of this, which he will 'make the beginning of an eighth day, which is the beginning of another world'. This, the author says, is why the Christians observe 'the eighth day' of the week with rejoicing. By giving Sunday the same name as the end time and emphasizing its joyful character, he thus draws out the implication of the title 'the Lord's day' as an anticipation of the age to come.[40] The designation 'eighth day' recurs in later Christian writings.[41] Justin Martyr, while not using that less easily understood term in his *First Apology* addressed to the Emperor Antoninus Pius, gave as the reason for worship on Sunday its being 'the first day, on which God, having transformed the darkness and matter, made the world', and as we saw earlier, like *Barnabas*, added that it was also the day of Christ's resurrection.[42]

Thus, the adoption of the Lord's day by early Christians was not as a replacement for the Jewish Sabbath understood as a divinely mandated day of rest. It was, however, a replacement for the Sabbath insofar as it became *the* day of the week when God's people were expected to assemble together for worship. The language used to describe it confirms that it was understood primarily not as a memorial of Christ's resurrection but as the key weekly expression of the constant eschatological readiness for the *parousia* which was intended to permeate the whole of a Christian's daily prayer and life.[43]

---

40 See further Bauckham, 'Sabbath and Sunday in the Post-Apostolic Church', pp. 262–4, 273.

41 See Justin Martyr, *Dialogue with Trypho* 41.4; 138.1; Tertullian, *De idolatria* 14; and Jean Daniélou, *The Bible and the Liturgy* (Notre Dame: University of Notre Dame Press 1956), pp. 255–81.

42 Justin Martyr, *First Apology* 67.8.

43 See further Paul F. Bradshaw, *Daily Prayer in the Early Church* (London: SPCK 1981/New York: Oxford University Press 1982; reprinted Eugene, OR: Wipf and Stock 2008), pp. 37–9, 57–9.

Chapter 2

Continuing traces of the Sabbath in later Christian practice

In his study of the origins of Sunday, Rordorf claimed that the observance of the Sabbath by Gentile Christians disappeared after the time of
Ignatius, and that it was a new regard for the Sabbath that re-emerged
from the end of the second century onward. He believed that he had
sufficiently demonstrated, chiefly on the basis of the Pauline epistles,
that the Gentile Christian churches originally did not observe the
Sabbath, and so if it had subsequently crept back into the churches of
Asia Minor, it would have been due to secondary influences (e.g.,
imitation of Jewish customs, astrological superstition). He was willing
to admit that it was a justifiable conjecture that there could have been a
direct line 'from the Sabbath observance of the churches in Asia Minor
to those of the Church at large in the third and fourth centuries', but
because the nature of the Sabbath observance was so markedly different
in these two cases, he doubted whether there was any connection
between them. He advanced as a possible hypothesis that the later
Christian observance might have developed out of the earlier tradition
of giving a spiritual interpretation to the Sabbath commandment.[1]
Bauckham rejected this conjecture, concurring with the argument put
forward earlier by Kenneth Strand[2] that since the spiritualized interpretation had been developed in opposition to Sabbath observance, it was
hard to see how actual observance of the Sabbath could have developed
out of it. Bauckham concluded that 'the Gentile-Christian Sabbath
observance of the third and fourth centuries would seem, in general, to

---

1 Willy Rordorf, *Sunday* (London: SCM Press/Philadelphia: Westminster Press 1968),
pp. 142–53.
2 K. A. Strand, 'From Sabbath to Sunday in the Early Christian Church: A Review of
Some Recent Literature. Part I: Willy Rordorf's Reconstruction', *Andrews University
Seminary Studies* 16 (1978), pp. 333–42, here at p. 338.

have been no longer the result of Jewish-*Christian* influence; it seems to have been rather a matter of popular Christian adoption of Jewish customs from their Jewish neighbors', and should probably be seen 'as an attempt by the church to contain judaizing tendencies by Christianizing the Sabbath'.[3] Gerard Rouwhorst reached a similar conclusion:

> Most of the Syriac sources do not bear any evidence of the continuing influence of the Sabbath or even of elements related to it. If they make mention of the weekly Jewish day of rest at all, it is only in a polemical sense and particularly with the intention to restrain Christians from observing that day. This fact in itself, of course, demonstrates that some Christians felt attracted by the Sabbath or rituals connected with it and celebrated it together with the Jews or, what seems more probable, had developed their own Christian Sabbath practices . . . The celebration of the Saturday/Sabbath appears only in one source, that is moreover relatively late, whereas several other sources which are, in addition, older, explicitly condemn it. This means that the antiquity of this tradition, as far as the majority of the Syriac Churches is concerned, is very unlikely.[4]

However, questions need to be raised about all these negative judgements. First, they are based primarily upon an argument from silence: we do not hear any more about Christian Sabbath observance after Ignatius' letters early in the second century until the beginning of the third. Yet that is not a very long period of time, and we have no reason to suppose that the observance of the Sabbath by others would have ceased immediately after Ignatius wrote, nor any indication that our third-century sources thought that what they were describing were entirely new developments. Thus if any gap ever existed between the alleged disappearance of Sabbath observance and its resumption, it would have had to have been very short indeed. Nor have we any grounds for believing, as many scholars apparently do, that Paul's influence on Gentile Christianity would have been so strong that hardly any of them would have been tempted to keep the Sabbath, and the few

---

3 Richard Bauckham, 'Sabbath and Sunday in the Post-Apostolic Church' in D. A. Carson (ed.), *From Sabbath to Lord's Day* (Grand Rapids: Zondervan 1982), pp. 261–2 and n. 72 (emphasis in original).
4 Gerard Rouwhorst, 'Jewish Liturgical Traditions in Early Syriac Christianity', *VC* 51 (1997), pp. 72–93, here at pp. 80, 84.

that were would have stopped doing so very quickly. All these scholars are willing to admit that Jewish-Christian communities did continue with their Sabbath practices, and so it would hardly be surprising if some Gentile Christians also did the same in areas where the Jewish-Christian influence remained strong. As we saw in the quotations above, Rouwhorst admitted as much on the basis of the polemics of other Christians against it (Justin Martyr, for example, while sharing the general criticism of the Jews for spending their Sabbaths in idleness, was prepared to tolerate Jewish Christians continuing to observe the Sabbath; it was only those who tried to compel Gentiles to do that too whom he opposed[5]) and even Rordorf was prepared to entertain the theoretical possibility of a direct line of influence from Asia Minor to wider Christianity, drawing back only because of the apparent difference in form between the two.

Rouwhorst's survey was also limited because he focused there exclusively on the Syrian sources. In a later essay where he addressed the subject more broadly, however, he referred to 'certain phenomena that will be best explained as traces or as echoes of the Sabbath'. Among these he mentioned the whole idea of having readings from a holy book in the Sunday Eucharist, which he thought could have no other root than the Sabbath day readings in the synagogue, and in particular the custom in the churches east of Antioch of having regular readings from the law and the Prophets. He also adopts a more positive attitude towards the material he had discussed in his earlier survey, concluding that it 'might be that the liturgical celebration of Saturday, at least in certain regions, originated from an attempt to integrate minorities of Christians who had remained faithful to some type of Sabbath observance into the larger Gentile Christian communities'.[6]

Nevertheless, the first signs of respect for the Sabbath after the time of Ignatius occur far away from Syria in North Africa. In his treatise on prayer, written in the early years of the third century, Tertullian speaks of some who are refraining from kneeling on the Sabbath:

---

5 Justin Martyr, *Dialogue with Trypho* 12.47.
6 Gerard Rouwhorst, 'The Reception of the Jewish Sabbath in Early Christianity' in P. Post, G. Rouwhorst, L. van Tongeren and A. Scheer (eds), *Christian Feast and Festival* (Louvain: Peeters 2001), pp. 255–61. See also his essay, 'The Reading of Scripture in Early Christian Liturgy' in Leonard V. Rutgers (ed.), *What Athens has to do with Jerusalem* (Louvain: Peeters 2002), pp. 305–31.

Concerning kneeling also prayer is subject to a diversity of observance, through a certain few who refrain from kneeling on the Sabbath, and this dissension is particularly on trial within the churches. The Lord will grant his grace that they may either yield or follow their opinion without offence to others. We, however, as we have received, only on the day of the Lord's resurrection ought to guard not only against this action, but every habit and office of anxiety; deferring even our business lest we give place to the devil.[7]

Although Tertullian describes those doing this as just 'a certain few', yet if the matter was 'on trial within the churches', then the numbers must have been significant enough to make it an issue. Moreover, in his treatise on fasting, written later during the period in which he was a Montanist, Tertullian accuses the Catholics of sometimes continuing the weekly Friday fast on Saturdays as well, a day that he says is 'never to be kept as a fast except at Pascha'.[8] In another treatise he describes the dispensation from fasting on Saturdays as something granted by God when the Sabbath was created.[9] It seems, therefore, that in his part of the world the established custom of the time was to treat the Sabbath with such respect that fasting was generally not allowed, just as on Sundays and unlike other weekdays. Some individuals, however, had begun to take that respect further still and were refusing even to kneel for prayer on that day, but on occasions the mainstream churches would go in the opposite direction and engage in fasting.

Although the form of respect for the Sabbath that is described does not amount to observing it in the same manner as Jewish Christians, yet it is hard to see where it might have originated other than from the older customs of Asia Minor. We need to bear in mind that it is exactly at the same time that we learn from Tertullian of the observance of the season of Pentecost among the Christians of his region,[10] a practice which once

---

7 Tertullian, *De oratione* 23.1–2.

8 Tertullian, *De ieiunio* 14. For the Friday fast, see below, pp. 29–35; and for the fast on the Saturday before Pascha, p. 52. It has been suggested that the occasional Saturday fasts among the Catholics may possibly have been those of the Ember Days known to us in later Roman sources: see Thomas J. Talley, 'The Origin of the Ember Days: An Inconclusive Postscript' in Paul De Clerck and Eric Palazzo (eds), *Rituels: Mélanges offerts à Pierre-Marie Gy, OP* (Paris: Cerf 1990), pp. 465–72.

9 Tertullian, *Adversus Marcionem* 4.12. According to Epiphanius, *Panarion* 42.3.3–4, the Marcionites fasted on the Sabbath to express their hatred for the Creator of the world.

10 See below, pp. 70–1.

again is not identical with the Jewish festival but must have some connection with it, and apparently once more stemming from Asia Minor. Because both of these are different from what Jews were doing, and yet appear connected in some way with it, it seems less a case of deliberately 'Judaizing' than of the preservation of certain elements from ancient traditions, even if other aspects had dropped away or been changed in the course of time. Rouwhorst's suggestion that the emergence of the Saturday customs could be explained as being an extension of the same practices in the Pentecost season begs the question as to why there was a desire to honour the Sabbath in particular in this way rather than any other day of the week.[11]

However, while Tertullian may have thought that Saturdays ought never to be kept as fast days, that is not what we find to have been the custom of the church at Rome. Could that have been the source of the North African tendency to fast on some Saturdays, as Rome and North Africa had a propensity to share a common liturgical tradition in antiquity? Fasting on Saturdays at Rome may already have been happening in the third century, if not earlier,[12] but it is confirmed by Innocent I in a letter to Decentius, Bishop of Gubbio, written at the beginning of the fifth century. He defends the practice at some length, asserting that 'if we fast on Friday because of the passion of the Lord, we ought not to omit the Sabbath, which is enclosed between the time of sadness and of joy . . . because both days reveal sadness for the apostles and those who had followed Christ'.[13] Augustine also discloses that not just Rome but also 'some other churches, though few, near to it or remote from it' treated the day in the same way.[14] This evidently included some churches in his own North Africa, but not the church in Milan, as he tells the story of his mother's concern about what to do

---

11 Gerard Rouwhorst, 'Continuity and Discontinuity between Jewish and Christian Liturgy', *Bijdragen* 54 (1993), pp. 72–83, here at p. 77, n. 21.

12 Hippolytus, *Commentarium in Dan.* 4.20.3, criticizes those who order a fast on the Sabbath and on the Lord's day, contrary to Christ's ordinance, but these thus appear to have been heretical groups rather than the Church at large.

13 Innocent I, *Ep.* 25.

14 Augustine, *Ep.* 36.27; see also 82.14. John Cassian also acknowledges that this was the practice both at Rome and among 'some people in some countries of the West', although he disapproves of it. On the other hand, he claims that the dispensation from fasting on Saturdays throughout the East had nothing to do with Judaism but was appointed by the apostles so that those who had fasted for five days in the week might have two days' respite (*De institutis coenobiorum* 3.9–10). Paulinus of Nola, *Vita Ambrosii* 38, also mentions the Saturday fast.

when visiting that city and of the advice given to him by its bishop, Ambrose:

> When my mother was with me in that city, although I, being as yet a catechumen, felt no concern about these questions, it caused her concern whether she ought to fast on the Saturday according to the custom of our own city or to eat according to the custom of the church of Milan. To free her from this perplexity, I put the question to the man of God named above. He answered, 'What can I recommend than what I myself do?' When I thought that by this response he meant nothing else but that we should eat on Saturdays – for I knew this to be what he did – he, following me, added: 'When I am here, I do not fast on Saturday; but when I am at Rome, I fast on Saturday. Whatever church you may come to, keep its custom if you do not wish to receive or give offence.' I reported this reply to my mother and it satisfied her, nor did she hesitate to comply with it; and I have myself followed it. But because it happens, especially in Africa, that one church, or the churches in one district, may have some who eat on Saturdays and others who fast, it seems to me that I should follow the custom of those to whom the government of the congregation of those people has been entrusted.[15]

Whether this variation in practice had always been so from the start, because Jewish influence had little effect on those churches, or was a step taken later by them as a deliberate anti-Jewish action (comparable to the Quartodeciman fast on the day of the Jewish Passover[16]) is impossible to say with any certainty. The Council of Elvira in Spain, held *c.* 306, directs in Canon 26 that a rigorous form of fasting be followed on Saturdays in order to correct the current practice. This might make it seem that there at least the fast had not existed from the outset, but it appears more likely that the intention is simply to increase the level of fasting from the less rigorous 'no food until the evening' to 'no food for the whole day' (cf. Canon 23).[17] Victorinus of Pettau, who was

---

15 Augustine, *Ep.* 36.32. He repeats the story in *Ep.* 54.3.
16 See Rouwhorst, 'The Reception of the Jewish Sabbath in Early Christianity', pp. 255–6; and for the paschal fast, below, pp. 42–3.
17 For a summary of the critical questions surrounding these canons, see Hamilton Hess, *The Early Development of Canon Law* (New York: Oxford University Press 2002), pp. 40–2.

martyred in 304, also insisted that fasting on Fridays should be rigorous, by which he seems to have meant carried over to Saturday, because he goes on to say, 'lest we should appear to observe any Sabbath with the Jews, which Christ himself, the Lord of the Sabbath, says by his prophets that "his soul hateth" [Isa. 1.13–14], which Sabbath he in his body abolished'.[18]

Third-century evidence from Eastern regions, on the other hand, as one might expect, suggests a closer connection with the Jewish roots than simply honouring the day by not fasting. On the one hand, the *Didascalia Apostolorum*, a Syrian church order strongly opposed to Jewish practices usually thought to have been composed in the third century, urges Jewish Christians to give up treating the Sabbath as equal in status to Sunday, making the standard argument that the Jewish Sabbath had been intended as a 'type' of the eschatological Sabbath rest, and that Jesus had fulfilled or abolished all such types by his coming.[19] On the other hand, sources originating in the region of Smyrna in Asia Minor imply that the Sabbath may have been observed more widely there than just by Jewish Christians. The *Martyrdom of Pionius* includes the following:

> On the second day of the sixth month, on the occasion of a great Sabbath and on the anniversary of the blessed martyr Polycarp, while the persecution of Decius was still on . . . It was Saturday and after they had prayed and taken the sacred bread with water . . .[20]

Although this may seem to indicate that some sort of eucharistic celebration was a regular feature of Saturdays in the middle of the third century when the Decian persecution took place, the date of the composition of the account is disputed. While some believe that at least parts of it are contemporaneous with the event, and may perhaps come from the hand of the martyr himself, even though there have been later interpolations,[21] others instead see inconsistencies in it and incline

---

18 Victorinus, *De fabrica mundi* 5. For fasting on Fridays, see below, pp. 29–35.

19 *Didascalia Apostolorum* 5.17.

20 *Martyrium Pionii* 2, 3: Greek text and ET in Herbert Musurillo, *The Acts of the Christian Martyrs* (Oxford: Clarendon Press 1972), pp. 136–67, here at pp. 136–7. For eucharistic celebrations involving water rather than wine, see Andrew McGowan, *Ascetic Eucharists* (Oxford: Clarendon Press 1999), pp. 143–250.

21 See Robin Lane Fox, *Pagans and Christians* (San Francisco: Harper & Row 1986), pp. 460–8, 471–2; E. L. Gibson, 'Jewish Antagonism or Christian Polemic: The Case of the *Martyrdom of Pionius*', *JECS* 9 (2001), pp. 339–58.

towards a date around 300.[22] Pionius also attacks in a speech those Christians who frequent synagogues (13.1—14.16), suggesting that this too was an issue in that region. A similar problem is highlighted by Origen, who cautions Christians not to partake of meals in both church and synagogue (*Selecta in Exod.* 12.46).

To the evidence of the *Martyrdom of Pionius* for Smyrna may perhaps be added that of the *Life of Polycarp*. Although this account has often been regarded as a fourth-century composition, Alistair Stewart-Sykes has recently argued that it should be dated in the third century.[23] It makes several allusions to gatherings on Saturdays: 'On the Sabbath, when prayer had been made on bended knee at great length, he stood up to read, as was his custom . . .'; 'Then, when the others had performed the appeals and exhortations fitting on the Sabbath and, on the Lord's day, the offerings and thanksgivings . . .'; 'The following Sabbath he said . . .'.[24] If this can be relied on as a third-century witness for Smyrna, it presents a picture of the existence of a regular assembly for the reading of Scripture and preaching there. Coupled with the other evidence listed above, this might lead to the conclusion that the more widespread observance of Saturdays attested for the Christian East in the fourth century was not so much a recent innovation but a continuation and development of practices that had persisted at least in some places from much earlier days.

What is clear is that there is evidence from a variety of sources and regions in the fourth century for the special liturgical observance of Saturdays. Indeed, the celebration of the Eucharist on Saturdays as well as Sundays was so common then that the ecclesiastical historian Socrates mistakenly believed that Alexandria and Rome, which had celebrations only on Sundays, must once have also had Saturday celebrations, but 'on account of some ancient tradition, have ceased to do this'.[25] The question at issue is whether these Saturday observances constitute a recently emergent phenomenon in a church which had not

---

22 See Musurillo, *The Acts of the Christian Martyrs*, p. xxix. More recently, however, Candida Moss, *The Other Christs: Imitating Jesus in Ancient Christian Ideologies of Martyrdom* (New York/London: Oxford University Press 2010), pp. 195–6, has argued again for a mid-third-century date.

23 Alistair Stewart-Sykes, *The Life of Polycarp* (Sydney: St Pauls Publications 2002), pp. 4–22.

24 *Vita Polycarpi* 22–24; ET from Stewart-Sykes, *The Life of Polycarp*, pp. 123–7.

25 *Historia ecclesiastica* 5.22. Athanasius, *Apologia contra Arianos* 11, confirms that Sunday was the only regular day for the Eucharist in Alexandria.

known them since the time of Ignatius, outside communities composed exclusively of Jewish Christians, or whether they in some way reflect continuity with the Church's ancient past, even if the celebration of the Eucharist itself on that day was a newer development out of an older service of the word. Rouwhorst represents the majority view when he suggests that there was a shift of policy from the opposition to Sabbath observance that can be seen in the *Didascalia* to one of accommodation that can be seen in the late-fourth-century *Apostolic Constitutions*. In this church order the observance of the Sabbath is enjoined, but for meditation on the law and not for idleness; because it is a memorial of creation there is to be no fasting on Saturdays, except once a year on the day of the Lord's burial; and even slaves are to be freed from work on both Saturdays and Sundays so that they might go to church for instruction in piety.[26] Rouwhorst suggests the likelihood that in Syria,

> in the third and in the beginning of the fourth century, there were groups of Jewish Christians . . . who observed the Lord's day as well as the Sabbath and used quite superficially Christianized Sabbath blessings. In the course of the fourth century some of their Sabbath customs were taken over by communities of the same region who thus far only had observed the Lord's day.[27]

Against this view Stewart-Sykes argues that there had been continuity of Sabbath observance from earlier times, that what Christians had disputed was not whether it should be kept at all, but how it should be observed – as a day for idleness, as they believed the Jews were now doing, or as a day for study of God's law.[28] Thus, the Council of Laodicea (*c.* 363) banned resting on the Sabbath, as that would have been a sign of Judaizing (Canon 29), but prescribed that the Gospels should be read with other Scriptures in public worship on that day (Canon 16). Stewart-Sykes also points out that in the *Life of Polycarp* his ordination is said to have taken place on the Sabbath, and this would have been because it was regarded as a day for episcopal teaching to take place, and that the same practice appears to underlie the directions for a bishop's ordination in the *Apostolic Constitutions*, as the enthronement of the new bishop there is to take place early in the morning, followed

---

26 *Apostolic Constitutions* 2.36, 7.23; 7.36; 8.33. See also 2.59.
27 Rouwhorst, 'Jewish Liturgical Traditions in Early Syriac Christianity', pp. 85–7.
28 Stewart-Sykes, *The Life of Polycarp*, p. 57.

by the celebration of the Eucharist, after the recitation of the ordination prayer on the previous day, that is, presumably Saturday.[29]

Evidence from Egypt points to the existence of an unusual practice that may shed some light on the observance of the day in earlier times. While the city of Alexandria may only have known a celebration of the Eucharist on Sundays, according to Socrates this was not the case in the surrounding area:

> The Egyptians in the neighbourhood of Alexandria, and the inhabitants of Thebaïs, hold their religious assemblies on the Sabbath, but do not participate of the mysteries in the manner usual among Christians in general: for after having eaten and satisfied themselves with food of all kinds, in the evening making their offerings, they partake of the mysteries.[30]

A similar custom is attested for certain monastic communities in Egypt. While some of them appear to have attended the Eucharist only on Sundays,[31] Cassian tells of the monks of lower Egypt assembling on both Saturdays and Sundays for communion 'at the third hour'.[32] More interestingly still, Pachomian sources describe as the normal custom a Sunday Eucharist celebrated in the monastery by a priest coming in from outside, and the monks also going to a nearby village for a Eucharist on Saturday evenings.[33] These reports suggest that the

---

29 Stewart-Sykes, *The Life of Polycarp*, pp. 61–4.

30 Socrates, *Historia ecclesiastica* 5.22; this account is repeated by Sozomen, *Historia ecclesiastica* 7.19; and Timothy of Alexandria in his *Canonical Responses* 13 also refers in passing to eucharistic celebrations on both Saturday and Sunday: see J. B. Pitra, *Iuris Ecclesiastici Graecorum Historia et Monumenta* 1 (Rome: Typis Collegii urbani 1864), p. 633.

31 See Palladius, *Lausiac History* 33.2 (where a priest and a deacon go to a community of women only on a Sunday); 59.2 (where a nun, Taor, does not go to the local church on Sunday with the rest of the community); Daniel 7 in *The Sayings of the Desert Fathers*, ed. Benedicta Ward (London: Mowbray 1975), p. 45.

32 *De institutus coenobiorum* 3.2. His statement is corroborated by the *Historia monachorum in Aegypto* 20.7; ET in Norman Russell, *The Lives of the Desert Fathers* (London: Mowbray 1981) p. 106.

33 See Armand Veilleux, *La Liturgie dans le cénobitisme pachômien au quatrième siècle*, Studia Anselmiana 57 (Rome: Herder 1968), pp. 228–32. On the other hand, the Rule of Pachomius itself refers only to the Sunday Eucharist (*Praecepta* 15–16). Veilleux believes that this can be explained by the fact that the section of the Rule that mentions the Sunday celebration is dealing with variations in the office on Sundays and feasts, and not specifically listing all the days on which the Eucharist took place (Veilleux, *La Liturgie*, pp. 233–4).

association of the Eucharist with a Sabbath evening meal may have continued here from earliest times, even after Sunday supplanted it elsewhere as the primary occasion for the celebration of the Eucharist. Finally, Socrates also tells of another custom about which we have no other evidence: 'At Cæsarea of Cappadocia and in Cyprus on Saturdays and Sundays in the evening after the lamplighting the presbyters and bishops interpret the Scriptures.'[34]

Although, therefore, there are signs that in some cases there was considerable unease about continuing to treat the Sabbath as in any way special among the other days of the week, presumably in order to maintain a sharp distinction from Judaism, in the majority of cases that day did continue to receive particular honour among Christians. It was not so much abolished as transformed – from a day of rest to a memorial of creation.

---

34 Socrates, *Historia ecclesiastica* 5.22.

Chapter 3

Sunday in the fourth century

With the Peace of Constantine in the fourth century came a significant change in the character of the Christian Sunday, because on 3 March in the year 321 the emperor promulgated a law requiring rest from work for everyone except farmers 'on the most honourable day of the Sun'. It is unclear whether in so doing he was responding to the wishes of Christians or acting on his own initiative. As we saw earlier, Christians had previously condemned as idleness the Jewish observance of the Sabbath by resting and had reinterpreted the biblical Sabbath rest as an eschatological event awaiting fulfilment in the age to come. There are no signs of a desire to anticipate that by a regular weekly day of rest on Sundays prior to the fourth century. The first known explicit example of regarding Sunday as the Christian equivalent of the biblical Sabbath comes from Eusebius of Caesarea writing after 330 CE – that is, after the promulgation of Constantine's law – and his emphasis is not on resting on that day but on devoting it to the priestly service of God. Through the prophets God had rebuked those who had spent the Sabbath day in feasting and drinking and disorder:

> That is why, rejecting those Sabbaths, the Word by the new covenant has changed and transferred the feast of the Sabbath to the rising of the light. He has given us an image of the true rest, the day of salvation, the Lord's day and the first day of light, on which the Saviour of the world, after all his deeds among men, and victorious over death, opened the gates of heaven, passing beyond the creation of the six days, and receiving the divine Sabbath and the blessed rest, when the Father said to him, 'Sit at my right hand, until I make your enemies your footstool.' On that day of light, the first day and the day of the true sun, we also gather after the interval of six days, when we celebrate the holy and spiritual Sabbaths – we who have been

redeemed through him from the nations throughout the world – and what the law ordained for the priests to do on the Sabbath we fulfil according to the spiritual law. For we offer spiritual sacrifices and oblations . . .[1]

Nevertheless, it is still possible that church leaders had played a part in bringing about Constantine's legislation out of a desire to make church attendance easier for Christians and to give them an equivalent of the Roman pagan festival holidays. On the other hand, there are very few signs of Christian attempts to prohibit work until the sixth century – Canon 29 of the Council of Laodicea and *Apostolic Constitutions* 8.33.1–2 seem to be the only exceptions in the fourth century. Officially at least, Sunday was still generally viewed as the day of worship rather than a day of rest. Nor can it have been Constantine's intention to create a Christian version of the Jewish Sabbath, since the form that his legislation took, including the exemption of farmers from its requirements because their opportunity to work was so heavily dependent upon the weather, followed the precedent of existing Roman legislation with regard to pagan holidays and not the prescriptions of the Old Testament, which did not permit any such exemptions.[2]

Interestingly, the issue of whether one should refrain from kneeling to pray on Sundays, clearly described as an established custom at least in North Africa by Tertullian at the beginning of the third century,[3] was apparently still a matter for dispute in some places in the early fourth century, as the Council of Nicaea, referring to the existence of some who knelt both on the Lord's day and during the season of Pentecost, found itself having to legislate for prayer to be made standing on those occasions (Canon 20).

By this time, however, the celebration of the Eucharist on Sunday mornings does seem to have been adopted universally and was not a matter of controversy. In addition to this, the day came to be marked

---

1 Eusebius of Caesarea, *Commentary on Ps. 91*, quoted from Richard Bauckham, 'Sabbath and Sunday in the Post-Apostolic Church' in D. Carson (ed.), *From Sabbath to Lord's Day* (Grand Rapids: Zondervan 1982), pp. 283–4.
2 A point made by Gerard Rouwhorst, 'The Reception of the Jewish Sabbath in Early Christianity' in P. Post, G. Rouwhorst, L. van Tongeren and A. Scheer (eds), *Christian Feast and Festival* (Louvain: Peeters 2001), p. 262.
3 See above, p. 17. The fifth-century Theodoret of Cyrrhus, *Quaestiones et responsiones ad orthodoxos* 115, claims that Irenaeus in the second century had affirmed standing for prayer on Sundays was an Apostolic custom (ET in Cantalamessa, p. 51).

from the fourth century onwards in a number of places by another rite linked specially to it, which we may call a vigil of the resurrection, since at its heart was the reading of a Gospel account of the Passion and resurrection of Christ. It appears to have originated in Jerusalem, in the very place where the resurrection was believed to have happened. According to the pilgrim Egeria, at cockcrow,

> the bishop enters, and goes into the cave in the Anastasis [the Church of the Resurrection]. The doors are all opened, and all the people come into the Anastasis, which is already ablaze with lamps. When they are inside, a psalm is said by one of the presbyters, with everyone responding, and it is followed by a prayer; then a psalm is said by one of the deacons, and another prayer; then a third psalm is said by one of the clergy, a third prayer, and the Commemoration of All. After these three psalms and prayers they take censers into the cave of the Anastasis so that the whole Anastasis basilica is filled with the smell. Then the bishop, standing in the sanctuary, takes the Gospel book and goes to the door, where he himself reads the account of the Lord's resurrection. At the beginning of the reading the whole assembly groans and laments at all that the Lord underwent for us, and the way they weep would move even the hardest heart to tears. When the Gospel is finished, the bishop comes out, and is taken with singing to the Cross, and they all go with him. They have one psalm there and a prayer, then he blesses the people, and that is the dismissal. As the bishop goes out, everyone comes to have his hand laid on them.[4]

That the Gospel reading must have included the Passion as well as the resurrection seems to be indicated by the groaning and weeping of the people while it was being read. This is the very first occasion on which the use of incense in Christian worship is recorded, and it is often thought that it had been introduced in order to represent the spices that the women took with them to the tomb on Easter Day. However, this interpretation may well be a later rationalization.[5] There is no mention of incense in the briefer account given of what is seemingly a derivation of this Jerusalem innovation included among the Sunday observances in *Apostolic Constitutions* 2.59:

---

4 Egeria, *Itinerarium* 24.9–11; ET from John Wilkinson, *Egeria's Travels* (3rd edn, Warminster: Aris & Phillips 1999), pp. 144–5.
5 See Clemens Leonhard, *The Jewish Pesach and the Origins of the Christian Easter* (Berlin/New York: de Gruyter 2006), p. 297, n. 482.

And on the day of our Lord's resurrection, which is the Lord's day, meet more diligently, sending praise to God that made the universe by Jesus, and sent Him to us, and condescended to let Him suffer, and raised Him from the dead. Otherwise what apology will he make to God who does not assemble on that day to hear the saving word concerning the resurrection, on which we pray thrice standing in memory of him who arose in three days, in which is performed the reading of the prophets, the preaching of the Gospel, the oblation of the sacrifice, the gift of the holy food?[6]

A similar office forms a part of the regular Sunday services in later Eastern rites, and although it was not preserved in full in the West, traces of it can be seen in some traditions, suggesting that it once had a more prominent place there too. All this seems to be the result of the influence that pilgrims to Jerusalem had in bringing about the imitation in their home communities of rites that they had experienced in the Holy City.[7]

---

6 ET from *ANF* 7, p. 423.

7 See Juan Mateos, 'La vigile cathédrale chez Egérie', *OCP* 27 (1961), pp. 281–312, here at pp. 302–10; and Rolf Zerfass, *Die Schriftlesung im Kathedraloffizium Jerusalems*, Liturgiewissenschaftliche Quellen und Forschungen 48 (Münster: Aschendorff 1968), pp. 121–7.

Chapter 4

The Christian week: Wednesday and Friday

The *Didache* directs its readers: 'Do not let your fasts be with the hypocrites, for they fast on the second day and the fifth day of the week, but you shall fast on the fourth and the day of preparation.'[1] Regular fasting each week was not something that was prescribed for Jews in the first century, but there are signs that some pious individuals were already choosing to fast on the second and fifth days of the week (Monday and Thursday), the traditional market days of Palestine.[2] Thus the 'hypocrites' mentioned here may well be Pharisees, who did engage in frequent public fasting (see Matt. 6.16; 9.14; Luke 18.12).[3]

At first sight it may look as if the compiler of the *Didache* was simply choosing two other days at random (Wednesday and Friday) in order to differentiate Jewish Christians from other Jews, especially as Friday, the day of preparation for the Sabbath, was one on which Jews would never usually fast. However, many years ago Annie Jaubert argued that religious days were not normally chosen arbitrarily, and drew attention to the solar calendar in use among the Jewish community at Qumran, in which she claimed that Sunday, Wednesday and Friday had a certain prominence, as constituting a possible source for the choice.[4] Attested in *1 Enoch*, the *Book of Jubilees*, as well as the Dead Sea Scrolls, this calendar consisted of exactly 364 days, 52 weeks of 7 days, with the consequence that festivals always fell on the same day of the week every year. The first

---

1 *Didache* 8.1.
2 See Clemens Leonhard, *The Jewish Pesach and the Origins of the Christian Easter* (Berlin/New York: de Gruyter 2006), pp. 131–5.
3 But cf. Jonathan A. Draper, 'Christian Self-Definition against the "Hypocrites" in Didache VIII' in Jonathan A. Draper (ed.), *The Didache in Modern Research* (Leiden: Brill 1992), pp. 223–44.
4 Annie Jaubert, 'Jésus et le calendrier de Qumrân', *New Testament Studies* 7 (1960), pp. 1–30.

day of the first month always began on the Wednesday following the
vernal equinox (or more precisely at sunset on the Tuesday evening)
because according to Genesis 1.14 the creation of the lights in the
firmament on the fourth day was to be 'for signs and for seasons and for
days and years'. Passover fell 14 days later, on a Tuesday evening/
Wednesday every year, Pentecost was always on a Sunday in the third
month, and the Day of Atonement on a Friday in the seventh month.[5]
Liturgical scholars have subsequently tended to conclude, therefore, that
while Wednesdays and Fridays were not marked either by fasting or by
any special liturgical assemblies on a weekly basis at Qumran so far as we
are aware, the Christian choice of these particular days in place of the
Pharisaic Jewish ones may have been influenced by the familiarity of
some early converts with that solar calendar. On the other hand, it is
important to note that James VanderKam has pointed to the existence of
a sufficiently large number of exceptions to the alleged liturgical prominence of Sundays, Wednesdays and Fridays in the solar calendar as to
cast doubts on the validity of Jaubert's conclusions.[6]

Other early Christian sources confirm that the practice of fast days
on Wednesdays and Fridays each week was not a peculiarity of the
Didache nor restricted to Jewish Christianity alone. Clement of Alexandria (*Stromateis* 7.12), Origen (*Homilia in Lev.* 10.2), and the
Didascalia (ch. 21) are all aware of the custom. The mid-second-century
Shepherd of Hermas uses the name 'station' for days of fasting (*Similitude*
5.1), the Latin word *statio* being a military term to denote a period of
sentry duty. Although this work does not specify which those days were,
Tertullian mentions keeping fasts on the fourth and sixth day of the
week (*De ieiunio* 14), and these he too calls stations, and says that prayer
is always made kneeling on those days (*De oratione* 23). He is the first to
refer to two practices associated with those days that would later
become common. The first occurs in his treatise on fasting, where he
defended the Montanist custom both of making days of fasting obliga-
tory and not voluntary, and of prolonging the fast beyond the ninth
hour of the day. Apparently, his Catholic opponents were using the New
Testament example of Peter and John going up to the Temple 'at the
hour of prayer, the ninth hour' (Acts 3.1) to justify concluding their

---

5 For further details, see James C. VanderKam, *Calendars in the Dead Sea Scrolls*
(London: Routledge 1998).
6 James C. VanderKam, 'The Origin, Character and Early History of the 364-Day
Calendar: A Reassessment of Jaubert's Hypotheses', *Catholic Biblical Quarterly* 41
(1979), pp. 390–411, here at pp. 399–402.

Wednesday and Friday fasts at that point in the day (*De ieiunio* 10). This suggests that the Catholics were holding some sort of act of worship at the conclusion of their fasts, and Tertullian confirms that this was also observed by the Montanists, even though it did not form the conclusion of their fasts: it was 'not as if we slighted the ninth hour, [an hour] which, on the fourth and sixth days of the week, we most highly honour'. He goes on to offer what he thinks is a better explanation than Peter and John's Temple visit for why this hour should be marked. The practice, he claims,

> comes from the death of the Lord; which death albeit it behoves to be commemorated always, without difference of hours yet are we at that time more impressively commended to its commemoration, according to the actual [meaning of the] name of Station. For even soldiers, though never unmindful of their military oath, yet pay a greater deference to Stations. And so the 'pressure' must be maintained up to that hour in which the orb – involved from the sixth hour in a general darkness – performed for its dead Lord a sorrowful act of duty; so that we too may then return to enjoyment when the universe regained its sunshine. If this savours more of the spirit of Christian religion, while it celebrates more the glory of Christ, I am equally able, from the self-same order of events, to fix the condition of late protraction of the Station; [namely], that we are to fast till a late hour, awaiting the time of the Lord's burial, when Joseph took down and entombed the body which he had requested. Thence [it follows] that it is even irreligious for the flesh of the servants to take refreshment before their Lord did.[7]

Although one might be tempted to think that Tertullian's explanation for the observance of the ninth hour is likely to have been the true origin of the custom, that is rendered less probable by the fact that it was apparently not used by the Catholics to justify their practice. Nevertheless, the fact that both Catholics and Montanists held some sort of worship assembly at that hour suggests that it must have been a long-established custom, and perhaps ultimately derived from a rabbinic tradition of gatherings to study the law on their weekly fast days, although these are thought to have been in the mornings and not at the ninth hour.

---

7 Tertullian, *De ieiunio* 10; ET from *ANF* 4, p. 109.

The second practice related to these days that Tertullian mentions is some sort of eucharistic service. In his treatise on prayer, he attempts to counter what was apparently a widespread objection to participation in this assembly, raised on the grounds that reception of the eucharistic bread would break the fast. Tertullian proposes the solution that people should attend the gathering but reserve the sacrament for later consumption, thus fulfilling both aspects of the day, worship and fasting:

> Similarly also on station days, many do not think that they should attend the sacrificial prayers, because the station would be undone by receiving the Lord's body. Does then the eucharist destroy a service devoted to God or bind it more to God? Surely your station will be more solemn if you have also stood at God's altar? If the Lord's body is received and reserved, each point is secured, both the participation in the sacrifice and the discharge of the duty. (*De oratione* 19)

What sort of liturgical assembly was this? Although the language used here ('sacrificial prayers', 'God's altar', 'the sacrifice') might suggest that a complete eucharistic celebration was taking place, Andrew McGowan believes that such words and phrases are quite consistent with Tertullian's language about prayer in general, and that therefore this need not indicate a full eucharistic rite but rather the distribution of consecrated bread at the conclusion of a morning gathering for prayer or for a service of the word.[8] It can hardly have been the same assembly that took place at the ninth hour, as *De oratione* was written before Tertullian became a Montanist, and so the fast would have ended by that point in the day and eucharistic reception would then have been no problem. However, Tertullian's proposed solution to the scruples felt by some was not widely adopted, but as we shall see when we examine fourth-century sources, the celebration of the Eucharist or distribution of communion was instead moved to the end of the day's fast.

Like Tertullian, other early Christian writers not unnaturally looked towards the final week of Jesus' life for a possible rationale for the observance of the fast days each Wednesday and Friday. The Syrian *Didascalia Apostolorum* presented a chronology of that week which located the arrest of Jesus on the Wednesday, but did not link this directly with the weekly fast days. However, Victorinus, Bishop of

---

8 Andrew McGowan, 'Rethinking Agape and Eucharist in Early North African Christianity', *SL* 34 (2004), p. 170.

Pettau in Austria, who was martyred in 304, did make the connection. He spoke in his *De fabrica mundi* of fasting on the fourth day of the week until the ninth hour, 'or even until the evening' or the next day, and claimed that it was on account of Jesus' capture by a quaternion of soldiers on this day, and 'on account of the majesty of his works – that the seasons also, wholesome to humanity, joyful for the harvests, tranquil for the tempests, may roll on', that the fourth day was a station. The sixth day, he said, was similarly observed on account of Christ's Passion.

When we move into the fourth century we have evidence that not only fasting but also the holding of special services generally marked those days of the week. The ecclesiastical historian Socrates reports that at Alexandria these were services of the word, as they probably had also been for Tertullian:

> on Wednesdays and Fridays, the scriptures are read, and the teachers interpret them; and all the usual services are performed in their assemblies, except the celebration of the mysteries. This practice in Alexandria is of great antiquity, for it appears that Origen most commonly taught in the church on those days.[9]

On the other hand, Origen himself claimed that in the third century at Alexandria larger crowds gathered for worship on Fridays and Sundays than on other days (*Homilia in Isa.* 5.2). It could just be that Friday, the day of the crucifixion, attracted greater devotion among people, but Harald Buchinger is inclined to believe that because both days are mentioned together, Friday's service, like Sunday, involved a celebration of the Eucharist.[10] However, that would be to cast doubts on the reliability of Socrates' evidence. An alternative possibility is that the Friday service of the word included the distribution of communion with bread and wine consecrated at a previous Sunday service – a practice that became widespread in later Eastern traditions,[11] and that by the fourth century this custom had extended to Wednesdays also at Alexandria,

---

9 Socrates, *Historia ecclesiastica* 5.22.

10 Harald Buchinger, 'Early Eucharist in Transition? A Fresh Look at Origen' in Albert Gerhards and Clemens Leonhard (eds), *Jewish and Christian Liturgy and Worship: New Insights into its History and Interaction* (Leiden: Brill 2007), pp. 207–27, here at pp. 210–11.

11 See Stefanos Alexopoulos, *The Presanctified Liturgy in the Byzantine Rite*, Liturgia condenda 21 (Louvain: Peeters 2009).

but is not mentioned by Socrates because it was not a 'celebration of the mysteries' but was subsumed under the category of 'all the usual services'.

Egeria describes services being held in Jerusalem at the ninth hour on Wednesdays and Fridays and fasting also being observed on those days – by catechumens as well as by the baptized – unless the feast of a martyr should coincide with them (*Itinerarum* 27.5). These gatherings took place on Sion, the ancient home of the Jerusalem church, and not at the Anastasis (the church of the resurrection) where all the other weekday services were held, suggesting that these were of greater antiquity. She also says that during the 50 days of Easter they were transferred to the morning, because there was no fasting then (*Itinerarum* 41). During Lent the same services occur, when 'all things are done that are customary to do at the ninth hour, except the oblation. For, so that the people may always be taught the law, both the bishop and the presbyter preach assiduously' (*Itinerarum* 27.6). It seems likely that the singular 'presbyter' is a scribal error and the plural was really meant. But what does she mean by 'except the oblation' (her normal term for the Eucharist)? It is thought by many that she was trying to say that during the rest of the year at Jerusalem this service was eucharistic, and only reverted to a pure service of the word in the Lenten season. It is possible, however, that she could have been contrasting Jerusalem practice, which had a service of the word all year round, and the custom with which she was familiar in her home country, where the service was instead regularly eucharistic.

Epiphanius of Salamis, the fourth-century monk and bishop of that metropolitan see in Cyprus, speaks of assemblies (*synaxes*) held on Wednesdays, Fridays and Sundays, which he believes to have been instituted by the apostles, but he does not make it clear whether these were all eucharistic or not. The Wednesday and Friday services were held at the ninth hour because of the fast, except during the Easter season when they took place in the morning, as in Jerusalem; and he also mentions that during the Lenten fast they were held every weekday – a custom also apparently adopted at Antioch.[12] Ambrose in Milan declares that the Eucharist was celebrated there at midday on 'most days', but on fast days there was not a full celebration and instead communion was

---

12 Epiphanius, *Adversus haereses* 3.22. For Antioch, see Rolf Zerfass, *Die Schriftlesung im Kathedraloffizium Jerusalems*, Liturgiewissenschaftliche Quellen und Forschungen 48 (Münster: Aschendorff 1968), pp. 133ff.

received at the conclusion of the fast just before the evening meal (*Sermones in psalmum 118* 8.48; 18.28) – doubtless the older of the two customs.

Finally, one other practice associated with Fridays should be noted – the observance of an all-night vigil every week in some places in the fourth century. This seems to have been primarily a monastic institution, or if it had originated at an earlier date, a custom that was being kept alive at that time chiefly by urban monastic communities. John Cassian provides a substantial description of its contents as practised in Palestinian monasteries:

> In the winter time, however, when the nights are longer, the vigils, which are celebrated every week on the evening at the commencing the Sabbath, are arranged by the elders in the monasteries to last till the fourth cock-crowing, for this reason, that after the watch through the whole night they may, by resting their bodies for the remaining time of nearly two hours, avoid flagging through drowsiness the whole day long, and be content with repose for this short time instead of resting the whole night . . . And so they divide them into an office in three parts, that by this variety the effort may be distributed and the exhaustion of the body relieved by some agreeable relaxation. For when standing they have sung three psalms antiphonally,[13] after this, sitting on the ground or in very low stalls, one of them repeats three psalms, while the rest respond, each psalm being assigned to one of the brethren, who succeed each other in turn; and to these they add three readings while still sitting quietly. And so, by lessening their bodily exertion, they manage to observe their vigils with greater attention of mind.[14]

This unit of three antiphonal psalms, three responsorial psalms, and three readings was doubtless repeated as many times as necessary throughout the night. Egeria describes a similar Friday night vigil in Jerusalem, but here apparently occurring only during Lent. It began

---

13 Of the meaning of antiphonal psalmody at this period, see Robert F. Taft, *The Liturgy of the Hours in East and West* (Collegeville: The Liturgical Press 1986; 2nd edn 1993), p. 139; Robert F. Taft, 'Christian Liturgical Psalmody: Origins, Development, Decomposition, Collapse' in Harold W. Attridge and Margot E. Fassler (eds), *Psalms in Community* (Atlanta: Society of Biblical Literature 2003), pp. 7–32, here at pp. 19–23.
14 John Cassian, *De institutis coenobiorum* 3.8; ET from *NPNF*, 2nd Series 11, pp. 216–17.

after the normal evening service and continued until the celebration of the Eucharist on Saturday morning, which was held at an earlier hour than in the rest of the year, before sunrise. This was done, she states, so that those who had been fasting all week at that season might break their fast a little sooner. All she says about its contents was that 'throughout the night they alternate responsorial psalms, antiphons, and various readings' (27.7–9). She gives no indication of who took part in it, but we may reasonably conclude that it was the especially devout and the members of monastic communities who constituted the great majority. Similar weekly vigils were continued in a number of later monastic traditions, in both West and East.[15]

Cassian believed that the practice had been observed uninterruptedly among Christians in the East since the time of the apostles: 'because, when our Lord and Saviour had been crucified on the sixth day of the week, the disciples, overwhelmed by the freshness of his sufferings, remained watching throughout the whole night, giving no rest or sleep to their eyes'.[16] While this derivation is highly unlikely, the absence of other evidence makes it impossible to ascertain the antiquity of the custom. Tertullian at the beginning of the third century uses the expression 'by day the station, by night the vigil' (*De oratione* 29) and elsewhere speaks of 'night assemblies', *nocturnae convocationes* (*Ad uxorem* 2.9), which sound as if they were more frequent than an annual paschal vigil. But beyond that, we have no other information. The probability seems to be that a weekly all-night vigil had come to be the practice of at least some Christians in some places, including North Africa, by the third century, but like many other things survived in the fourth century as the custom only of especially ascetic individuals and of urban monastic religious communities.

---

15 See Otto Heiming, 'Zum monastischen Offizium von Kassianus bis Columbanus', *ALW* 7 (1961), pp. 89–156, here at pp. 107–8.

16 Cassian, *De institutis coenobiorum* 3.9; ET from *NPNF*, 2nd Series 11, p. 217.

Easter and Pentecost

Chapter 5

The Quartodeciman celebration

Early Christian sources reveal two quite distinct modes of celebrating Easter, or Pascha as it was known (the term also used for the Passover). The one which ultimately became universal was to keep the feast on the Sunday after the Jewish Passover and eventually to focus its celebration upon the resurrection of Jesus Christ, which – according to the testimony of the four canonical Gospels – had taken place on the first day of the week. The other ancient form of the celebration is attested chiefly in second-century sources deriving from Asia Minor and parts of Syria east of Antioch. This tradition made Easter a memorial of the death of Jesus and situated the feast instead at the time of the Passover itself, during the night from 14 to 15 of the Jewish month of Nisan, the first month of spring. Because of their attachment to this day, those who followed this latter custom were called 'Quartodecimans' (i.e., 'four-teeners') by other Christians. The traditional scholarly consensus tended to be that the Sunday celebration was the older of the two (perhaps going back all the way to the Apostolic age itself, even though it is only explicitly attested from the second century onwards) and was the one observed by the mainstream of the Christian tradition from the first. The Quartodeciman custom was judged to be no more than a second-century local aberration from this norm, brought about by an apparently common tendency among some early Christians to 'Judaize', a practice already criticized by St Paul in the first century.[1]

In the second half of the twentieth century, however, the tide began to turn and many scholars now believe that the Quartodeciman practice began at a much earlier date as a Jewish-Christian adaptation of the

---

1 See, for example, A. A. McArthur, *The Evolution of the Christian Year* (London: SCM Press 1953), pp. 98–107; Josef Jungmann, *The Early Liturgy to the Time of Gregory the Great* (Notre Dame: University of Notre Dame Press 1959), pp. 25–6.

Passover,[2] while others have gone further and argued that the celebration of Easter on a Sunday was a considerably later development than is often supposed – that it was not adopted at Rome until about the year 165, although it may have emerged in Alexandria and Jerusalem somewhat earlier.[3] Prior to this time, these churches would actually have known no annual Easter observance at all. This theory effectively reverses the conclusions reached by the majority of earlier scholars: Quartodecimanism is not some local aberration from a supposed normative practice dating from Apostolic times, but is instead the oldest form of the Easter celebration.

It was traditionally assumed that the Jewish Passover meal in the first century would have followed substantially the same pattern as we find in sources from later centuries. However, more recent scholarship has cast serious doubts upon this assumption too, and today most Jewish scholars agree that many of the customs described in the later literature only came into being after the destruction of the Jerusalem Temple in the year 70. The primary act prior to this time was the sacrifice of the Passover lambs during the afternoon of 14 Nisan, each of which was then consumed by a group of participants within the precincts of the city of Jerusalem. That meal would have included the eating of *matzah* (unleavened bread) and bitter herbs, and often also the drinking of wine. More than that cannot be assumed to have existed at this early date.[4] Although after the destruction of the Temple some Jews may have tried to continue the sacrifice at other locations, the majority, including Jewish Christians, had to adapt to a festival that no longer included either the sacrifice or the eating of a lamb. The focus now fell on a meal that developed other highly symbolic overtones, which were sharply different for Christians than for Jews who were not Christians.[5] So

---

2 Among early proponents of this view, see Bernhard Lohse, *Das Passafest der Quartadecimaner* (Gütersloh: Bertelsmann 1953); Joachim Jeremias, *The Eucharistic Words of Jesus* (London: SCM Press 1966), pp. 122–3.

3 See below, pp. 49–51.

4 See Joshua Kulp, 'The Origins of the Seder and Haggadah', *Currents in Biblical Research* 4 (2005), pp. 109–34, esp. pp. 112–13 and the scholars cited there.

5 For the Jewish development of the feast, and especially how it may have been influenced by what Christians were doing, see Joseph Tabory, 'Towards a History of the Paschal Meal', and Israel J. Yuval, 'Easter and Passover as Early Jewish-Christian Dialogue' in Paul F. Bradshaw and Lawrence A. Hoffman (eds), *Passover and Easter: Origin and History to Modern Times* (Notre Dame: University of Notre Dame Press 1999), pp. 62–80, 98–124; but cf. the critical comments by Kulp, 'The Origins of the Seder and Haggadah', pp. 119–25.

how did the Quartodeciman Christians celebrate their version of the feast?

Their Pascha is known to us from several sources, but until the twentieth century information from which to reconstruct it was limited almost entirely to the original documents cited by the fourth-century church historian Eusebius when he was recording the dispute that broke out around 195 between the Quartodecimans and those churches which were by then keeping Easter on Sunday, as to which of them was correct.[6] In this dispute, in order to demonstrate the antiquity of the Quartodeciman practice, the Asian bishops, led by Polycrates, listed a number of their predecessors reaching back to Apostolic times who, they claimed, celebrated Pascha on 14 Nisan. Beyond that, however, little can be learned from here about the nature of the celebration. Subsequently, however, more texts have come to light.

First, there is the *Epistula Apostolorum*, a second-century document now extant only in Coptic and Ethiopic translations, but based on a missing Greek original. Once thought by some to be of Egyptian origin, there is now general agreement that it comes from Syria or Asia and makes a brief reference to a Quartodeciman celebration, although this is not explicitly stated.[7] In the Coptic version Jesus instructs the apostles to 'remember my death. Now when the Passover [Pascha] comes, one of you will be thrown into prison . . .' Jesus will release him and 'he will spend a night of watching with [you] and stay with you until the cock crows. But when you have completed the memorial that is for me and my *agape*, he will again be thrown into prison . . .'[8] Although some commentators have assumed that the 'memorial' and the *agape* meal were two separate events here rather than two ways of speaking about the same event – the Easter Eucharist/*agape* celebrated in remembrance of Jesus – that is not the most natural interpretation of the text. Because the term 'Eucharist' came to be used to refer to what was consumed

---

6 Eusebius, *Historia ecclesiastica* 5.23–5; ET in Cantalamessa, pp. 33–7.
7 See C. Hill, 'The *Epistula Apostolorum*: An Asian Tract from the Time of Polycarp', *JECS* 7 (1999), pp. 1–53. The attempt by Karl Gerlach, *The Antenicene Pascha: A Rhetorical History*, Liturgia condenda 7 (Louvain: Peeters 1998), pp. 97–8, to argue that it refers to a Sunday celebration rather than a Quartodeciman one is rejected as unconvincing by Gerard Rouwhorst, 'Liturgy on the Authority of the Apostles' in Anthony Hilhorst (ed.), *The Apostolic Age in Patristic Thought* (Leiden: Brill 2004), pp. 63–85, here at p. 69, n. 14.
8 ET from Cantalamessa, p. 38.

rather than to the rite itself, other names, including *agape*, were more often used to denote the eucharistic meal.[9]

It has also been commonly supposed that the watch or vigil lasted until cockcrow and then the celebration began, but once again, especially if the Ethiopic version is a reliable guide to the original, it appears more likely that the celebration *ended* at cockcrow[10] (although it has to be admitted that some later sources do speak of an Easter celebration beginning then[11]). Some confirmation of this timing is provided by a Syrian text entitled *Diataxis*, a fragment of which was known to Epiphanius of Salamis in the fourth century and cited by him.[12] This directs that, while the Jews eat their Passover meal (which would have begun at sunset), Christians are to 'be fasting and mourning for them, because they crucified the Christ on the day of the festival, and when they mourn by eating unleavened bread with bitter herbs, you should feast'. Thus the Christians would have begun their celebration when the Jewish one ended, which would have been by midnight if the rule given in the Mishnah (*Pesahim* 10.9) were operative.[13] Although Jews did not view the Week of Unleavened Bread, which began after the Passover meal, as a time of mourning, it seems that the Christians had developed the idea that it was, in order to create a parallelism between the two activities.

Also according to the same passage in the Mishnah, Jews were to fast from the time of the evening sacrifice (*c.* 3 p.m.) onwards in order to be better prepared to eat the Passover meal. This would in effect mean not eating after breakfast until the evening meal, as normal practice in the ancient world was to eat only two meals a day, breakfast and dinner in the late afternoon. The Christians no doubt continued this same custom with regard to their paschal fast, but came to extend it later into

---

9 On the identity between Eucharist and *agape* in early Christianity, see Andrew B. McGowan, 'Naming the Feast: *Agape* and the Diversity of Early Christian Meals', *SP* 30 (1997), pp. 314–18.

10 Variants in the Ethiopic version include 'celebrate the remembrance of my death, which is the Pascha . . . ; and 'when you complete my *agape* and my memorial at the crowing of the cock . . .'. ET in Wilhelm Schneemelcher (ed.), *New Testament Apocrypha* 1 (2nd edn, Cambridge: James Clarke & Co./Louisville: Westminster John Knox Press 1991–2), pp. 249–84, here at p. 258.

11 See below, pp. 56–7.

12 Epiphanius, *Panarion* 70.11.3; ET in Cantalamessa, p. 82. See also Rouwhorst, 'Liturgy on the Authority of the Apostles', pp. 81–4.

13 See Gerard Rouwhorst, 'The Quartodeciman Passover and the Jewish Pesach', *QL* 77 (1996), pp. 152–73, here at pp. 163–4.

the evening in order to distinguish themselves from other Jews and kept a vigil together during those extended hours. Alistair Stewart-Sykes, modifying a theory put forward by Cyril Richardson, has suggested that the mid-second-century dispute at Laodicea between two groups of Quartodecimans may have been a disagreement over whether the Christian meal was to be postponed to this later hour or eaten at the same time as the Jews.[14]

Although the *Didascalia Apostolorum* is not itself a Quartodeciman text, an older Quartodeciman layer that subsequently has been reworked to fit a Sunday Pascha appears to underlie part of it, and this too indicates that the Christians were to fast and keep vigil while the Jews ate their Passover.[15] According to the *Didascalia*, the purpose of this pre-paschal fast, which is also mentioned by Eusebius and Ephrem the Syrian,[16] was to be a sign of mourning for the death of Jesus and a time of intercession for the Jews.[17] Gerard Rouwhorst believes that both these explanations for the fast were not peculiar to this source but were shared more generally by Quartodecimans, although the intercession may have functioned more as prayer *against* the Jews than *for their conversion* in other Quartodeciman circles, because other sources from that tradition, like early Christian literature in general, are marked by a strongly anti-Jewish tone.[18] Stewart-Sykes notes that the anonymous sermon *In Sanctum Pascha*, once erroneously attributed to Hippolytus of Rome, hints that the fasting is intended as preparation for the paschal Eucharist, and plausibly suggests that this may be a pointer to the original basis for the practice.[19] The motivations given in other sources are probably therefore subsequent rationalizations.

Two other important sources that shed some light on Quartodeciman practices are the *Peri Pascha* of Melito of Sardis, usually dated

---

14 Alistair Stewart-Sykes, *The Lamb's High Feast: Melito,* Peri Pascha *and the Quartodeciman Paschal Liturgy at Sardis* (Leiden: Brill 1998), pp. 155–60, 169–72; Cyril Richardson, 'A New Solution to the Quartodeciman Riddle', *Journal of Theological Studies* 24 (1973), pp. 74–84. See Eusebius, *Historia ecclesiastica* 4.26.3; ET in Cantalamessa, p. 46.

15 *Didascalia Apostolorum* 5.20.10; ET in Cantalamessa, p. 83.

16 Eusebius, *Historia ecclesiastica* 5.23–4 (see also below, p. 52); Ephrem, *De ieiunio* 5.

17 *Didascalia Apostolorum* 5.13–14, 19.2–3; ET in Sebastian Brock and Michael Vasey (eds), *The Liturgical Portions of the Didascalia*, Grove Liturgical Study 29 (Nottingham: Grove Books 1982), pp. 26, 28.

18 See Rouwhorst, 'The Quartodeciman Passover and the Jewish Pesach', pp. 161, 168–9.

19 *In Sanctum Pascha* 32; Stewart-Sykes, *The Lamb's High Feast*, p. 162.

c. 165 and regarded as a homily delivered during the paschal celebration, and *In Sanctum Pascha*, referred to above, which shows
considerable affinity to Melito's work, especially with regard to its
paschal theology, even though it does not explicitly profess to be of
Quartodeciman origin.[20] Because both of these are largely devoted to a
typological explanation of Exodus 12, and Melito actually begins by
stating that this passage has just been read, we would probably be
justified in seeing it as having been a regular reading during the vigil
that preceded the Easter Eucharist. This seems to have been a uniquely
Christian innovation, as its reading did not form part of the Jewish
Passover but simply the telling of the story of the exodus.[21] None of our
sources give any indication of what other readings might have been
included at this early date, and Rouwhorst's suggestion that the Passion
narrative was one of them is simply speculative, although he may be
right when he proposed that hymns and prayers might also have helped
fill out the vigil.[22]

The typological interpretation that is found in these two works as
well as in the *Twelfth Demonstration* of Aphraates and the *Paschal Hymns*
of Ephrem (both dating from the early fourth century) understands the
Passover lamb as prefiguring Christ's crucifixion and the exodus as fore-
shadowing Christ's liberation of humanity. The image of Christ as the
Passover lamb is found in 1 Corinthians 5.7[23] and also underlies John's
Gospel. There Jesus is identified as 'the Lamb of God' near the
beginning (John 1.36) and then is said to have died on the cross on the
day of the preparation of the Passover (i.e., 14 Nisan) at the hour when
the lambs for the feast were being slaughtered (John 19.14ff.). In

---

20 Texts in Alistair Stewart-Sykes, *Melito of Sardis: On Pascha* (Crestwood, NY: St
Vladimir's Seminary Press 2001); and Pierre Nautin (ed.), *Homélies pascales I*, Sources
chrétiennes 27 (Paris 1950). See also Rouwhorst, 'The Quartodeciman Passover and the
Jewish Pesach', pp. 156–7; Stewart-Sykes, *The Lamb's High Feast*, who argues that
Melito's work is a Haggadah rather than a homily; and for critical views, Lynne H.
Cohick, *The Peri Pascha Attributed to Melito of Sardis* (Providence, RI: Brown Judaic
Studies 2000); Clemens Leonhard, *The Jewish Pesach and the Origins of the Christian
Easter* (Berlin/New York: de Gruyter 2006), pp. 42–55.
21 See Rouwhorst, 'The Quartodeciman Passover and the Jewish Pesach', p. 172 and
n. 94.
22 Rouwhorst, 'The Quartodeciman Passover and the Jewish Pesach', pp. 162–3.
Stewart-Sykes, *The Lamb's High Feast*, p. 176, doubts that the Passion narrative was read
during the vigil 'since this concerns the fulfilment of the paschal hope'.
23 See Gerlach, *The Antenicene Pascha*, pp. 32–9, for discussion of whether or not this
verse implies the existence of a Christian Passover celebration.

addition, the soldiers are said to have refrained from breaking the legs of the dead Jesus and so fulfilled the Scripture requiring that no bone of the Passover lamb be broken (John 19.32–36; cf. Exod. 12.46; Num. 9.12). Although the central emphasis of the Quartodeciman celebration thus fell on remembrance of the death of Christ rather than his resurrection – and indeed the Quartodecimans even claimed that Pascha (which in reality is simply a transliteration of the Aramaic form of the Hebrew *pesach*) was derived from the Greek verb *pathein*, 'to suffer'[24] – it was not on Christ's Passion in isolation but rather on that event in the context of the whole redemptive act, from his Incarnation to his glorification: 'This is the one made flesh in the virgin, who was hanged on a tree, who was buried in the earth, who was raised from the dead, who was exalted to the heights of heaven.'[25] Rouwhorst, however, disputes the common view that the Quartodeciman celebration also had a strongly eschatological character. He does not deny that, especially in its earliest phase, expectation of the *parousia* may have featured in the vigil and eucharistic meal, but he argues that, if so, it must have lost this quite quickly as it has left no trace in the written sources.[26]

Finally, we may pay attention to one other second-century text that may possibly embody traces of a Quartodeciman tradition and certainly shows some commonality with Melito's *Peri Pascha*.[27] The fragmentary *Gospel of Peter* states that the disciples fasted and grieved from the time that Christ died 'until the Sabbath' (27). As the Sabbath began at nightfall that day, this would mean for only three hours. If the phrase were understood as denoting 'up to and including the Sabbath',[28] the period would be longer, but that interpretation has been dismissed by Rouwhorst on the grounds that the Greek preposition cannot support it.[29] He points to

---

24 See Melito of Sardis, *Peri Pascha* 46; ET in Cantalamessa, p. 43.

25 Melito, *Peri Pascha* 70; ET from Stewart-Sykes, *Melito of Sardis: On Pascha*, p. 56. See also Rouwhorst, 'The Quartodeciman Passover and the Jewish Pesach', pp. 164–6.

26 Rouwhorst, 'The Quartodeciman Passover and the Jewish Pesach', pp. 166–8; Gerard Rouwhorst, 'How Eschatological was Early Christian Liturgy?', *SP* 40 (2006), pp. 93–108, here at pp. 96–103. For a contrary view, see Stewart-Sykes, *The Lamb's High Feast*, pp. 182–6. The earliest Christian sources to affirm unambiguously that the vigil was kept in expectation of the return of Christ belong to the fourth century: Lactantius, *Divinae institutiones* 7.19.3; Jerome, *Commentarium in Matt.* 4; ET in Cantalamessa, pp. 94, 99.

27 See Othmar Perler, 'L'évangile de Pierre et Méliton de Sardes', *Revue biblique* 71 (1964), pp. 584–90.

28 As does Raymond E. Brown, *The Death of the Messiah* (London: Chapman/New York: Doubleday 1994), pp. 1340f.

29 Rouwhorst, 'Liturgy on the Authority of the Apostles', pp. 70–1.

another passage in *Gospel of Peter* 58–9, after the empty tomb has been discovered, when the disciples are said to be still fasting and grieving on the
'last day of the Unleavened Bread'. As the Week of Unleavened Bread
would have begun on the day on which Jesus died, this would have meant
the Friday one week later, with the disciples ending their fast at the
beginning of the Sabbath that evening.[30] However, this would conflict
with the canonical accounts of the resurrection known to the author of the
Gospel of Peter, and hence Rouwhorst suggests that the key to the problem
is to be found in those later Syrian sources that designate the week
preceding Pascha – essentially a week of fasting and grieving for Christians
– as the 'Week of Unleavened Bread'. He believes that the original practice
would have been for the Week of Unleavened Bread to be kept as a fast by
the Christians of that region at the same time as other Jews were celebrating it, beginning immediately after the Quartodeciman Pascha. It would
then have moved to Holy Week when Pascha was later transferred to
Sunday.[31] Rouwhorst's argument has, however, been rejected by Leonhard,
who argues that the work does not presuppose a Quartodeciman Pascha or
provide evidence for the existence of a post-Pascha week of fasting.[32]

   This is all we can learn about the content of the Quartodeciman celebration, but a word needs to be said about exactly when it took place.
The determination of the correct date for the celebration of the Passover
each year was a difficult enough matter for Jewish Diaspora communities. Strictly speaking, they depended upon the sighting of the new
moon in Jerusalem, which occurred on average every 29½ days, making
each new month either the thirtieth or thirty-first day after the old one.
By the time that Passover arrived, two weeks later, communities far from
Jerusalem would still not know which of the two days had been declared
the new moon. Sometimes, too, the decision to insert an extra month
into the Jewish year might be made so late that very distant Diaspora
communities would not know about it in time, and so would celebrate
their Passover a month early.[33] Having the date of Easter dependent
upon the determination of the Passover presented an even greater

---

30 A solution also proposed by Gerlach, *The Antenicene Pascha*, pp. 192–3, and by
J. Dominic Crossan, *The Cross that Spoke* (San Francisco: Harper & Row 1988), p. 25.
31 Rouwhorst, 'Liturgy on the Authority of the Apostles', pp. 70–1.
32 Leonhard, *The Jewish Pesach and the Origins of the Christian Easter*, pp. 224–9.
33 See T. C. G. Thornton, 'Problematical Passovers. Difficulties for Diaspora Jews and
Early Christians in Determining Passover Dates during the First Three Centuries A.D.',
SP 20 (1989), pp. 402–8.

problem for early Christians. While some seemingly felt no embarrass-
ment in having to ask their Jewish neighbours when they should
celebrate their festival, others found this demeaning and so sought alternative solutions, in particular the compilation of their own paschal
tables.[34]

Even the Quartodecimans, though supposedly tied to 14 Nisan, were
not immune to this difficulty, and thus in both Asia Minor and Cappadocia we find some communities attempting to solve the problem by
adapting the observance to their local calendar rather than persevering
with ascertaining the Jewish date each year. Those in Asia assigned the
celebration to the fourteenth day of Artemisios, the first month of
spring in their calendar, which was the equivalent of 6 April in our own
reckoning of the year,[35] and those in Cappadocia to the fourteenth day
of Teireix, their first month of spring and the equivalent of 25 March.[36]

The Quartodeciman sources not only reveal the wide geographical
area in which a Quartodeciman celebration originally flourished, but by
the dates of their composition also indicate the time after which it began
to decline and to be superseded by a celebration held in the night
between Holy Saturday and Easter Day. In Asia this happened in the
first part of the third century, while in the Syriac-speaking regions the
practice continued to exist for another century until the Council of
Nicaea in 325 legislated that all Christians should keep the feast on the
Sunday. Although this met with some opposition, the number of
churches persisting in following the old date after the middle of the
fourth century was very small indeed.[37]

---

34 See below, pp. 57–9.
35 Thomas Talley, *The Origins of the Liturgical Year* (New York: Pueblo 1986; 2nd edn,
Collegeville, The Liturgical Press 1991), pp. 7–9; also Thomas Talley, 'Afterthoughts on
The Origins of the Liturgical Year' in Sean Gallagher *et al.* (eds), *Western Plainchant in the
First Millennium* (Aldershot: Ashgate 2003), pp. 1–10, here at pp. 2–3.
36 Thomas J. Talley, 'Further Light on the Quartodeciman Pascha and the Date of the
Annunciation', *SL* 33 (2003), pp. 151–8, here at pp. 155–6.
37 See Rouwhorst, 'The Quartodeciman Passover and the Jewish Pesach', p. 157; and
for the Council of Nicaea, below, p. 59.

Chapter 6

The date of the festival

It is not difficult to understand why leaders of communities of early Christians that did not at first observe an annual commemoration of the death and resurrection of Christ might have desired to adopt the practice that they saw among the Quartodecimans. Nor is it hard to appreciate why they would have preferred to locate this innovation on the Sunday immediately following the Passover rather than on the actual feast itself: as Sunday was already the occasion of their regular weekly celebration of the paschal mystery, it would obviously be easier to develop that existing liturgical day than to persuade congregations to embrace a completely new event, and one that was associated with Jewish practice, from which many churches were then trying to distance themselves.

Although the existence of this Sunday celebration is only first explicitly recorded in the sources cited by Eusebius in connection with the paschal controversy in the late second century, several scholars have continued to defend the position that it was at least as ancient as the Quartodeciman observance.[1] Eusebius himself claimed that it was 'in accordance with Apostolic tradition', but it should be noted that this was simply his own opinion (though also shared by fifth-century church historians) and not part of the older sources that he quotes.[2] Those

---

1 These include Bernard Lohse, *Das Passafest der Quartadecimaner* (Gütersloh: Bertelsmann 1953), pp. 113–18; J. van Goudoever, *Biblical Calendars* (Leiden: Brill 1961), pp. 124–9, 164–75; Willy Rordorf, 'Zum Ursprung des Osterfestes am Sonntag', *Theologische Zeitschrift* 18 (1962), pp. 167–89; Cantalamessa, pp. 10–11; and most recently, Karl Gerlach, *The Antenicene Pascha: A Rhetorical History*, Liturgia condenda 7 (Louvain, Peeters 1998), p. 407.

2 Eusebius, *Historia ecclesiastica* 5.23.1; see also 5.25.1; ET in Cantalamessa, pp. 33, 37. Similar claims are made by Socrates, *Historia ecclesiastica* 5.22; Sozomen, *Historia ecclesiastica* 7.19.1.

sources merely show that it had become a widespread custom by the second half of the second century and make no claim as to its greater antiquity. There were in existence, Eusebius said, letters of various synods of bishops held at the time:

> from those who were then assembled in Palestine under the presidency of Theophilus, bishop of the diocese of Cæsarea, and Narcissus, of that of Jerusalem; likewise from those at Rome, another [letter] bearing the name of Bishop Victor, about the same question; and one from the bishops of Pontus under the presidency of Palmas, since he was the eldest; and one from the dioceses of Gaul which were under Irenæus' supervision. Furthermore, [a letter] from those of Osrhoene [= Edessa] and the cities of that region, and personal [letters] from Bacchylus, bishop of the church of the Corinthians, and from very many more, who expressed one and the same opinion and judgment and voted the same way.

Their unanimous verdict was 'that the mystery of the Lord's resurrection from the dead should never be celebrated on any other day than the Lord's day, and that on that day alone should we observe the close of the paschal fasting' – Eusebius' words, it should be noted, and not a quotation from an original document. However, he does reproduce an extract from the statement agreed at the synod of Palestinian bishops (*c.* 180) mentioned in the quotation above, in which those bishops assert that the church of Alexandria also observed the feast on Sunday and that letters were regularly exchanged between themselves and that church so that they were in agreement on the date each year.[3] Nevertheless, the very fact that it was necessary for the question to be so extensively debated at that time is itself evidence for how widely established was the opposing Quartodeciman tradition.

An important consideration with regard to the antiquity of the Sunday celebration of Easter is the date when Christians first began to observe the weekly Lord's day, as they could not have chosen that occasion for their annual feast before Sunday had become established as a regular weekly occasion for worship. As we have noted earlier in this book,[4] there is no firm evidence for that to have happened before the end of the first century. If this was the case, then the Quartodeciman

---

3 Eusebius, *Historia ecclesiastica* 5.23.3; 23.2; 25.1; ET from Cantalamessa, pp. 34, 37.
4 Above, pp. 7–9.

practice does appear to have preceded it by a considerable period of time.

Some scholars would date the emergence of the Sunday Pascha much later still, on the basis of the language used in the paschal controversy at the end of the second century. Eusebius records that Victor of Rome attempted to excommunicate all the churches that were persisting in the Quartodeciman observance, but other bishops disagreed with his action and wanted to maintain peace and unity. Irenaeus then wrote on behalf of the bishops of Gaul. While concurring that the Sunday celebration was the only right practice, he urged Victor not to excommunicate the others for observing another ancient custom, because

> such variation in the observance did not begin in our own time but much earlier, in our forefathers' time. Incorrectly, as it would seem, they kept up an ignorant custom of their own that they had made for posterity. And nonetheless, they were all at peace . . . In their number were the presbyters before Soter, who headed the church of which you are now the leader – namely, Anicetus and Pius, Hyginus and Telephorus, and Xystus. They themselves did not observe, nor did they permit those with them to do so, and in spite of the fact that they were not observant, they were at peace with those who came to them from the dioceses in which it was observed.[5]

Crucial to the interpretation of this passage is the meaning to be given to the verb 'observe' (τηρεῖν) in this context. The traditional opinion, still maintained by a number of scholars today, is that it should be understood as 'observe 14 Nisan',[6] but others have argued that it actually means 'observe Pascha', that is, that those who did not 'observe' did not keep Pascha at all.[7] If so, that would mean that before the time of Bishop Soter, that is, before about 165, no annual Easter observance at Rome existed on either day. Yet even these scholars are prepared to admit that the Sunday observance might well have been adopted a little earlier than this in some other churches, especially those of Alexandria

---

5 Eusebius, *Historia ecclesiastica* 5.24.9–14; ET from Cantalamessa, pp. 35–6.

6 In addition to the scholars already cited above in n. 1, see also Christine Mohrmann, 'Le conflit pascal au IIe siècle: note philologique', *VC* 16 (1962), pp. 154–71; Gerard Rouwhorst, 'The Quartodeciman Passover and the Jewish Pesach', *QL* 77 (1996), p. 158, n. 42.

7 See for example Karl Holl, *Gesammelte Aufsätze zur Kirchengeschichte II: Der Osten* (Tübingen: Mohr 1928), pp. 204–24; Wolfgang Huber, *Passa und Ostern* (Berlin:

and Jerusalem. If the claim by Epiphanius can be trusted, that the controversy over the paschal date began after the bishops of Jerusalem were no longer 'of the circumcision', that would make it around 132. At that time, following the Bar Kochba revolt, Jews (and Jewish Christians) were expelled from the city and the leadership of the Jerusalem church passed into the hands of Gentiles. They would no doubt have wanted to distance that church from Judaism and so very likely could have been the ones to introduce for the first time then a Sunday Pascha in place of the Quartodeciman observance, a development that was subsequently imitated elsewhere.[8]

The theory that the Sunday celebration was derived from the Quartodeciman one, whenever it was that the latter came into existence, helps to explain several otherwise somewhat puzzling features of the general early Christian observance of Easter, not the least of which is the meaning that was given to it. For, not only in Quartodeciman circles but also at first among those who kept the feast on Sunday, the original focus of the celebration was not on the resurrection of Christ, as one might have expected if it had always been associated with the Sunday, but on his death. Thus, for example, Irenaeus in Gaul in the late second century says:

> The passages in which Moses reveals the Son of God are innumerable. He was aware even of the day of his passion: he foretold it figuratively by calling it Pascha. And on the very day which Moses had foretold so long before, the Lord suffered in fulfilment of the Pascha.[9]

Töpelmann 1969), pp. 45ff.; Marcel Richard, 'La question pascale au IIe siècle', *L'Orient syrien* 6 (1961), pp. 179–212; Thomas J. Talley, *The Origins of the Liturgical Year* (New York: Pueblo 1986; 2nd edn, Collegeville: The Liturgical Press 1991), pp. 13–27. Talley (pp. 6–7) attempts to claim that the *Epistula Apostolorum* contains an explicit defence of the Quartodeciman Pascha against Christians who did not celebrate Pascha at all; but Gerard Rouwhorst, 'Liturgy on the Authority of the Apostles' in Anthony Hilhorst (ed.), *The Apostolic Age in Patristic Thought* (Leiden: Brill 2004), pp. 69–70, n. 15, thinks that this is speculative. See also Alistair Stewart-Sykes, *The Lamb's High Feast: Melito, Peri Pascha and the Quartodeciman Paschal Liturgy at Sardis* (Leiden: Brill 1998), p. 205, n. 288.
8 Epiphanius, *Panarion* 70.9; see Holl, *Gesammelte Aufsätze zur Kirchengeschichte II*, pp. 215ff.; Talley, *The Origins of the Liturgical Year*, pp. 24–5.
9 Irenaeus, *Adversus haereses* 4.10.1; ET from Cantalamessa, p. 50. See also Rouwhorst, 'The Quartodeciman Passover and the Jewish Pesach', p. 159.

While this seems a perfectly natural orientation for a feast originally situated on the Jewish Passover to have taken, it appears to be a less obvious path for the Sunday celebration, if it were not originally derived from the Quartodeciman custom.

A second feature that seems to suggest that the Sunday Pascha derives from an older Quartodeciman observance is the apparent universality of fasting on Holy Saturday. As we saw earlier in the book when discussing signs of the continuing influence of the Sabbath on early Christianity,[10] many churches refused to allow any fasting to take place on a Saturday, except for the one Saturday in the year that preceded Easter. It is easier to see how this major departure from the norm could have come into existence if there were already a well-established tradition of fasting during the day on 14 Nisan in preparation for the Quartodeciman celebration that night: when Pascha was moved to the Sunday, the fast day would have accompanied it and displaced the usual prohibition with regard to that day. This in turn helps to explain the remark by Irenaeus in his letter to Victor concerning the paschal controversy, that the disagreement did not merely concern the day of Pascha but also the length of the preparatory fast.

> For some think it necessary to fast for one day, others two, others even more days; and others measure their day as lasting forty hours, day and night. And such variation in the observance did not begin in our time but much earlier, in our forefathers' time.[11]

Those who fasted for one day would be the Quartodecimans; those fasting for two days would be some of those observing Sunday as Pascha, because the Saturday fast would then have been preceded by the normal weekly Friday fast;[12] and those fasting for 40 hours would have joined those two days together in a continuous fast from Friday morning to Saturday night, without breaking it for a meal on Friday evening. This is also the first reference to the development among some of a regime of fasting for 'even more days' in preparation for the feast, a

---

10 See pp. 17–20.

11 Eusebius, *Historia ecclesiastica* 5.24.12–13; ET from Cantalamessa, p. 36.

12 For the regular Friday fast, see above, pp. 29–34. In the *Apostolic Tradition* attributed to Hippolytus the normal pre-paschal fast is said to be two days, but as a concession, those who are sick (or pregnant?) may limit their fast to the Sabbath alone (33.1–2); see Paul F. Bradshaw, Maxwell E. Johnson and L. Edward Phillips, *The Apostolic Tradition: A Commentary* (Minneapolis: Fortress Press 2002), pp. 172–5.

practice that seems also to have been known to Tertullian and becomes increasingly common in later sources.[13] It may possibly owe its origin to the transfer of an original period of fasting by Quartodecimans during the Week of Unleavened Bread after Pascha, which may be alluded to in the *Gospel of Peter*, to a week of fasting before Pascha when that feast came to be celebrated on a Sunday and followed by the 50 festal days of Pentecost.[14] However, a six-day fast from Monday until the end of the Saturday night vigil is first explicitly mentioned in the third century by Dionysius of Alexandria and by the Syrian *Didascalia Apostolorum*.

Dionysius, in a letter written about the middle of the century, indicates that he was aware of a variety of practices, some people fasting for the full six days, others for two, three, or four days, and some none at all, but he appears to imply that either six days or just the Friday and Saturday were more usual. In the same passage he deals with what was obviously a related topic – when the fast and vigil should end so that eating could begin. Again there was variety. While noting that the church at Rome waited until the hour of cockcrow to end the paschal fast, a practice he described as 'generous and painstaking', he acknowledged the existence of two other customs: some finished before midnight, and these he censured as 'remiss and wanting in self-restraint', and others stopped between those two points, and these he said should not be treated 'altogether severely'. Although he disapproves of the former, they may not in fact have been merely lax but possibly a remnant still keeping to the original Jewish time of the Passover meal, and those in between seem to be in line with what had been the more usual Quartodeciman custom.[15] What is particularly interesting is that Dionysius links the question to the time of Christ's resurrection because, he says, there was general agreement that one ought not to start the feast until after that, even though the canonical Gospels fail to specify a precise hour at which it happened.[16] This is a clear indication

13 Although in *De ieiunio* 2.2 (ET in Cantalamessa, p. 92) Tertullian asserts that his Catholic opponents regard the Friday and Saturday of the Pascha as the only legitimate days for fasting, later in the same work (13.1) he implies that they actually fast for more days, contrary to their professed principles.

14 See above, p. 46, and for Pentecost, below, pp. 69–74.

15 For the possibility of the existence a tradition of eating at the same time as the Jews, see Stewart-Sykes' view of the Laodicean dispute, above, p. 43; and for the more usual Quartodeciman practice, above, p. 42.

16 *Epistula ad Basilidem* 1; ET in Cantalamessa, pp. 60–1. Athanasius in the fourth century interprets the six days as a recapitulation of the six days of creation: *Epistulae Festales* 1; ET in Cantalamessa, p. 70.

that, as a natural consequence of the transfer of the celebration of Pascha to Sunday, its primary focus had begun to shift from the Passion to the resurrection. Tertullian provides an even earlier indication of this trend in North Africa when he states that the Catholics there had begun to understand the reason for the Friday and Saturday fast to be because it was the time 'when the bridegroom is taken away' (Mark 2.20; Luke 5.35).[17]

It has already been remarked earlier that, underlying part of *Didascalia Apostolorum*, appear to be prescriptions for a Quartodeciman observance. These have been re-worked by one or more later hands (how many is a matter of scholarly dispute) to accommodate a Sunday Pascha, resulting in a complex and somewhat confusing appearance, including an idiosyncratic chronology for the final week of the life of Jesus. Rouwhorst has argued that this section of the church order did not reach its final state until the fourth century and not the third as most others have supposed.[18] He also claims that because the text makes such a strong appeal to the example of the apostles in order to justify both a full week of fasting and also the Friday–Saturday fast, both of these fasts must have been innovations and were here being defended against Quartodecimans who practised neither of these customs.[19] Thus as it now stands, the church order attempts to find a basis for the six-day fast by asserting that Judas was paid for his betrayal 'on the tenth day of the month, on the second day of the week', and so it was as though Jesus had already been seized on that day, in fulfilment of the requirement in Exodus 12.3 and 6 to take a lamb on the tenth day of the month and keep it until the fourteenth. It then continues:

> Therefore you shall fast in the days of the Pascha from the tenth, which is the second day of the week; and you shall sustain yourselves with bread and salt and water only, at the ninth hour, until the fifth day of the week. But on the Friday and on the Sabbath fast wholly,

17 *De ieiunio* 2.2 and 13.1. Tertullian also speaks of the Easter vigil lasting 'the whole night' (until cockcrow?) in *Ad uxorem* 2.4.2, as does Lactantius at the beginning of the fourth century, referring to 'watching until morning' in *Divinarum institutionum* 7.19.3; ET in Cantalamessa, pp. 91, 94.

18 Gerard Rouwhorst, *Les Hymnes pascales d'Ephrem de Nisibe* 1 (Leiden: Brill 1989), pp. 157–90. A fourth-century date is also supported by Alistair Stewart-Sykes, *The Didascalia Apostolorum: An English Version with Introduction and Annotation* (Turnhout: Brepols 2009), pp. 49–55.

19 Rouwhorst, 'Liturgy on the Authority of the Apostles', pp. 77–9.

and taste nothing. You shall come together and watch and keep vigil all the night with prayers and intercessions, and with reading of the Prophets, and with the gospel and with psalms, with fear and trembling and with earnest supplication, until the third hour in the night after the Sabbath; and then break your fasts . . .[20]

This passage is interesting in several respects. First, the biblical prescriptions about the timing of the Passover have been adapted to fit a quite different chronology from the original Quartodeciman one. Obviously in most years the 'second day of the week' and the actual 'tenth day of the month' cannot have coincided, but the author expects the readers to understand the Monday of the paschal week as being the symbolical equivalent of the tenth day.

Second, although six days of fasting are prescribed, a distinction is still maintained between the older two-day fast and the other days of the week: bread, salt and water are permitted after the ninth hour on Monday through Thursday, but nothing at all on the last two days. The particular importance of these final days is also emphasized a little later in the text, where the above prescriptions are reiterated:

Especially incumbent on you therefore is the fast of the Friday and the Sabbath; and likewise the vigil and watching of the Sabbath, and the reading of the Scriptures, and psalms, and prayer and intercession for them that have sinned, and the expectation and hope of the resurrection of our Lord Jesus, until the third hour in the night after the Sabbath. And then offer your oblations; and thereafter eat and make good cheer, and rejoice and be glad, because that earnest of our resurrection, Christ, is risen . . .[21]

Third, as this second extract makes clear, the Saturday night celebration is becoming focused on the resurrection rather than of the death of Christ or of the whole paschal mystery, a development already noted in Dionysius' letter, and so Friday and Saturday in turn become memorials of Christ's death and burial (although apparently not yet marked by any particular liturgical provisions), as the *Didascalia* goes on to say: 'Fast then on the Friday, because on that day the People killed themselves in crucifying our Saviour; and on the Sabbath as well, because it is the

20 *Didascalia Apostolorum* 5.18–19.1; ET from Cantalamessa, p. 83.
21 *Didascalia Apostolorum* 5.19.6–7; ET from Cantalamessa, p. 83.

sleep of the Lord, for it is a day which ought especially to be kept with fasting . . .'[22]

Fourth, because the term Pascha is still understood to refer to the Passion of Christ, it is used to denote the period of the memorial of Christ's suffering and death. Thus, in the first extract, 'the days of the Pascha' correspond to the week of fasting and therefore *end* at what later Christians would call Easter Day. Tertullian too in North Africa uses the expression *die Paschae* in the singular with reference to a day when there was general fasting (and the kiss of peace was omitted) and presumably therefore to the Saturday,[23] whereas Cyprian half a century later appears to have begun to use the word to denote the Sunday itself.[24]

Finally, the fast concludes at 'the third hour in the night after the Sabbath'. Several commentators have assumed that the day is being counted as beginning at midnight here,[25] and so the third hour would have been around 3 a.m., the equivalent of cockcrow commended by Dionysius. However, Rouwhorst has insisted that the Jewish reckoning of the day was being followed in this text, and therefore around 9 p.m. is meant.[26] Whichever method was intended, it would have necessitated continuing the fast into what was thought of as the beginning of Sunday, something that was normally not allowed, and so the text goes on to permit an exception to that rule.[27] The compiler also manages to calculate that Jesus fulfilled the saying in Matthew 12.40 that 'the Son of Man will be three days and three nights in the heart of the earth' by counting the time from the sixth to the ninth hour on Friday as the first day and the three hours of darkness that followed as the first night, the time from the ninth to the twelfth hour and the night of the Sabbath as the second day and night, and the Sabbath day and the three hours of the following night as the third.[28]

---

22 *Didascalia Apostolorum* 5.19.9–10; ET from Sebastian Brock and Michael Vasey (eds), *The Liturgical Portions of the Didascalia*, Grove Liturgical Study 20 (Nottingham: Grove Books 1982), p. 28.

23 Tertullian, *De oratione* 18.7. Cantalamessa, p. 90, understands the expression to refer to Good Friday, but this seems less likely. Elsewhere (*De ieiunio* 13.1) Tertullian uses the word Pascha to cover the fast days of both Friday and Saturday.

24 See Cyprian, *Epistulae* 21.2; 41.1 and 7; 56.3.

25 See, for example, Cantalamessa, p. 182, note f.

26 Rouwhorst, *Les Hymnes pascales d'Ephrem de Nisibe* 1, pp. 173–80.

27 *Didascalia* 5.20.12; ET in Cantalamessa, pp. 83–4.

28 *Didascalia* 5.14; ET in Brock and Vasey, *The Liturgical Portions of the Didascalia*, p. 26.

Variation in the hour of the celebration that we can observe in these sources persisted into the fourth and fifth centuries. Although the early conclusion of the vigil that we find in the *Didascalia* (if Rouwhorst's interpretation is correct) does seem to have faded away – perhaps because it could not be reconciled with the presumed hour of Christ's resurrection, especially if communities had begun to reckon the day beginning at midnight – some churches continued to adhere to cockcrow, while others concluded the vigil at midnight, with correspondingly different convictions about the time when Christ had risen that justified their particular practice. Thus, while the *Testamentum Domini*, a church order usually thought to have originated in Syria, associates daily midnight prayer with the time of Christ's resurrection (2.24), in the *Apostolic Constitutions*, also from Syria at around the same time, the fasting and paschal vigil are to continue until cockcrow, which is understood as daybreak on the first day of the week, the time when Christ rose (5.18–19). Although Egeria gives no indication of the hour when the Easter vigil at Jerusalem ended, the weekly resurrection vigil there, as we have seen,[29] began at cockcrow. On the other hand, the Armenian Lectionary (dating from the first half of the fifth century and reproducing the readings, feasts and a number of the rubrics of the church at Jerusalem) states that the Easter vigil ended and the Eucharist began at midnight.[30] While Augustine admits that the precise hour during the night at which Christ rose is unknown, the vigil in North Africa continued until cockcrow.[31] In contrast, Jerome was familiar with a vigil that ended at midnight, which he believed to be an Apostolic custom arising from a Jewish tradition that 'tells us that the Messiah will come at midnight'.[32]

Even though these differences in the hour of celebration may have continued, there was growing agreement from the middle of the third century onwards that Easter should be celebrated on the Sunday following the Jewish Passover. But this did not put an end to calendrical problems. We have already mentioned in the previous chapter the difficulties involved in knowing when Passover would fall each year. Some Christians tried to solve this by calculating for themselves the date of the first full moon after the spring equinox and computing the date of

---

29 Above, p. 27.
30 See John Wilkinson, *Egeria's Travels* (3rd edn, Warminster: Aris & Phillips 1999), p. 270.
31 Augustine, *Sermo Guelferbytanus* 1.10; 5.4.
32 Jerome, *Commentarium in Matt.* 4; ET from Cantalamessa, p. 99.

Easter from that. However, because the science of astronomy was much less exact then than it is today, a variety of tables for finding the date of Easter were produced by different groups of Christians, with the consequence that the feast was often celebrated on divergent dates in different parts of the world.

For example, the earliest such table that is known to us is one reported by Eusebius to be the work of a third-century Bishop Hippolytus and is found engraved on the base of a statue at Rome alleged to be that of Hippolytus.[33] In order to predict the date of Easter, this combines two of the eight-year lunar cycles devised by Greek astronomers and creates seven series of a 16-year cycle, beginning in the year 222. Eusebius also reports that Dionysus of Alexandria in the middle of the third century sent out annual letters to announce what was to be the date of Easter – a practice already referred to above in connection with the second-century paschal controversy and one continued by the later bishops of that church – and that he too used an eight-year cycle.[34] Another widely known table was based on a cycle of 28 years, and out of this was formed a more accurate version based on 84 years, which gained only one day over the real moon in about 63 years, and came into use later in Rome and North Africa. Anatolius of Laodicea, who died *c.* 282, in order to compute the date of Easter used a 19-year lunar cycle that had been known in both Babylon and Greece since at least the fourth century BCE and lost just one day in about 286 years, and his table became the basis of all those used thereafter by the church at Alexandria.[35]

---

33 Eusebius, *Historia ecclesiastica* 6.22. For the statue, see Margherita Guarducci, 'La statua di "Sant'Ippolito"' in *Ricerche su Ippolito*, Studia Ephemeridis Augustinianum 13 (Rome: Institutum Patristicum Augustinianum 1977), pp. 17–30; Margherita Guarducci, 'La "Statua di Sant'Ippolito" e la sua provenienza' in *Nuove ricerche su Ippolito*, Studia Ephemeridis Augustinianum 30 (Rome: Institutum Patristicum Augustinianum 1989), pp. 61–74.

34 Eusebius, *Historia ecclesiastica* 7.20. For the second-century practice, see above, p. 49.

35 For further details of these and other tables, see Anscar Chupungco, *Shaping the Easter Feast* (Washington, DC: The Pastoral Press 1992), pp. 43–5; C. W. Jones, *Bedae Opera de Temporibus* (Cambridge, MA: Mediaeval Academy of America 1943), pp. 11–77; Daniel P. McCarthy and Aidan Breen, *The ante-Nicene Christian Pasch, De ratione paschali: The Paschal Tract of Anatolius, Bishop of Laodicea* (Dublin: Four Courts Press 2003); Alden A. Mosshammer, *The Easter Computus and the Origins of the Christian Era*, Oxford Early Christian Studies (Oxford/New York: Oxford University Press 2008).

After the Council of Nicaea, therefore, the Emperor Constantine directed that all churches were to keep the feast on the same day, re-affirming a decision that had already been made for churches in the West at the Council of Arles in 314, when it had been agreed that the Bishop of Rome should send out letters announcing the date of Easter each year.[36] Constantine cites the scandal of Christians celebrating the feast on different days as a reason for this decree, but it appears that such variation was less of a concern than were the Quartodeciman and Syrian practices of continuing to use the Jewish reckoning to set the date of their celebration. The letter argued that lack of accuracy in Jewish calendrical calculation sometimes resulted in the Passover – and hence Easter – being celebrated prior to the actual spring equinox, and that this was a grave error. But the real motivation was clearly a desire to distance Christianity from Judaism: 'it seemed unsuitable that we should celebrate that holy festival following the custom of the Jews'.[37]

Nevertheless, this decision did not put an end to variation, as some groups of Christians persisted in their traditional customs, and in any case no particular table to compute the date of Easter appears to have been prescribed by Constantine. Thus, the churches of Alexandria and Rome continued to use different tables from one another and assigned the equinox to different dates, 21 March in the case of the former and 25 March in the case of the latter. Another contrast between them was what should be done when the full moon fell on a Sunday: should Easter be kept on that day or on the following Sunday? As a result, in the year 387, Easter was observed at Alexandria and in northern Italy on 25 April, in Gaul on 21 March, and at Rome on 18 April.[38] It took many centuries for such discrepancies finally to be resolved.

---

36 Canon 1; ET in Cantalamessa, p. 94.
37 Constantine, *Ep. ad ecclesias* 18; ET from Cantalamessa, p. 63.
38 Ambrose, *Ep.* 23. For details, see Chupungco, *Shaping the Easter Feast*, pp. 45–6, 70–1.

Chapter 7

The development of the *triduum*

We have observed in the preceding chapter how the celebration of Pascha on a Sunday caused the focus of the feast to begin to shift from the death of Christ to his resurrection, and the significance of the Friday and Saturday from simply a preparatory fast to a commemoration of his death and entombment, albeit without any indication that these days as yet received any special liturgical expression of this understanding. Alongside this development in the third century, and in conjunction with it, a shift in the interpretation of the meaning of Pascha, from 'passion' to 'passage' – the passage from death to life – started to emerge, apparently beginning in Alexandria. Towards the end of the second century Clement of Alexandria had described the Passover as being humanity's passage 'from all trouble and all objects of sense';[1] and Origen in the middle of the third century developed this concept by challenging the traditional interpretation of Pascha:

> Most, if not all, of the brethren think that the Pascha is named Pascha from the passion of the Savior. However, the feast in question is not called precisely Pascha by the Hebrews, but *phas[h]* . . . Translated it means 'passage'. Since it is on this feast that the people goes forth from Egypt, it is logical to call it *phas[h]*, that is, 'passage'.[2]

While Clement had spoken of the Jewish observance as having begun 'on the tenth day' of the month, Origen clearly viewed the paschal events as having extended over three days, in fulfilment of Hosea 6.2, even if they were not yet liturgically celebrated in this way:

---

1 *Stromateis* 2.11.51.2; ET from Cantalamessa, p. 52.
2 *Peri Pascha* 1; ET from Cantalamessa, p. 53.

Now listen to what the prophet says: 'God will revive us after two days, and on the third day we shall rise and live in his sight.' For us the first day is the passion of the Savior; the second on which he descended into hell; and the third, the day of resurrection.[3]

At the same time, however, he could still speak of Easter Day as 'the Sunday which commemorates Christ's passion'.[4]

Fourth-century Christians gave this new interpretation a mixed reception. While some accepted it readily, others, especially in the West, continued to adhere to the older notion that the word meant 'passion'.[5] Even as late as the fifth century Augustine had to contend vigorously against the persistence of this false etymology among his contemporaries.[6] Others instead combined the understanding of Pascha as 'passage' with the older focus on Christ's sacrifice. So, for example, Athanasius, in his annual letter to the Christians of Egypt to announce the date when Easter would fall that year, could on one occasion describe the feast as a transition from death to life, and on another refer to the sacrifice of Christ.[7] A similar combination of themes can be seen in Didymus of Alexandria:

When the spiritual spring arrives and the month of the first fruits is at hand, we keep the Crossing-Feast, called in the Hebrew tongue Pascha. On this day Christ has been sacrificed, in order that, consuming his spiritual flesh and his sacred blood, 'we should feast with the unleavened bread of sincerity and truth'.[8]

---

3 *Homilia in Exod.* 5.2; ET from Cantalamessa, p. 55.

4 Origen, *Homilia in Isa.* 5.2.

5 See, for example, Ambrosiaster, *Quaestiones Veteris et Novi Testamenti* 96.1; 116.1; *Commentarius in xiii epistulas Paulinas*, on 1 Corinthians 5.7; Gregory of Elvira, *Tractatus de libris SS. Scripturarum* 9.9, 16, 20, 22; Chromatius of Aquila, *Sermones* 17A; ET in Cantalamessa, pp. 98–9, 104–5, 107. Even though Chromatius was familiar with a liturgically celebrated *triduum* in his church, he still continued to understand the paschal vigil as commemorating the death, repose in the tomb, descent into hell, and resurrection of Christ (see *Sermones* 16 and 17).

6 Augustine, *Enarrationes in Psalmos* 120.6; *In Johannis evangelium tractatus* 55.1; ET in Cantalamessa, pp. 109–10.

7 Athanasius, *Ep. festales* 5, 42; ET in Cantalamessa, pp. 70, 72.

8 *Commentarium in Zach.* 5.88; ET from Cantalamessa, p. 79. The biblical quotation is from 1 Corinthians 5.7.

This fusion of the two ideas is also found among a number of Western theologians in the late fourth century, including Ambrose and Augustine himself. [9]

These factors appear to have been responsible for the widespread emergence of the idea of the feast as being a three-day unity (Greek, τριήμερον; Latin *triduum*), comprising the commemoration of the death of Christ on Friday, his burial in the tomb on Saturday, and his resurrection on Sunday,[10] although in the East the memorial of Christ's repose in death on the Sabbath, the day of rest, was often joined with that of his descent into Hades.[11] The concept of the *triduum* did not immediately catch on everywhere, however, and there are signs in some places of a reluctance to make the transition from the single unitive feast. So, for example, in northern Italy, while in some cities before the end of the fourth century Easter was focused upon the resurrection of Jesus, with his death being commemorated on Good Friday, in others there was a continuing emphasis on the Passion in the celebration of the paschal feast itself;[12] and even in the fifth century Theodoret of Cyrrhus could speak of the 'day of the saving passion, in which we solemnize the memory both of the passion and of the resurrection of the Lord'.[13]

The liturgical embellishment of the three days with ceremonies that gave particular expression to each of the specific themes is generally

---

9 See, for example, Ambrose of Milan, *De Cain et Abel* 1.8.31; *Ep.* 1.9–10; *De sacramentis* 1.4.12; Gaudentius of Brescia, *Tractatus* 2.25–6; ET in Cantalamessa, pp. 95–6, 106. For Augustine, see the passages referred to in n. 6 above. But compare Maximus of Turin, whose homilies reveal a gradual progression of thought during his episcopate, until he can affirm unequivocally the concept of Pascha as 'passing over' in *Sermones* 54.1; ET in Cantalamessa, p. 108.

10 See, for example, for the East, Basil of Caesarea, *Homilia* 13.1; Gregory of Nazianzus, *Oratio* 1.3–4; Gregory of Nyssa, *De tridui spatio*; Pseudo-Chrysostom, *Homilies on the Holy Pascha* 7.4; ET in Cantalamessa, pp. 75–8; for the West, Ambrose, *Ep.* 23.12–13; Augustine, *Ep.* 55.14, 24; ET in Cantalamessa, p. 109.

11 The earliest clear witness to the observance of this day as the descent into Hades is in Amphilochius, Bishop of Iconium from 373 to 394, *Oration 5, For Holy Saturday* 1: 'Today we celebrate the feast of our Savior's burial. He, with the dead below, is loosing the bonds of death and filling Hades with light and waking the sleepers . . .' (ET from Cantalamessa, p. 77). See further Aloys Grillmeier, 'Der Gottessohn im Totenreich: soteriologische und christologische Motivierung der Descensuslehre in der älteren christlichen Überlieferung', *Zeitschrift für Katholische Theologie* 71 (1949), pp. 1–53, 184–203.

12 See, for example, Zeno of Verona, who seems to associate both the death and resurrection of Christ with the Easter vigil: *Treatise on the Pascha* 1.57; ET in Cantalamessa, pp. 94–5.

13 Theodoret of Cyrrhus, *Cure for the Greek Illnesses* 9.24; ET in Cantalamessa, p. 81.

thought to have begun in Jerusalem in the late fourth century in response to the crowds of pilgrims who began to flock there and often joined in the celebration of the sacred season in the very places where the events of Christ's Passion and resurrection were believed to have taken place. These liturgical innovations now stretched to the whole of the week before Easter and also to other parts of the year.[14] We are fortunate in having a detailed description from the pilgrim Egeria, who visited the Holy City in the 380s. From this it is clear that the discovery of the true cross had led to the introduction of an occasion on the morning of Good Friday for its public display and veneration by all who wished, beginning at 8 a.m.:

> The bishop's chair is placed on Golgotha Behind the Cross, where he now stands, and he takes his seat. A table is placed before him with a cloth on it, the deacons stand round, and there is brought to him a gold and silver box containing the holy Wood of the Cross. It is opened, and the Wood of the Cross and the Title are taken out and placed on the table . . . Thus all the people go past one by one. They stoop down, touch the holy Wood first with their forehead and then with their eyes, and then kiss it, but no one puts out his hand to touch it. Then they go on to a deacon who stands holding the Ring of Solomon, and the Horn with which the kings were anointed. These they venerate by kissing them, and till noon everybody goes by, entering by one door and going out through the other.[15]

The main service of the day, however, was an extensive liturgy of the word that began at midday in the courtyard between the Cross and the Anastasis:

> They place the bishop's chair Before the Cross, and the whole time between midday and three o'clock is taken up with readings. They are all about the things Jesus suffered: first the psalms on this subject, then the Apostles [the Epistles or Acts] which concern it, then passages from the Gospels. Thus they read the prophecies about what

---

14 For the ceremonies of the rest of Holy Week, see below, pp. 114–19.

15 Egeria, *Itinerarium* 37.1–3; ET from John Wilkinson, *Egeria's Travels* (3rd edn, Warminster: Aris & Phillips 1999), pp. 155–6. Wilkinson fails to note that there is a lacuna in the text before the words 'till noon', and he also inadvertently repeats the phrase 'till midday' at the end of the sentence.

the Lord would suffer, and the Gospels about what he did suffer . . . and between all the readings are prayers, all of them appropriate to the day . . . Then, when three o'clock comes, they have the reading from St John's Gospel about Jesus giving up the ghost, and, when that has been read, there is a prayer, and the dismissal.[16]

Although a service of the word took place on every Friday in the year at Jerusalem, it was normally at 3 p.m. rather than midday, and hence both the change of time and the choice of readings reflect the particular significance of the day.[17] In addition to the other normal daily services on this day, there was one more act of devotion to commemorate the final event of Good Friday: after evening prayer, the community went to the Anastasis where 'they read the Gospel passage about Joseph asking Pilate for the Lord's body and placing it in a new tomb. After the reading there is a prayer, the blessings of the catechumens and then the faithful, and the dismissal.'[18] This was followed by a vigil during the night, as on all Fridays in Lent.[19]

It is questionable as to how far we should speak of these Jerusalem practices as being 'imitated' elsewhere. Not only, as indicated above, was there at first an apparent reluctance in some places to adopt the *triduum* at all, what actually went on in other parts of the world, and especially in the West, did not closely resemble the particular customs of the Holy City. While the veneration of the cross captured popular imagination and spread to other churches of the East, no attempt was made to copy every one of the other practices in exact detail everywhere. Even the dissemination of this particular devotion was impeded at first by the need to obtain a fragment of the true cross from the Jerusalem church, although Cyril of Jerusalem acknowledges that even in his time small pieces of the wood were being distributed throughout the world.[20] Thus we hear of public veneration of a fragment of the cross at Antioch on Good Friday and of other relics of the Passion, most notably the lance which was said to have pierced Christ's side, at Constantinople during

---

16 Egeria, *Itinerarium* 37.5–7; ET from Wilkinson, *Egeria's Travels*, p. 156.

17 The Armenian Lectionary lists the specific readings used: eight from the Old Testament, eight from the New, and four from the Gospels. See Wilkinson, *Egeria's Travels*, p. 187.

18 Egeria, *Itinerarium* 37.8; ET from Wilkinson, *Egeria's Travels*, pp. 156–7.

19 See above, pp. 35–6.

20 Cyril of Jerusalem, *Catechesis* 13.4.

the last three days of Holy Week.[21] At Rome, on the other hand, while the Good Friday liturgy from quite early times seems to have included readings appropriate to the day,[22] it was otherwise indistinguishable from any Friday in the year, and it is not until the end of the seventh century that there is evidence of the adoption of the veneration of the cross on that day, a development perhaps influenced by the practice at Constantinople or derived directly from Jerusalem.[23] The papal liturgy involved an elaborate procession with the relic to the Church of the Holy Cross, its veneration, and then the traditional service of the word followed. It is interesting to note that the ritual directions speak of the arrival at the church as being 'at Jerusalem', suggesting that the procession was seen as a symbolic pilgrimage to the Holy City. In other churches at Rome there was no procession, and the veneration followed rather than preceded the service of the word. Later, the ceremony spread throughout the West, with ordinary wooden crosses being used where relics were lacking.[24]

At Jerusalem there were no special services on the Saturday, and with regard to the paschal vigil, Egeria simply says that they kept it 'like us', but with one addition: the newly baptized were taken immediately to the Anastasis where after a hymn the bishop said a prayer for them before returning to the Martyrium (the great church on Golgotha). There the Eucharist was celebrated, but immediately after the dismissal, the whole congregation returned to the Anastasis, 'where the resurrection Gospel is read' and the Eucharist celebrated for a second time.[25] Apart from the resurrection Gospel reading, which was a feature of every Sunday morning's liturgy in the Jerusalem tradition,[26] the second

---

21 For Constantinople, see Robert F. Taft, 'Holy Week in the Byzantine Tradition' in Maxwell E. Johnson (ed.), *Between Memory and Hope: Readings on the Liturgical Year* (Collegeville: The Liturgical Press 2000), pp. 155–81, here at pp. 160–2, and esp. n. 32.

22 Although extant sources for the Roman readings are all much later, it appears to be an older tradition that in preparation for Easter the accounts of the Passion from three of the four Gospels were chosen to be read successively on the three days in the preceding week on which a liturgy of the word would normally have occurred: Sunday (Matthew), Wednesday (Luke), and Friday (John), Mark being omitted because it was understood to be an abbreviation of Matthew.

23 For the latter possibility, see G. Römer, 'Die Liturgie des Karfreitags', *Zeitschrift für katholische Theologie* 77 (1955), pp. 39–93, here at pp. 71–2.

24 See further Patrick Regan, 'The Veneration of the Cross' in Johnson, *Between Memory and Hope*, pp. 143–53.

25 Egeria, *Itinerarium* 38.1–2; ET in Wilkinson, *Egeria's Travels*, p 157.

26 See above, p. 27.

celebration of the Eucharist did not include a liturgy of the word, according to the Armenian Lectionary.[27] Why the Eucharist should have been repeated at all is not clear: was it so that the resurrection could be celebrated on the very site where it had happened?[28] We encounter a similar repetition on Holy Thursday and on the day of Pentecost.[29] The only source for the contents of a paschal vigil from a significantly earlier date than this is the *Didascalia*, which speaks simply of the reading of the Prophets, Psalms and Gospel, with prayers and intercessions. By 'Prophets' it is likely that the Hebrew Scriptures in general are meant, since they were all seen as being prophetic of the Christ-event, and indeed further on the author uses the term 'Scriptures' instead when describing the vigil.[30]

Later sources supply details of the readings that were used at the vigil. There is considerable variation from place to place both in the number of readings and in the particular biblical texts used, suggesting that no widespread ancient tradition of reading specific passages appropriate to the occasion had been inherited. So, for example, the Armenian Lectionary provides 12 readings from the Old Testament, with 1 Corinthians 15.1–11 and Matthew 28.1–20 as the Epistle and Gospel for the Eucharist which followed.[31] Talley pointed out that the first three readings (the story of creation, Genesis 1.1—3.24; the account of the binding of Isaac, Genesis 22.1–18; and the narrative of the Passover, Exodus 12.1–24) constituted three of the four themes in a 'Poem of the Four Nights' in an expanded Targum on Exodus (the fourth being the coming of the Messiah), and suggested that they established a line of continuity with the Jewish Passover tradition, but Leonhard has subsequently demonstrated at length that this expansion is a later composition and does not have any connection with the Christian Easter.[32] At Verona in northern Italy only six Old Testament readings

27 See Wilkinson, *Egeria's Travels*, p. 188.
28 This is the suggestion of Gabriel Bertonière, *The Historical Development of the Easter Vigil and Related Services in the Greek Church*, OCA 193 (Rome: Pontifical Oriental Institute 1972), pp. 68–70.
29 See below, pp. 74, 117.
30 *Didascalia* 5.19.1 and 6; ET in Cantalamessa, p. 83. See also above, p. 55.
31 Wilkinson, *Egeria's Travels*, pp. 188, 193.
32 Thomas J. Talley, *The Origins of the Liturgical Year* (New York: Pueblo 1986; 2nd edn, Collegeville: The Liturgical Press 1991), pp. 3, 47–50; Clemens Leonhard, *The Jewish Pesach and the Origins of the Christian Easter* (Berlin/New York: de Gruyter 2006), pp. 309–14, 317–423.

were employed at the paschal vigil at the end of the fourth century (Gen. 1; Exod. 12; 14; Isa. 1; 5; Dan. 3); of these, the readings from Isaiah have no parallel in the Jerusalem series.[33] There is no extant list of vigil readings associated with Rome prior to the eighth-century Gelasian Sacramentary, which has a series of ten, but as that book shows signs of some Gallican influence, Bernard Botte argued that the earliest known Roman practice was to have six readings, as was the case in northern Italy, although the passages chosen were somewhat different (Gen. 1; 22; Exod. 14; Deut. 31; Isa. 4; and Bar.).[34] If correct, this means that neither Exodus 12 nor Daniel 3 was originally part of this tradition, although both are commonly found in other later Western lectionaries and Exodus 12 was read on Good Friday at Rome.

Finally, one other element in the vigil deserves to be mentioned: the lighting of the paschal candle. By the fourth century, daily evening worship throughout the year in many places began with a ceremonial lighting of the evening lamp, the *Lucernarium*, in which were recalled the gifts of the natural light of the day, the lamps to illuminate the night, and above all the light of Christ. The evening service that began the paschal vigil would have been no exception to this rule, but the ceremony inevitably took on a special significance in this particular context, and later centuries attached it to the vigil itself rather than to evening prayer and saw it as symbolizing the light of Christ risen from the dead, although Rome was very slow to incorporate the practice because its daily worship traditions were dominated by monastic forms that lacked a *Lucernarium*. While in Western traditions it remained at the very beginning of the vigil, in the East it was later moved to the end of the readings instead, where it constituted a dramatic climax and led into the Easter eucharistic celebration.[35]

---

33 For further details, see Gordon P. Jeanes, *The Day Has Come! Easter and Baptism in Zeno of Verona*, ACC 73 (Collegeville: The Liturgical Press 1995); S. Gros, 'La vigile pascale à Vérone dans les années 360–380', *Ecclesia Orans* 18 (2001), pp. 11–23.

34 Bernard Botte, 'Le choix des lectures de la veillée pascale', *Questions liturgiques et paroisssales* 33 (1952), pp. 65–70, here at p. 66. Herman Schmidt, *Hebdomada Sancta* (Rome: Herder 1957), pp. 844–6, came to a similar conclusion, apparently independently, although he inserted Isaiah 54 in place of Baruch. Talley, *The Origins of the Liturgical Year*, pp. 51–3, misunderstood Schmidt to mean that there were seven readings.

35 See Patrick Regan, 'Paschal *Lucernarium*: Structure and Symbol', *Worship* 82 (2008), pp. 98–118; Bertonière, *The Historical Development of the Easter Vigil and Related Services in the Greek Church*, pp. 29–58; A. J. MacGregor, *Fire and Light in the Western Triduum*, ACC 71 (Collegeville: The Liturgical Press 1992), pp. 299–308.

Thus, not only had the occasion observed as the Christian Passover changed from 14/15 Nisan to the Sunday following, but its character too had been transformed in the course of the fourth century. From a primary emphasis on the sacrifice of Christ, the paschal lamb, it had shifted to an exclusive focus on his resurrection, with first the *triduum* and then the other days of Holy Week gradually emerging to commemorate the various events connected with the last days of his life.

Chapter 8

Pentecost: the great fifty days

According to Leviticus 23.15–16, the Feast of Weeks was to take place on the fiftieth day after the ceremony of the waving of the omer of barley, which itself was to take place 'on the day after the Sabbath' after Passover (23.11). Within early Judaism there was a debate about how 'the day after the Sabbath' was to be interpreted. Did it mean the day after the next weekly Sabbath that followed the Passover, or did 'Sabbath' here mean either the first or the seventh day of the festival of Unleavened Bread, which were appointed as days of rest when no work was to be done? The *Book of Jubilees*, however, understood it to be the Sabbath that followed the conclusion of the seven days of the Feast of Unleavened Bread. As *Jubilees* was following the solar calendar later adopted at Qumran, in which Passover always fell on a Wednesday, the conclusion of the feast would occur on the following Wednesday, and the next Sabbath would be on 25 Nisan. Because there were 30 days in each of the first two months of the year, counting 50 days from the next day (Sunday) would result in the Feast of Weeks always being on the fifteenth day of the third month, a Sunday.[1]

The earliest references to Pentecost (the Greek word for 'fiftieth') in Christian sources are to what is obviously this Jewish feast, rather than a specifically Christian one (Acts 2.1; 20.16; 1 Cor. 16.8). Similarly, when the *Epistula Apostolorum* claims that the coming of 'the Father' will occur between Pentecost and the feast of Unleavened Bread, it is widely agreed that this is referring merely to points on the Jewish calendar and does not indicate the existence of any specifically Christian

---

1 See above, pp. 29–30, and James C. VanderKam, *Calendars in the Dead Sea Scrolls* (London: Routledge 1998), pp. 31 and 55.

feast.[2] It is not until towards the end of the second century that the earliest attestation of a Christian observance as such occurs, and in contrast to Jewish practice, it consists of a 50-day period beginning on Easter Day rather than a feast on the day of Pentecost alone. It was regarded as a time of rejoicing, and every day was treated in the same way as a Sunday, that is, with no kneeling for prayer or fasting, which seems to suggest that it had originated as an extension of Easter Day. This practice is attested in three sources from different parts of the world at this period: the *Acts of Paul* from Asia Minor;[3] Irenaeus of Lyons (who may have brought it from Asia Minor) in a lost work on the Pascha, at least according to the fifth-century Theodoret of Cyrrhus;[4] and Tertullian in North Africa. There is also an allusion to the season by Origen later in the third century (*Homilia in Lev.* 2.2), as well as in what seems to be quite an ancient section of the so-called *Apostolic Tradition* (33.3) and in a few other sources. Rouwhorst has questioned the trustworthiness not only of these latter sources but also of the citation attributed to Irenaeus, and so concluded that the only parts of the world in which we can have any certainty that the season was being observed at this time are North Africa, Egypt and Caesarea, and only in some communities in Asia Minor, as none of our other sources from that region mention it.[5]

Tertullian deals with Pentecost most fully in his treatise on baptism, where he describes it as 'a most joyous period' (*laetissimum spatium*) for conferring baptisms,

> because the Lord's resurrection was celebrated among the disciples and the grace of the Holy Spirit was inaugurated and the hope in the Lord's coming indicated, because it was then, when he had been taken back into heaven, the angels told the apostles that he would

---

2 See Cantalamessa, p. 39. Gerard Rouwhorst, 'How Eschatological was Early Christian Liturgy?', *SP* 40 (2006), pp. 99–100, has shown that this appears to be the original reading of the text and not 'between Pascha and Pentecost', as some have previously supposed.

3 *Acta Pauli* 1 in Wilhelm Schneemelcher (ed.), *New Testament Apocrypha* 2 (2nd edn, Cambridge: James Clarke & Co./Louisville: Westminster John Knox Press 1991–2), p. 251. See further Clemens Leonhard, *The Jewish Pesach and the Origins of the Christian Easter* (Berlin/New York: de Gruyter 2006), pp. 183–5.

4 *Quaestiones et Responsiones ad orthodoxos* 115; ET in Cantalamessa, p. 51.

5 Gerard Rouwhorst, 'The Origins and Evolution of Early Christian Pentecost', *SP* 35 (2001), pp. 309–22, here at pp. 312–15.

come exactly as he had gone up into heaven – meaning, of course, during the Pentecost.[6]

As Pascha is still understood at this time as focusing principally on the death of Jesus, it is evident that the whole 50-day season celebrated the resurrection, Ascension and gift of the Spirit, and looked for Christ's coming in glory.

Because we have no earlier explicit testimony to the Christian obser-vance of the season than those cited above, it is something of a mystery as to why it would emerge apparently from nowhere at this time and yet spread quite rapidly to various parts of the ancient world. While its name is obviously derived from the New Testament, its form and meaning are so markedly different from the Jewish observance that it is not easy to attribute it wholly to that source, even though Georg Kretschmar, followed by Robert Cabié, presented a detailed case for the celebration of the Ascension on the fiftieth day linked to the theme of the Covenant being of ancient Palestinian provenance, and Talley made a valiant attempt to argue that it was not just the day of Pentecost that was sacred to Jews but the whole period between Passover and Pentecost.[7]

Rouwhorst examined Kretschmar's argument in detail and exposed the flaws in it, but summarily dismissed the view of some recent biblical scholars that the day of Pentecost was already being kept as a time of covenant renewal and of the reception of new members by some Jewish communities in the first century, which might possibly help explain an early Christian choice of the season as a baptismal occasion.[8] Instead he tentatively suggested that the commemoration of the Ascension on the fiftieth day 'might . . . have had the character of a farewell ceremony' and 'might go back to the tradition of Jerusalem'. At the same time he advanced the hypothesis that the Christian observance of the 50 days

6 Tertullian, *De baptismo* 19.2; ET from Cantalamessa, p. 91. See also *De oratione* 23.2; *De ieiunio* 14.2 (ET in Cantalamessa, pp. 90, 92); *De corona* 3.4. That Tertullian consis-tently uses Pentecost to mean 50 days and not the fiftieth day, see Robert Cabié, *La Pentecôte: L'évolution de la Cinquantaine pascale au cours des cinq premiers siècles* (Paris: Desclée 1965), pp. 40–1; but for a more nuanced judgement, Cantalamessa, p. 22.
7 Georg Kretschmar, 'Himmelfahrt und Pfingsten', *Zeitschrift für Kirchengeschichte* 66 (1954–5), pp. 209–53, here at pp. 217–22; Cabié, *La Pentecôte*, pp. 131–3; Thomas J. Talley, *The Origins of the Liturgical Year* (New York: Pueblo 1986, 2nd edn, Collegeville: The Liturgical Press 1991), pp. 59–60.
8 See further below, pp. 76–7.

could have begun in Egypt, where Alexandrian Jews appear to have been the first to give a new meaning to the Jewish festival, as the commemoration of the Covenant at Sinai, after the destruction of the Temple prevented its continued observance as a harvest festival. In a similar manner to Talley, he drew attention to an alleged parallel Jewish and Christian tendency to view the fiftieth day as being the 'seal' or conclusion of a period and not just an isolated feast.[9] He appears to lack much firm ground for his theories, however, and Leonhard has resolutely criticized the whole notion that the Christian season of Pentecost had any antecedents prior to the late second century.[10]

The continuing observance of the 50 days is more widely attested in fourth-century sources, but it may not have become quite as universal as is generally supposed. Thus Canon 20 of the Council of Nicaea refers to some who kneel on Sundays and in the days of Pentecost, ordering them to desist; and Canon 43 of the Spanish Council of Elvira (305) seeks to correct what it describes as a corrupt practice and insists that all should celebrate 'the day of Pentecost'. On the basis of a variant reading in two manuscripts, Cabié interprets the corrupt practice as being a recent innovation of prematurely terminating the Easter season on the fortieth day, but it is not impossible that the canon is seeking to introduce the celebration of Pentecost to churches which had not previously known it.[11]

What is even more significant is that neither the *Didascalia* nor Aphraates and Ephrem in East Syria in the first half of the fourth century make the slightest allusion either to a 50-day season or to any observance on the fiftieth day, but are only cognisant of a single week of celebration following Easter.[12] Elsewhere, too, this week receives special emphasis within the 50-day season, which may perhaps be an indication that this shorter period was at one time the only extension of the Easter festival not just in Syria but other places as well. So, for example, Egeria says that the Jerusalem church celebrated 'the eight days of Easter . . . like us', and the

---

9 Rouwhorst, 'The Origins and Evolution of Early Christian Pentecost', pp. 315–22.

10 Leonhard, *The Jewish Pesach and the Origins of the Christian Easter*, pp. 159–82.

11 ET in Cantalamessa, p. 94; Cabié, *La Pentecôte*, pp. 181–2.

12 Cabié, *La Pentecôte*, p. 153, n. 1 and 154, n. 3. See also Rouwhorst, 'The Origins and Evolution of Early Christian Pentecost', p. 311. Talley, *The Origins of the Liturgical Year*, pp. 56–7, cites similar testimony from the homilies of Asterius the Sophist, a Cappadocian writing between 335 and 341, but they are now thought to be the work of an otherwise unknown Asterius writing later in the fourth or early in the fifth century. See Wolfram Kinzig, *In Search of Asterius: Studies on the Authorship of the Homilies on the Psalms* (Göttingen: Vandenhoeck & Ruprecht 1990).

services throughout the eight days followed 'the same order as people do everywhere else'.[13] This included the daily instruction of all the newly baptized in 'the mysteries', that is, the meaning of the rites of baptism and Eucharist in which they had just participated; and there are in existence the text of these lectures not only from Jerusalem but also from other places.[14] Egeria also describes the newly baptized (together with any of the faithful who wished) assembling for a special service of hymns and prayers each afternoon. A further service was held on Easter Day after evening prayer, when John 20.19–25 was read, and this was repeated a week later, when the reading was John 20.26–31, both being done at the very place, day and time that the events described in those readings were said to have happened.[15] As with Pentecost, it is not immediately obvious why this eight-day celebration should have emerged. The biblical precedent of the week-long feast of Unleavened Bread (Exod. 12.14–20), the account of the disciples meeting together seven days after the resurrection (John 20.26–29), and also the early Christian understanding of Sunday as the eighth day (above, p. 13), may all have played a part.

In any case, the integrity of the 50 days does not appear to have been so deeply rooted that it was able to resist erosion in the course of the fourth century in response to the influence of the chronology of the Acts of the Apostles. While the church in Egypt seems to have been able to maintain the uninterrupted continuity of the season throughout the fourth and fifth centuries,[16] this was not so elsewhere. In addition to the

---

13 Egeria, *Itinerarium* 39.1. Translators have generally treated the word *sero* in the Latin text as authentic and rendered it 'till a late hour', even though there is no sign that the services went on any later on the weekdays at this season than in the rest of the year. John Wilkinson, *Egeria's Travels* (3rd edn, Warminster: Aris & Phillips 1999), p. 157, however, has now accepted its emendation to *octo*, 'eight', but failed to remove the phrase 'till a late hour' from his translation.

14 Egeria, *Itinerarium* 47; ET in Wilkinson, *Egeria's Travels*, p. 163. ET of the lectures from Jerusalem and Milan, and also those from Antioch and Mopsuestia for the same week, though not focused on the rites in these last two instances because that teaching had been done before the baptism, is in E. J. Yarnold, *The Awe-Inspiring Rites of Initiation* (2nd edn, Edinburgh: T. & T. Clark/Collegeville: The Liturgical Press 1994). Although Egeria states that the lectures were given every day in Jerusalem, the surviving set, usually presumed to be the work of Cyril, consists of only five. Cyril says (*Catecheses* 18.33) that they began on the Monday, and they may also have been omitted on the Wednesday and Friday: see Charles (Athanase) Renoux, 'Les catéchèses mystagogiques dans l'organisation liturgique hiérosolymitaine du IVe et du Ve siècle', *Le Muséon* 78 (1965), pp. 355–9; Talley, *The Origins of the Liturgical Year*, pp. 55–6.

15 Egeria, *Itinerarium* 39.3–40.2; ET in Wilkinson, *Egeria's Travels*, p. 158.

16 See Cabié, *La Pentecôte*, pp. 61–76.

existence in many places of a special emphasis on the first week of the season, in Constantinople, Rome, Milan and Spain the fiftieth day itself came to be celebrated as a commemoration of the gift of the Spirit, while in other places – including Jerusalem – both the Ascension and the gift of the Spirit were celebrated together on that day.[17] As one might expect, at Jerusalem, in addition to the normal Sunday services, a second Eucharist was celebrated on Sion, where it was believed that the descent of the Spirit had occurred, and then in the afternoon another non-eucharistic service at the Imbomon, the presumed site of the Ascension. After evening prayer on Eleona, there were further services in the Martyrium, the Anastasis, at the Cross and on Sion, ending about midnight.[18] Egeria also records a special observance that was held at Bethlehem on the fortieth day, but this does not seem to have been connected with the Ascension, although what it actually was remains a mystery.[19]

However, towards the end of the fourth century a separate feast of the Ascension on the fortieth day did emerge in a number of places, including Antioch, Nyssa and northern Italy, and became almost universal early in the fifth century.[20] There are also traces of the existence in some places of a 'mid Pentecost' festival.[21] Although some churches still continued to keep the whole 50 days as a festal season, even when punctuated in this way, others resumed the regular weekly fasts after the fortieth day, because 'the bridegroom had been taken away', while still others (at least according to Filastrius, Bishop of Brescia in northern Italy in the late fourth century) fasted even before the Ascension.[22]

---

17 Cabié, *La Pentecôte*, pp. 117–38.

18 Egeria, *Itinerarium* 43; ET in Wilkinson, *Egeria's Travels*, pp. 159–60.

19 Egeria, *Itinerarium* 42; ET in Wilkinson, *Egeria's Travels*, p. 159. For one suggestion, see Talley, *The Origins of the Liturgical Year*, pp. 63–5.

20 Details in Cabié, *La Pentecôte*, pp. 185–97; Talley, *The Origins of the Liturgical Year*, pp. 66–9.

21 First attested in the fourth century in the East by Amphilochius, Bishop of Iconium, and in the fifth century in the West by Peter Chrysologus, Bishop of Ravenna; see Cabié, *La Pentecôte*, pp. 100–5.

22 See Cabié, *La Pentecôte*, pp. 247–9.

Chapter 9

Initiation at Easter

It is often supposed that early Christians would have administered baptism as the first part of their regular Sunday Eucharist,[1] largely on the basis of what Justin Martyr appears to indicate in the account of Christian worship in his *First Apology*, although it should be noted that Justin does not explicitly say that the baptismal Eucharist he describes in chapters 61 and 65 did take place on a Sunday. In any case, this supposition overlooks the fact that from the *Didache* onwards (7.4) a period of at least one or two days of fasting was generally prescribed prior to baptism. Except at Rome and in parts of North Africa, however, fasting was prohibited on all Saturdays apart from the day before Easter,[2] and so Sunday baptisms elsewhere would normally have been impossible. Thus, we might expect that the conclusion of an already existing period of fasting, such as those that came to precede festivals, would quite naturally have become regular occasions for baptism, regardless of the specific meaning of that festival.

Tertullian in North Africa at the end of the second century is the first Christian writer to suggest that Easter was a particularly suitable occasion for the celebration of baptism:

The Pascha affords a more [than usually] solemn day for baptism, since the passion of the Lord, in which we are baptized, was accomplished [then] . . . After this, the Pentecost is an extremely happy period for conferring baptisms, because the Lord's resurrection was

---

1 See, for example, Willy Rordorf, *Sunday* (London: SCM Press/Philadelphia: Westminster Press 1968), pp. 264–71; Thomas J. Talley, *The Origins of the Liturgical Year* (New York: Pueblo 1986; 2nd edn, Collegeville: The Liturgical Press 1991), p. 37.
2 See above, pp. 14–19.

celebrated among the disciples and the grace of the Holy Spirit was inaugurated and the hope in the Lord's coming indicated.

However, he goes on to say that 'every day is the Lord's [day]; every hour and every time is suitable for baptism. If there is a question of solemnity, it has nothing to do with the grace.'[3] He thus expresses a preference – but only a preference – for baptism at Easter.

It is hard to avoid the conclusion that the reference to being baptized into 'our Lord's passion' is an allusion to Romans 6.3 ('all of us who have been baptized into Christ Jesus were baptized into his death'), especially as Tertullian expounds the baptismal theology of Romans 6 in his *De resurrectione carnis* 47, and appears to be alluding to it in the phrase *symbolum mortis* in *De paenitentia* 6. However, that is not to say that it was necessarily the influence of Paul's theology that had initially given rise to the preference for baptism at Easter, as it would in any case have been a natural choice as an occasion for baptism because it was already preceded by at least two days of fasting, Friday and Saturday. It seems possible, therefore, that it was this practical consideration that led to Easter originally being adopted as one of the usual times in the year for the administration of baptism in North Africa, and what Tertullian was doing was giving a *post factum* reason for preferring this occasion to others. This notion is perhaps strengthened by the fact that Tertullian finds it necessary to add to the Lord's Passion a second biblical justification for baptizing at this time – that when Jesus told his disciples to go and prepare a place to celebrate the Passover, they would meet a man carrying water (Mark. 14.13; Luke 22.10) – apparently implying that a paschal theology of baptism was as yet not so deep-rooted.

It is usually assumed that the provision for baptism during the season of Pentecost was intended to cater for those who for whatever reason (for instance, sickness or menstruation) had been unable to receive baptism at Easter, even though they had undergone the preparation for it at that time, as it is difficult to reconcile a 50-day season in which fasting was not permitted with a time of full baptismal preparation that included fasting. On the other hand, it is possible that baptism at Pentecost has much more ancient roots. James VanderKam has built upon the arguments of other scholars and argued that the day of Pentecost was already being kept as a time of covenant renewal and of the reception of new members by some Jewish communities in the first

---

3 Tertullian, *De baptismo* 19.1–3; ET from Cantalamessa, p. 91.

century and that this understanding of the feast underlies the account of the outpouring of the Spirit on the day of Pentecost in Acts 2.[4] It appears conceivable, therefore, that baptism on the day of Pentecost might actually belong to an early stratum – even an Apostolic or at least a Jerusalem stratum – of the liturgical tradition,[5] and that the continuing observance of an annual feast of Pentecost among *some* Christians may be as old as their observance of Pascha, even though we have no explicit references to it at an early date. If this were the case, then the emergence at the end of the second century of a 50-day season with provision for baptism during it may have been a partial appropriation of this tradition in churches that had not previously observed the day of Pentecost at all, just as a Sunday Pascha was adopted in churches that had not previously observed that feast. This would also explain why some churches apparently took up this season while others did not, and why some of them kept a fast before the day of Pentecost.[6] Moreover, if the emergence of the feast of the Epiphany happened as early as is claimed by some scholars, then that too would also quite naturally have become another regular baptismal occasion before the priority of baptism at Easter began to assert itself more widely.[7]

Apart from Tertullian, the only other source to express a similar preference for paschal baptism at an early date is a commentary on the book of Daniel by a certain Hippolytus in the third century, traditionally associated with Rome although uncertainty surrounds the actual provenance of the author:

'Once, while they were watching for an opportune day, she went in as before with only two maids, and wished to bathe in the garden, for it was very hot' [Dan. 13.15 LXX]. What kind of day is opportune if

4 James C. VanderKam, 'The Festival of Weeks and the Story of Pentecost in Acts 2' in Craig A. Evans (ed.), *From Prophecy to Testament: The Function of the Old Testament in the New* (Peabody, MA: Hendrickson 2004), pp. 185–205; 'Sinai Revisited' in Matthias Henze (ed.), *Biblical Interpretation at Qumran* (Grand Rapids: Eerdmans 2005), pp. 44–60. See also above, p. 71.
5 See further Maxwell E. Johnson, 'Tertullian's *"Diem baptismo sollemniorem"* Revisited: A Tentative Hypothesis on Baptism at Pentecost' in M. E. Johnson and L. E. Phillips (eds), *Studia Liturgica Diversa: Essays in Honor of Paul F. Bradshaw* (Portland: The Pastoral Press 2004), pp. 31–44.
6 See above, pp. 72–4, and especially the references on p. 72 to the need for the Council of Nicaea to insist on standing throughout the season of Pentecost and for the Council of Elvira to require the celebration of the day of Pentecost.
7 See below, pp. 137–9, 146.

not that of the Pascha? On that day the bath is made ready for those going to be burnt and Susanna while she is being bathed is presented to God as a pure bride . . .[8]

While no theological justification is given for the preference for baptism at Easter in this source, there is a possibly an allusion to the baptismal theology of Romans 6 in an earlier (mid-second-century) text from Rome, the *Shepherd of Hermas*, where mention is made of believers receiving 'the seal' by descending into the water dead and arising alive.[9] On the other hand, while Carolyn Osiek is of the opinion this is 'unmistakably a reference to baptism', she points out that it differs significantly from Romans 6: 'The language of death and life is similar to Pauline language but is not exactly the same: here, death is the pre-baptismal state, not the dying process that is symbolically enacted in the course of baptism.'[10]

Some would add to this the evidence of the church order known as the *Apostolic Tradition* and attributed to Hippolytus. Not only, however, is the authenticity of this document now seriously questioned, and hence its reliability as a witness to early Roman liturgical customs,[11] but it is not explicit about the occasion of baptism: it only states that candidates are to bathe 'on the fifth day of the week' (Thursday), fast 'on the day of preparation of the Sabbath' (Friday), and assemble 'on the Sabbath' (Saturday) for a final exorcism by the bishop, before spending the whole night in vigil and being baptized at cockcrow.[12] While these directions are consistent with baptism at Easter, they do not necessarily require that conclusion to be drawn, and because the paschal season is mentioned elsewhere in the document (ch. 33), there would seem to be no reason why Easter would not have been specified here as the occasion for baptism if that indeed was what was meant. Hence those scholars who understand the text to be referring to a vigil that took place

---

8 Hippolytus, *Commentarium in Dan.* 1.16; ET from Cantalamessa, p. 60. On the identity of Hippolytus, see J. A. Cerrato, *Hippolytus between East and West: The Commentaries and the Provenance of the Corpus* (Oxford: Oxford University Press 2002).

9 *Similitude* 9.16.

10 Carolyn Osiek, *The Shepherd of Hermas: A Commentary* (Minneapolis: Fortress Press 1999), p. 238.

11 See Paul F. Bradshaw, Maxwell E. Johnson and L. Edward Phillips, *The Apostolic Tradition: A Commentary* (Minneapolis: Fortress Press 2002), pp. 1–6, 13–15.

12 *Apostolic Tradition* 20.5–21.1. See also Bradshaw, Johnson and Phillips, *The Apostolic Tradition: A Commentary*, pp. 110–11, 174–5.

whenever in the year baptism was administered may be correct,[13] but if so, at least this part of the text must have originated in an ecclesiastical setting like Rome or parts of North Africa where it was permitted to fast on other Saturdays in the year besides Easter.

From time to time attempts have been made to argue that the early Quartodeciman celebration of Pascha included the administration of baptism.[14] In an article published in 1973, however, while trying to present the most favourable case possible for an early date for the adoption of the paschal season for baptism, Stuart Hall was forced to admit how indefinite were the alleged allusions to paschal baptism in early sources,[15] and some years later in his edition of the *Peri Pascha* of Melito of Sardis he concluded that the case for paschal baptism in the second century was an unproven supposition.[16] Raniero Cantalamessa, too, expressed serious reservations about the suggestion that paschal baptism was practised among the Quartodecimans: the allusions to baptism in Quartodeciman sources dealing with Pascha do not refer explicitly to the actual administration of baptism on that occasion, and so that practice should not automatically be assumed to underlie them.[17] And more recently Stewart-Sykes has reached similar negative conclusions.[18]

There are, therefore, only two firm witnesses to the existence of a preference for baptism at Easter rather than at other times of the year prior to the fourth century, one from North Africa and the other possibly from Rome – two centres of primitive Christianity which frequently resemble one another and differ from the rest of the Church with regard to their liturgical practices. Nevertheless, scholars have often tended to assume that paschal baptism became widespread (some would say universal) during the third century. Such a conclusion is unwarranted. Not only is there a complete absence of such testimony

13 See, for example, Cantalamessa, p. 158, note a.

14 See, for example, Karl Gerlach, *The Antenicene Pascha: A Rhetorical History*, Liturgia condenda 7 (Louvain: Peeters 1998), pp. 61–5.

15 Stuart Hall, 'Paschal Baptism' in E. A. Livingstone (ed.), *Studia Evangelica* 6, Texte und Untersuchungen 112 (Berlin: Akademie-Verlag 1973), pp. 239–51.

16 S. G. Hall (ed.), *Melito of Sardis: On Pascha and Fragments* (Oxford: Clarendon Press 1979), p. xxviii.

17 Raniero Cantalamessa, *L'Omelia 'In S. Pascha' dello pseudo-Ippolito di Roma* (Milan: Vita e pensiero 1967), pp. 285–7.

18 Alistair Stewart-Sykes, *The Lamb's High Feast: Melito, Peri Pascha and the Quartodeciman Paschal Liturgy at Sardis* (Leiden: Brill 1998), pp. 176–82.

from other sources, but there is virtually nothing in the baptismal theology articulated by the Christian literature of this period which would have given any encouragement to such a practice. Christian writers tended to associate baptism with the concept of new birth, as in John 3, rather than with Romans 6. In such a theological climate, therefore, there would have been no reason to see Easter as any more appropriate for baptism than any other time of the year.

Besides North Africa and possibly Rome, only at Alexandria prior to the fourth century does any use seem to have been made of St Paul's imagery of baptism into the death and resurrection of Christ. While Clement of Alexandria referred to death in connection with baptism, but not explicitly to Paul's imagery,[19] Origen frequently drew on it,[20] and especially in his *Peri Pascha*, written after his move to Caesarea. Scholars have suggested that Origen's use of Romans 6 may well have played some role in the emphasis on this text for interpreting baptism that arose in the fourth century.[21] Buchinger similarly argues that Origen played a highly instrumental part in establishing a theological foundation to undergird the fourth-century trend towards the normativity of Easter baptism, although was not himself familiar with the actual practice of baptism at that festival.[22]

In any case, whatever may have been the case at Caesarea, one place where it appears that a preference for paschal baptism may well have been unknown before the middle of the fourth century is in the patriarchate of Alexandria. Talley, building upon the work of René-Georges Coquin, presented evidence for the existence in Egypt from early times of a 40-day fast in imitation of Jesus' fasting in the wilderness, which did not take place immediately before Easter but began on the day after 6 January, observed by the Alexandrian church as the celebration of the baptism of Jesus, and thus was situated in the correct chronological sequence of the Gospel accounts. He argued that this season functioned

---

19 Clement of Alexandria, *Excerpta* 77.
20 For example, in his *Homilia in Exod.* 5.2 (ET in Cantalamessa, p. 55), Origen links the three days of the Pascha with the threefold mystery of being baptized into Christ's death, being buried with him, and rising with him on the third day. See also Origen, *Contra Celsum* 2.69; *Commentarium in Evangelium Joannis* 1.27; *Homilia in Jer.* 1.16; 19.14; *In Jesu Nav.* 4.2.
21 See Maxwell E. Johnson, *Liturgy in Early Christian Egypt*, Alcuin/GROW Joint Liturgical Study 33 (Cambridge: Grove Books 1995), p. 7, n. 8.
22 Harald Buchinger, 'Towards the Origins of Paschal Baptism: The Contribution of Origen', *SL* 35 (2005), pp. 12–31. See also Harald Buchinger, *Pascha bei Origenes* (Innsbruck: Tyrolia-Verlag 2005).

as the final period of preparation for baptism in this region, with the rite itself being celebrated at the very end of the 40 days, whenever that happened to fall.[23]

There are even signs that a similar practice may once have existed in northern Italy. In the fourth century Ambrose refers to the enrolment of catechumens for paschal baptism at Milan as taking place at Epiphany,[24] and the same day seems to have been chosen at nearby Turin: Maximus addresses two sermons preached on the days immediately after Epiphany to catechumens apparently preparing for baptism at Easter.[25] Since elsewhere at this time candidates were enrolled at the beginning of Lent, is the northern Italian custom the vestige of an older tradition of baptizing 40 days after Epiphany?[26]

Testimony to a seemingly universal tradition of regarding Easter as the preferred occasion for baptism, therefore, emerges quite suddenly in the second half of the fourth century, much in the same way as does the evidence for the season of Lent a little earlier in the same century.[27] This suggests the possibility that there might have been some link between the emergence of these two liturgical phenomena. Could it be that both alike are results of post-Nicene attempts to bring the divergent customs of different churches into some sort of conformity? As we shall see in a later chapter, Alexandria (and perhaps other places) appear originally to have observed a pre-baptismal fast of 40 days unconnected to Easter; in North Africa (and Rome?) there was a tradition that regarded Easter as the preferred occasion for baptism, but preceded only by a shorter fast, of perhaps three weeks' duration; and other churches were familiar with the same three-week preparation for baptism but did not associate it with any particular period of the year. The arrangement which then became universal in the fourth century, of a preference for baptism at Easter preceded by 40-day season of fasting and preparation, would thus have been a post-Nicene amalgamation of these variant practices.

Nevertheless, paschal baptism does not seem ever to have become the normative feature of ancient Christianity that contemporary enthusiasts for liturgical reform would like it to have been. Even after its emergence in the fourth century, there were some significant differences in its status in different parts of the ancient world. In northern Italy, for

---

23 See below, pp. 99–101.

24 Ambrose, in *Expositio Evangelium S. Lucae* 4.76.

25 Maximus, *Sermones* 13; 65.

26 See Talley, *The Origins of the Liturgical Year*, p. 217.

27 See below, pp. 99ff.

example, it was apparently intended to be the one and only occasion in the year for the conferral of the sacrament. Ambrose reminded his hearers that in the Old Testament the high priest entered the inner sanctuary of the Temple only once a year. 'What is the purpose of all this? To enable you to understand what this inner tabernacle is, into which the high priest led you, where the custom is for him to enter *once a year*: it is the baptistery . . .'[28] Some confirmation of the exclusive character of paschal baptism in this region is provided by Maximus at Turin in the early fifth century. In a sermon preached on the feast of Pentecost he drew attention to the similarities between that feast and Easter, noting that both occasions were preceded by a Saturday fast and a vigil of prayer through the night, but made no mention of the celebration of baptism as being common to both;[29] and in another Pentecostal sermon he took up the same theme and remarked that 'at Easter all the pagans are usually baptized, while at Pentecost the apostles were baptized [with the Holy Spirit][30].' In this sermon, however, he seems to contradict what he said in the previous sermon about fasting on the Saturday before the feast of Pentecost by affirming that there was an unbroken period of 50 days during which no fasting took place.[31] It seems impossible to imagine, therefore, that Maximus can have been familiar with the practice of baptism at Pentecost and failed to refer to it here. Similarly, for both Ambrose and Maximus, a major theme of the feast of the Epiphany was the baptism of Christ, and yet neither ever alludes to a custom of baptizing converts on that occasion.[32]

At Rome, on the other hand, according to a letter of Pope Siricius to Himerius of Tarragona written in 385, both Easter and the day of Pentecost were the regular occasions for baptism. Siricius acknowledged that his fellow bishops elsewhere (probably in northern Spain, where the letter is directed) permitted the administration of baptism at Christmas, Epiphany, and on the feasts of apostles and martyrs. But 'with us and with all the churches'(!) these two feasts were the only days

---

28 Ambrose, *De sacramentis* 4.1–2; ET from E. J. Yarnold, *The Awe-Inspiring Rites of Initiation* (2nd edn, Edinburgh: T. & T. Clark/Collegeville: The Liturgical Press 1994), p. 128 (emphasis added).

29 Maximus, *Sermones* 40.1.

30 Maximus, *Sermones* 44.4.

31 See Robert Cabié, *La Pentecôte: L'evolution de la Cinquantaine pascale au cours des cinq premiers siècles* (Paris: Desclée 1965), pp. 141–2.

32 See Hieronymus Frank, 'Die Vorrangstellung der Taufe Jesu in der altmailändischen Epiphanieliturgie und der Frage nach dem Dichter des Epiphaniehymnus Illuminans Altissimus', *ALW* 13 (1971), pp. 115–32.

in the year for the regular celebration of the sacrament.[33] Pope Leo in 447 similarly wrote to the bishops of Sicily expressing astonishment that baptism could be celebrated at Epiphany, contrary to the tradition of the apostles: because of its connection with the resurrection, baptism belonged to Easter and also to the feast of Pentecost, which commemorated the coming of the Holy Spirit and was linked to Easter. Moreover, did not St Peter baptize 3,000 people on the day of Pentecost? And because, according to the Apostolic rule, baptism should be preceded by exorcism, fasting and instruction, only these two occasions should be kept.[34] Leo's sermons, however, make it clear that regular fasting was not resumed at Rome until the feast of Pentecost was over,[35] which suggests that the preparation of baptismal candidates for Pentecost must have taken place during Lent together with that of the candidates for paschal baptism. In other words, Pentecost was still understood here as only an 'overflow' from Easter and not a baptismal day in its own right.

Nevertheless, we need to treat the Roman evidence for the normative character of baptism at Easter and Pentecost with some caution. The letters of Siricius and Leo both reveal that in other parts of the West Epiphany and other festivals were regarded as regular occasions for the conferral of the sacrament; and in another letter written in 459 Leo also referred to certain bishops from central Italy who celebrated baptism on the feasts of the martyrs.[36] Augustine knew Easter and Pentecost as regular baptismal occasions, but also acknowledged the existence of baptismal celebrations at other times in the year.[37] Thus, the alleged 'Apostolic tradition' did not apparently extend beyond Rome and northern Italy, and even at Rome itself it was certainly not absolute. For in the very same letter to Himerius, Siricius admitted that infants and those in danger of dying were not to wait until one of the two occasions but should be baptized with all haste; and Innocent I at the end of the fourth century claimed that not a day passed at Rome on which 'the divine sacrifice or the office of baptism' did not take place.[38] Even after

---

33 Siricius, *Ep. ad Himerium* 1.2.3. Cabié, *La Pentecôte*, p. 120, argues that Pentecost is to be understood here as referring to the fiftieth day alone and not to the whole Easter season.

34 Leo, *Ep.* 16.

35 Leo, *De Pentecoste* 2.9; *Sermones* 78–81.

36 Leo, *Ep.* 168.

37 Augustine, *Sermones* 210.2. For baptism at Pentecost, see Augustine, *Sermones* 266, 272; and Cabié, *La Pentecôte*, p. 206. Ambrosiaster, *In Eph.* 4, also refers to baptism at other times of the year.

38 Innocent I, *Ep. ad Victricium* 9.

making allowance for some degree of exaggeration in this remark, it would seem that, whatever the theory, in actual reality the celebration of baptism must have been a fairly frequent occurrence in that city and by no means merely a single annual event.

We can also document similar traditions in the East to those in the West that were condemned by Siricius and his successors. Gregory of Nazianzus, in a sermon preached in 381, rejects excuses made by catechumens that they want to wait for Epiphany, Easter or Pentecost to be baptized on the grounds that it was better to be baptized close to the baptism of Christ, or to receive the new life on the day of Christ's resurrection, or to honour the manifestation of the Spirit. Gregory himself recommends them not to delay their baptism and thereby avoid the risk of dying unbaptized.[39] This passage reveals that not only was Epiphany an established occasion for baptism in Cappadocia along with Easter and Pentecost, but that there was here no limitation on baptism at any time in the year. Jerusalem also seems to have been familiar with a tradition of reserving baptism to these same three feasts in the first half of the fourth century,[40] although the sources from later in the century – the baptismal catecheses of Cyril of Jerusalem and the diary of the pilgrim Egeria – make mention only of Pascha as a baptismal occasion. Similarly, Basil of Caesarea, while acknowledging that every time was 'opportune for being saved through baptism', claimed that the day of Pascha was more opportune because it was 'a memorial of the resurrection, and baptism is a power for resurrection'.[41] We should also note that John Chrysostom 20 years later (*c.* 400/401) rejected Pentecost as a baptismal occasion at Constantinople.[42] Because he was forced to argue the case, however, this may mean that the restriction was a relatively recent innovation, as Robert Cabié has suggested,[43] or at least an attempt to stop a widespread custom from being adopted in that city.

Finally, we should note that baptism at the paschal season did not everywhere mean baptism within the Easter vigil itself. Indeed, Cantalamessa has warned against assuming that Tertullian was necessarily

---

39 Gregory of Nazianzus, *Oratio XL, In sanctum baptisma* 24.
40 See Abraham Terian, *Macarius of Jerusalem, Letter to the Armenians, A.D. 335*, AVANT: Treasures of the Armenian Christian Tradition 4 (Crestwood, NY: St Vladimir's Seminary Press 2008), p. 83.
41 Basil of Caesarea, *Homilia* 13.1; ET from Cantalamessa, p. 75.
42 John Chrysostom, *In Acta Apostolorum homilia* 1.6.
43 Cabié, *La Pentecôte*, pp. 202–3.

referring to the vigil when he spoke of baptism at Pascha.[44] Moreover, when some time in the middle of the fourth century Alexandria finally transferred its older post-Epiphany 40-day fast culminating in the celebration of baptism to a location immediately before Easter, it apparently did not incorporate the baptismal rite within the paschal vigil. Although witnesses to the Alexandrian tradition are rather limited and not entirely reliable, it seems that the baptisms may have taken place at first on the Saturday morning before Easter, and later, when a further week was prefixed to the Lenten season, were moved back to the end of the previous week, so that they still came at the conclusion of 40 days.[45]

Something similar may once have been the case at Constantinople, although the evidence is far from clear. The ninth- and tenth-century sources there include provision for a full baptismal liturgy both on the morning of what was known as Lazarus Saturday (one week before Easter and at the end of the 40-day Lenten season) and also at the paschal vigil itself. Furthermore, one tenth-century typikon, *Hagios Stavros* 40, directs the patriarch to perform the baptisms after the morning office on Holy Saturday. Juan Mateos suggested that the two Saturday morning celebrations were introduced in order to reduce the numbers to be baptized at the vigil,[46] but Talley thought it more probable that the Holy Saturday morning celebration had been added as a more convenient occasion for the baptism of infants, with the other two older celebrations being thereafter retained in the liturgical books but rarely, if at all, being found in practice.[47] Even if Talley is correct, that still leaves the question as to which of the other two occasions – Lazarus Saturday morning and the paschal vigil – was the original, since it seems improbable that both can claim equal antiquity at Constantinople. If the custom of baptizing at the vigil was established first, then Mateos's suggestion that a second baptismal occasion one week earlier was subsequently needed in order to cope with overwhelming numbers

---

44 Cantalamessa, *L'Omelia 'In S. Pascha' dello pseudo-Ippolito di Roma*, pp. 283–4. See also Talley, *The Origins of the Liturgical Year*, p. 35.

45 See Paul F. Bradshaw, 'Baptismal Practice in the Alexandrian Tradition: Eastern or Western?' in Paul F. Bradshaw (ed.), *Essays in Early Eastern Initiation*, Alcuin/GROW Joint Liturgical Study 8 (Nottingham: Grove Books 1988), pp. 5–17, here at pp. 8–9 = Maxwell E. Johnson (ed.), *Living Water, Sealing Spirit: Essays on Christian Initiation* (Collegeville: The Liturgical Press 1995), pp. 82–100, here at pp. 86–9.

46 Juan Mateos (ed.), *Le Typicon de la Grande Église* 2, OCA 166 (Rome: Pontifical Oriental Institute 1963), p. 63, n. 2.

47 Talley, *The Origins of the Liturgical Year*, pp. 188–9.

seems the only plausible explanation. The reverse possibility – that the custom of baptizing on Lazarus Saturday morning at the conclusion of the 40-day Lent was introduced first, in imitation of Alexandrian practice, but that later it was necessary to add the celebration of baptism at the Easter vigil in order to bring the Constantinopolitan church into line with liturgical practice elsewhere – is attractive, but open to objections. On the other hand, it is interesting to note that the last day on which candidates for baptism at the paschal season were permitted to enrol in the catechumenate at Constantinople was exactly three weeks before Lazarus Saturday – and that is precisely the duration of the original period of final preparation for baptism found in many parts of the ancient church.[48]

In conclusion, therefore, it seems very probable that prior to the middle of the fourth century preference for paschal baptism was merely a local custom of the Roman and North African churches, and even when it was more widely adopted at that time, there is clear evidence that in many parts of the ancient world other festivals in the liturgical year challenged the exclusive claims of the paschal season, to say nothing of signs of the continuing acceptance of the legitimacy of baptisms at any time of the year. Whatever the *theory* may have been in some places, therefore, it looks as though baptism at Easter was never the normative *practice* in Christian antiquity that many have assumed. The most that can be said is that it was an experiment that survived for less than 50 years. Like the seed sown on rocky ground, it endured for a while but eventually withered away.

---

48 See Maxwell E. Johnson, 'From Three Weeks to Forty Days: Baptismal Preparation and the Origins of Lent', *SL* 20 (1990), pp. 185–200 = Johnson, *Living Water, Sealing Spirit*, pp. 118–36; and below, pp. 92–5.

Lent and Holy Week

Chapter 10

The emergence of Lent and Holy Week

It was once commonly assumed that the 40-day period of pre-paschal preparation for baptismal candidates, penitents and the Christian community in general, known as 'Lent' (*Quadragesima* or *Tessarakoste*, i.e., 'forty'), had its origin as a gradual backwards development of the short preparatory and purificatory fast held before the annual celebration of Pascha.[1] According to this standard theory, the one- or two-day fast before Pascha (as attested by Tertullian in *De ieiunio* 13–14) became extended to include:

- the entire week, later called 'Great Week' or 'Holy Week', beginning on the preceding Monday;
- a three-week period (at least in Rome) including this 'Holy Week'; and, finally,
- a six-week, 40-day preparation period assimilating those preparing for Easter baptism to the 40-day temptation of Jesus in the desert.

That this pre-paschal period finally became 40 days in length in the fourth century has traditionally been explained by an appeal to a shift in world-view on the part of the immediate post-Constantinian Christian community. That is, instead of an eschatological orientation to the imminent *parousia* of Christ little concerned with historical events, sites and time, the post-Constantinian context of the fourth century reveals a

---

1 See Adolf Adam, *The Liturgical Year: Its History and Meaning after the Reform of the Liturgy* (New York: Pueblo 1981), pp. 91ff.; Gregory Dix, *The Shape of the Liturgy* (London: Dacre 1945), pp. 347–60; Patrick Regan, 'The Three Days and the Forty Days' in Maxwell E. Johnson (ed.), *Between Memory and Hope: Readings on the Liturgical Year* (Collegeville: The Liturgical Press 2000), pp. 125–41; Pierre Jounel, 'The Year' in A.-G. Martimort *et al.* (eds), *The Church at Prayer* 4 (Collegeville: The Liturgical Press 1986), pp. 31–150, here at pp. 65–72.

Church whose liturgy has become principally a historical remembrance and commemoration of the *past*; a liturgy increasingly splintered into separate commemorations of historical events in the life of Christ. As the primary and most influential proponent of this theory of fourth-century 'historicism', Gregory Dix explained it thus:

> The step of identifying the six weeks' fast with the 40 days' fast of our Lord in the wilderness was obviously in keeping with the new histori-cal interest of the liturgy. The actual number of '40 days' of fasting was made up by extending Lent behind the sixth Sunday before Easter in various ways. But the association with our Lord's fast in the wilderness was an idea attached to the season of Lent only *after* it had come into existence in connection with the preparation of candidates for baptism.[2]

As Robert Taft and John Baldovin have demonstrated,[3] however, the historical situation cannot be explained adequately as a simple interpre-tive shift from a pre-Nicene eschatological orientation to a fourth-century historical one. 'Eschatology' and 'history' are not mutually exclusive. As we have already seen with the Quartodeciman Pascha,[4] both eschatological orientation *and* the celebration of Pascha on the exact date of Christ's Passion, 14 Nisan, could go together. Recent scholarship on Lent, most notably by Talley[5] and even more recently by Nicholas Russo,[6] has necessitated revising previous theories based on this assumption of historicism. We can no longer speak of a *single* origin for Lent but, rather, of multiple origins for this period, which in the fourth-century post-Nicene context become universally standardized and fixed as the '40 days' that have characterized pre-paschal prepara-tion ever since.

---

2 Dix, *The Shape of the Liturgy*, p. 354.

3 Robert Taft, 'Historicism Revisited', in Robert Taft, *Beyond East and West: Problems in Liturgical Understanding* (2nd edn, Rome: Edizioni Orientalia Christiana 1997), pp. 42–9; John Baldovin, *The Urban Character of Christian Worship*, OCA 228 (Rome: Pon-tifical Oriental Institute 1987), pp. 90–3.

4 See above, pp. 39–45.

5 Thomas J. Talley, *The Origins of the Liturgical Year* (New York: Pueblo 1986; 2nd edn, Collegeville: The Liturgical Press 1991), pp. 163–238; and 'The Origin of Lent at Alexandria', in Thomas J. Talley, *Worship: Reforming Tradition* (Washington, DC: The Pastoral Press 1990), pp. 87–112 = Johnson, *Between Memory and Hope*, pp. 183–206.

6 Nicholas Russo, 'The Origins of Lent' (PhD dissertation, University of Notre Dame 2009).

Whenever and however Easter came to be universally celebrated on a Sunday in Christian antiquity, third-century sources indicate that the two-day fast on the Friday and Saturday before the celebration of Pascha was becoming a six-day pre-paschal fast in Alexandria and Syria.[7] Although this extension has often been interpreted as the initial stage in the development of the 40-day Lent (since this week is included in the overall calculation of Lent in later liturgical sources), this six-day preparatory fast is better interpreted as the origin of what would come to be called 'Holy Week' or 'Great Week' throughout the churches of the ancient world. Talley observed that within the later Byzantine tradition Lazarus Saturday and Palm Sunday divide Lent, which precedes them, from the six-day pre-paschal fast of Great Week, which follows, and these days were known already in fourth-century Jerusalem.[8] Rather than being related specifically to the origins of Lent, therefore, the two-day (or one-week) fast in these third-century sources (with the possible exception of *Apostolic Tradition* 20[9]) seems to have been an independent preparation of the faithful for the imminent celebration of Pascha itself. Already in the pre-Nicene *Didascalia Apostolorum*, this fast is related, chronologically, to events in the last week of Jesus' life. In other words, the *Holy Week* fast, properly speaking, is not *Lent* but a pre-paschal fast alone, which overlaps with, but should not be confused with, that longer preparatory period that comes to be known as Lent.

---

7 On this see above, pp. 52–5.
8 Talley, *The Origins of the Liturgical Year*, pp. 176–214. See also Talley, 'The Origin of Lent at Alexandria,' pp. 97–108.
9 See above, pp. 78–9.

Chapter 11

Three weeks and forty days

The fifth-century Byzantine historian Socrates describes his understanding of the variety of Lenten observances throughout the Christian
churches of his day:

> The fasts before Easter will be found to be differently observed
> among different people. Those at Rome fast three successive weeks
> before Easter, excepting Saturdays and Sundays. Those in Illyrica and
> all over Greece and Alexandria observe a fast of six weeks, which they
> term 'the forty days' fast'. Others commencing their fast from the
> seventh week before Easter, and fasting three five days only, and that
> at intervals, yet call that time 'the forty days' fast'. It is indeed surpris-
> ing to me that thus differing in the number of days, they should both
> give it one common appellation; but some assign one reason for it,
> and others another, according to their several fancies.[1]

What is most intriguing about Socrates' statement is his reference to a
three-week Lenten fast at Rome. Since he corrects himself about
Saturdays as non-fasting days in Rome later in this work and since
Athanasius (in his Festal Letter of 340[2]), Jerome (in a letter to Marcella
in 384[3]) and Pope Siricius (in a letter to Himerius of Tarragona in 385[4])
refer to an established pattern of a 40-day Lent there too, his statement
is inaccurate as a fifth-century description. Nevertheless, his reference to
'three successive weeks' of fasting appears to be corroborated by later
sources of the Roman liturgy. Such evidence includes:

---

1 Socrates, *Historia ecclesiastica* 5.22; ET from *NPNF* 2nd Series 2, p. 131.
2 *The Festal Epistles of S. Athanasius* (Oxford: Parker 1854), p. 100.
3 *Ep.* 24.4 (*PL* 22:428).
4 *PL* 13:1131–47.

- the provision of three *missae pro scrutiniis* (masses for the scrutinies of baptismal candidates) assigned to the third, fourth and fifth Sundays of Lent in the Gelasian Sacramentary (seventh century);
- the course reading of the Gospel of John during the last three weeks of Lent (beginning in the Würzburg Capitulary, the earliest Roman lectionary, *c.* 700, on the Friday before the third Sunday in Lent and reaching its conclusion on Good Friday); and
- the titles *Hebdomada in mediana* (week in the middle) and *Dominica in mediana* (Sunday in the middle), applied, respectively, to the fourth week and fifth Sunday of Lent in various *ordines Romani* (ceremonial and rubrical guides) and Roman lectionaries.

In the light of all this, Socrates' inaccurate fifth-century description may well indicate the remnant of a well-ingrained three-week Lenten period in Rome some time earlier. Such, at least, was the conclusion of Antoine Chavasse from his analysis of the Johannine readings of the last three weeks of Lent,[5] which he was able to reconstruct as an independent set of lections that he believed must once have constituted an original three-week Lenten period, including Holy Week. Chavasse noted that the series of Johannine readings during the last three weeks of Lent in early Roman lectionaries and in the Tridentine *Missale Romanum* began with John 4.5–32 on the Friday of Lent III. For some reason, however, it placed John 9.1–38 (Wednesday of Lent IV) and John 11.1–45 (Friday of Lent IV) *before* John 8.46–59 (Sunday of Lent V), and John 10.22–38 (Wednesday of Lent V) with the continuation of John 11 (47–54) on the Friday of Lent V. On this basis he attempted to reconstruct an earlier shape for this Johannine series, which he believed would have corresponded to the three *missae pro scrutiniis* in the Gelasian Sacramentary. According to his reconstruction, John 4.5–32, John 9.1–38 and John 11.1–54 would have been read, respectively, on the third, fourth and fifth Sundays in Lent in the time of Leo the Great.

---

5 See Antoine Chavasse, 'La structure du Carême et les lectures des messes quadragesimales dans la liturgie romaine', *La Maison-Dieu* 31 (1952), pp. 76–120; 'La préparation de la Pâque, à Rome, avant le Ve siècle. Jeûne et organisation liturgique' in *Memorial J. Chaine* (Lyon: Facultés catholiques 1950), pp. 61–80; and 'Temps de préparation à la Pâque, d'après quelques livres liturgiques romains', *Recherches de science religieuse* 37 (1950), pp. 125–45. For a more detailed summary and discussion of Chavasse's work, see Maxwell E. Johnson, 'From Three Weeks to Forty Days: Baptismal Preparation and the Origins of Lent', *SL* 20 (1990).

Even so, at an earlier stage of development this would have constituted a short lectionary series for the Sundays of an original three-week Lenten period, including Holy Week. The reason that this series of readings appears in a different sequence in later Roman sources, according to Chavasse, is that the baptismal scrutinies along with their readings became shifted to weekdays (ultimately, seven in number) in the later Roman tradition.[6] Along similar lines, Talley also concluded that Socrates' reference may reflect an earlier, if not fifth-century, Roman practice.[7]

The possibility of an original three-week Lent is not limited to Rome. On the basis of a detailed structural analysis of the contents of the fifth-century Armenian Lectionary, a lectionary generally understood to reflect fourth-century Jerusalem practice, Mario F. Lages argued that early Jerusalem practice, too, knew an original three-week Lenten preparation period of catechumens for paschal baptism.[8] This lectionary includes a canon of Lenten readings with concluding psalmody assigned to Wednesday and Friday gatherings at Sion and a list of 19 catechetical biblical readings assigned to Lenten catechesis, which parallel the pre-baptismal catecheses of Cyril of Jerusalem. Lages also pointed to the introductory rubric in the ninth- or tenth-century Armenian rite of baptism and to a pertinent rubric in the fifth-century Georgian Lectionary. The Armenian baptismal rubric reads in part:

> The Canon of Baptism when they make a Christian. Before which it is not right to admit him into church. But he shall have hands laid on beforehand, *three weeks or more* before the baptism, in time sufficient

---

6 Thanks to the work of Chavasse, this is precisely the sequence of Sunday Gospel readings assigned to the third, fourth and fifth Sundays in Lent in Series A of the current Roman Lectionary. To these Sundays have been attached the three scrutinies of adult catechumens in the current Roman *Rite of Christian Initiation of Adults*. See also here the recent essay by Dominic Serra, 'New Observations about the Scrutinies of the Elect in Early Roman Practice', *Worship* 80 (2006), pp. 511–27.

7 Thomas J. Talley, *The Origins of the Liturgical Year* (New York: Pueblo 1986; 2nd edn, Collegeville: The Liturgical Press 1991), p. 167.

8 Mario F. Lages, 'Étapes de l'évolution de carême à Jérusalem avant le Ve siècle. Essai d'analyse structurale', *Revue des Études Armeniénnes* 6 (1969), pp. 67–102; and 'The Hierosolymitain Origin of the Catechetical Rites in the Armenian Liturgy', *Didaskalia* 1 (1967), pp. 233–50. See also Maxwell E. Johnson, 'Reconciling Cyril and Egeria on the Catechetical Process in Fourth-Century Jerusalem' in Paul F. Bradshaw (ed.), *Essays in Early Eastern Initiation*, Alcuin/GROW Joint Liturgical Study 8 (Nottingham: Grove Books 1988), pp. 24–6. For the Armenian Lectionary, see Charles (Athanase) Renoux, *Le Codex arménien Jérusalem 121* 2, Patrologia Orientalis 36 (Turnhout: Brepols 1971).

for him to learn from the Wardapet [Instructor] both the faith and the baptism of the Church.[9]

And the Georgian Lectionary, while listing the same 19 catechetical readings as Cyril and the Armenian Lectionary, specifically directs that catechesis is to begin with these readings on the Monday of the fifth week in Lent, that is, exactly *19* days (or approximately three weeks) before paschal baptism.[10]

That is not all: this early three-week Lenten period in Rome and Jerusalem was customary in other liturgical traditions as well. A similar three-week period of final preparation for baptismal candidates is discernible from an analysis of the last three weeks of the 40-day Lent in North Africa, Naples, Constantinople and Spain.[11] For Spain, in particular, this three-week period appears to be confirmed by the first canon of the Second Council of Braga (572), which directs that bishops 'shall teach that catechumens (as the ancient canons command) shall come for the cleansing of exorcism twenty days before baptism, in which twenty days they shall especially be taught the Creed, which is: I believe in God the Father Almighty . . .'.[12] And, at Constantinople, the extant typika of the ninth- and tenth-century Byzantine Liturgy specify that no one might enter the pre-baptismal catechumenate any later than *three weeks* before Lazarus Saturday (the day before Palm Sunday), the day on which the patriarch himself presided at baptism in the little baptistery of Hagia Sophia.[13] Still today, Christians of the Byzantine tradition sing a baptismal *troparion* (entrance hymn) based on Galatians 3.27 on Lazarus Saturday. An almost identical pattern of three weeks of preparation before Palm Sunday appears also in the early medieval sources for the Ambrosian Rite in Milan.[14] What Socrates says about the 'three successive weeks' of pre-paschal fasting at Rome, therefore, may well be seen as the memory of an early Christian practice which was much more universal than Roman in its scope.

On the basis of this discernible pattern in Christian liturgical sources, Lawrence Hoffman suggested that this practice has its ultimate roots in

---

9 *DBL*, p. 74 (emphasis added).
10 Michel Tarschnischvili, *Le Grand Lectionnaire de l'Église de Jérusalem* 1, Corpus Scriptorum Christianorum Orientalium 188 (Louvain 1959), p. 68.
11 Johnson, 'From Three Weeks to Forty Days', pp. 191–3.
12 *DBL*, p. 158.
13 See above, pp. 85–6.
14 See *DBL*, pp. 184–5, 198–9.

Judaism.[15] Hoffman notes that, according to rabbinic sources, the feast of Passover itself is preceded by lectionary readings (Exod. 12 or Num. 19) on the third Sabbath prior to its arrival that stress either preparation for the Passover sacrifice or the necessity of being cleansed from impurity. The Exodus 12 reading, he notes further, was cited by Chavasse as an early reading for Good Friday at Rome and the prophetic reading of Ezekiel 36.25–36 (accompanying Num. 19 according to the Tosefta) appears on the Wednesday of Lent IV in early Roman lectionaries, that is, two and a half weeks before Easter. According to Hoffman, therefore, the early three-week Lent – at least in Jerusalem and Rome – was 'a Christian application of Judaism's insistence that one count back three weeks from Passover in order to cleanse oneself and prepare for the sacrifice of the Paschal lamb'.[16] If Hoffman is correct, then, as Talley writes, 'this could well suggest that the three-week preparation for Pascha antedates its employment as the framework for baptismal preparation'.[17]

The strength and appeal of Hoffman's theory are that it appears to provide a firm rationale for the Christian choice of a three-week period of preparation. The problem, however, is that when we first see whatever evidence there is for this three-week 'Lent' (with the exception of Socrates' general reference to fasting), it is already closely associated with the final preparation of catechumens for baptism; and not always clearly associated with *Easter* baptism.

---

15 Lawrence A. Hoffman, 'The Jewish Lectionary, the Great Sabbath, and the Lenten Calendar: Liturgical Links between Christians and Jews in the First Three Christian Centuries' in J. Neil Alexander (ed.), *Time and Community* (Washington, DC: The Pastoral Press 1990), pp. 3–20. See also Stéphane Verhelst, 'Histoire de la durée du Carême à Jérusalem', *QL* 84 (2003), pp. 23–50, who argues that the three-week and eight-week Lenten patterns in Jerusalem both have their roots in Judaism, the three-week period having its origins before Pascha, but transferred to before the commemoration of the destruction of the Temple on the 9 of Av (August) with a seven-week period following it. Later, the seven-week period, called the Ninevite Fast, was moved from its associations with the 9 of Av and was located ten weeks before Pascha. Here, as elsewhere, Verhelst's theory rests upon an assumption that the commemoration of the destruction of the Temple was an annual celebration among the Jerusalem Christians and so important that it actually gave rise to two 'Lenten' seasons, an earlier three-week one and a later eight-week one, or a combination thereof. While there may be something to this, it strikes us as too speculative to warrant acceptance.

16 Hoffman, 'The Jewish Lectionary, the Great Sabbath, and the Lenten Calendar', p. 14.

17 Talley, *The Origins of the Liturgical Year*, p. 167.

The Armenian baptismal rubric, for example, stresses three weeks of preparation for baptism without specifying when that baptism is to take place. But the early Syrian and Armenian traditions favoured baptism in relationship to Epiphany, not Easter, since they understood Christian initiation as the *mimesis* of the Jordan event interpreted in the light of the rebirth imagery of John 3 rather than the paschal imagery of Romans 6.[18] The three-week period of preparation was therefore more probably associated with catechumenal preparation for baptism without having anything to do specifically with Easter.[19] Similarly, thanks again to the work of Talley, it is now a commonly accepted hypothesis that prior to the post-Nicene context of the fourth century, the Alexandrian tradition knew neither Easter baptism nor a pre-paschal 'Lent' longer than the *one* week of the paschal fast. And, it must be noted, the reference to 'three weeks' in the Constantinopolitan liturgy is actually a reference in the typika to the enrolment of baptismal candidates exactly three weeks before the celebration of baptism on Lazarus Saturday (the day before Palm Sunday and a full week before Easter), a day which in current Byzantine usage still contains the vestige of a baptismal liturgy in its entrance antiphon.[20]

Because of the primary association of this three-week period with baptismal preparation, the real question, therefore, is whether or not this period must necessarily be connected to Easter and, consequently, to a pre-paschal *Lent*. Talley stated that 'Pascha was becoming the preferred time for baptism in many parts of the Church' in the third century,[21] but a much different conclusion has been offered in a previous chapter.[22] As we have seen, the most that can be said about Easter baptism before the fourth century is that there is a preference expressed for this practice, a preference limited to third-century North Africa (Tertullian) and possibly Rome (Hippolytus' *Commentary on Daniel*), with its possible celebration on other days by no means excluded. Only in the post-Nicene context of the fourth century does

---

18 See below, Chapter 16.

19 For further discussion, see Lawrence A. Hoffman and Maxwell E. Johnson, 'Lent in Perspective: A Summary Dialogue' in Paul F. Bradshaw and Lawrence A. Hoffman (eds), *Passover and Easter: The Symbolic Structuring of Sacred Seasons* (Notre Dame: University of Notre Dame Press 1999), pp. 55–70.

20 See Talley, *The Origins of the Liturgical Year*, pp. 189, 203–14. See also above, p. 95.

21 Talley, *The Origins of the Liturgical Year*, p. 167.

22 See above, pp. 75–86.

paschal baptism become a near universal Christian *ideal*. Even then, however, it does not appear to become the only or dominant custom outside of Rome or northern Italy. The letter of Pope Siricius to Himerius of Tarragona, one of the earliest Roman references to a 40-day Lent, reveals a variety of baptismal occasions in Spain (i.e., Christmas, Epiphany and the feasts of apostles and martyrs). Evidence from Leo I demonstrates that Epiphany was also a baptismal day in Sicily and that the feasts of martyrs were baptismal occasions elsewhere in Italy. And a sermon of Gregory of Nazianzus shows, similarly, that Epiphany baptism was a common practice in Cappadocia. These examples, along with those of Alexandria and Constantinople referred to above, lead to the conclusion that baptism at Easter was never the normative *practice* in Christian antiquity that many have assumed.

What, then, may be concluded about Socrates' three weeks and the origins of Lent? As we have seen, it is primarily within the context of final baptismal preparation where references to this three-week period are discerned. But what is most striking is that not all of these sources refer to *Easter* baptism. We seem therefore to have a three-week period of (final) catechetical preparation for baptism that only later gets associated with Easter. It becomes 'Lent' simply because Easter gradually becomes the preferred day for Christian initiation. Whenever baptism occurred, it was preceded, as the Armenian baptismal rubric says, by 'three weeks or more' of preparation. For those churches (North Africa and Rome) that 'preferred' to celebrate initiation at Easter, we may speak of this three-week period as a kind of primitive 'Lent'. For those that did not have such an early preference, this three-week period was not 'Lent' but merely a final catechetical baptismal preparation for whenever baptism itself was to occur. Only when paschal baptism becomes the normative ideal – in the second half of the fourth century – do these variations become blurred, harmonized, and thus brought into universal conformity as part of the newly developed pre-paschal *Quadragesima* or *Tessarakoste*.

Chapter 12

The development of Lent

The pre-paschal Lent of 40 days, like the universal ideal of paschal baptism itself, also appears to be a fourth-century post-Nicene development. Talley wrote:

> [T]he Council of Nicaea is something of a watershed for the fast of forty days. Prior to Nicaea, no record exists of such a forty-day fast before Easter. Only a few years after the council, however, we encounter it in most of the church as either a well-established custom or one that has become so nearly universal as to impinge on those churches that have not yet adopted it.[1]

From where, then, does this 40-day fast as a pre-paschal preparation period emerge?

Following the initial work of Anton Baumstark and René-Georges Coquin,[2] it was Talley himself who provided what, until recently, has been the standard answer to this question by directing scholarly attention to Alexandria. Within this tradition, neither Easter baptism nor a pre-paschal fast of more than one week was customarily known at the earliest stages. And there are references in the sources of this tradition to a 40-day fast separate from this one-week pre-paschal fast. These references appear in Origen's *Homilies on Leviticus* 10.2, in the context of remarks concerning the reconciliation of penitent apostates in Peter of Alexandria's *Canonical Epistle* (c. 305), and in the *Canons of*

---

1 Thomas J. Talley, *The Origins of the Liturgical Year* (New York: Pueblo 1986; 2nd edn, Collegeville: The Liturgical Press 1991), p. 168.
2 Anton Baumstark, *Comparative Liturgy* (London: Mowbray 1958), p. 194; René-Georges Coquin, 'Une réforme liturgique du concile de Nicée (325)?' in *Comptes Rendus* (Paris: Académie des Inscriptions et Belles-lettres 1967), pp. 178–92.

Hippolytus (c. 336–40), the earliest document derived from the so-called *Apostolic Tradition*:

- (Origen): They fast, therefore, who have lost the bridegroom; we having him with us cannot fast. Nor do we say that we relax the restraints of Christian abstinence; for we have the *forty days consecrated to fasting*, we have the fourth and sixth days of the week, on which we fast solemnly.[3]
- (Peter I of Alexandria, Canon 1): for they did not come to this of their own will, but were betrayed by the frailty of the flesh; for they show in their bodies the marks of Jesus, and some are now, for the third year, bewailing their fault: it is sufficient, I say, that from the time of their submissive approach, *other forty days* should be enjoined upon them, to keep them in remembrance of these things; *those forty days* during which, though our Lord and Saviour Jesus Christ had fasted, He was yet, after He had been baptized, tempted by the devil. And when they shall have, during these days, exercised themselves much, and constantly fasted, then let them watch in prayer, meditating upon what was spoken by the Lord to him who tempted Him to fall down and worship him: 'Get behind me, Satan; for it is written, Thou shalt worship the Lord thy God, and Him only shalt thou serve.'[4]
- (*Canons of Hippolytus* 12): *during forty days* they [the catechumens] are to hear the word and if they are worthy they are to be baptized.[5]
- (*Canons of Hippolytus* 20): The fast days which have been fixed are Wednesday, Friday, *and the Forty*. He who adds to this list will receive a reward, and whoever diverges from it, except for illness, constraint, or necessity, transgresses the rule and disobeys God *who fasted on our behalf.*[6]

While in two of these sources the 40 days of fasting are explicitly related to Jesus' own post-baptismal temptation in the desert, none of them

---

3 ET from Talley, *The Origins of the Liturgical Year*, p. 192 (emphasis added).
4 ET from *ANF* 6, p. 269 (emphasis added).
5 Paul F. Bradshaw, *The Canons of Hippolytus*, Alcuin/GROW Joint Liturgical Study 2 (Nottingham: Grove Books 1987), pp. 17–18 (emphasis added). It is to be noted, however, that Russo would instead translate the phrase as 'after forty days', implying that the hearing of the word only began when that period was over: see Nicholas Russo, 'The Origins of Lent' (PhD dissertation, University of Notre Dame 2009), p. 332.
6 Bradshaw, *The Canons of Hippolytus*, p. 25 (emphasis added).

speak of this period in relationship to Easter and only one of them to baptismal preparation. It would be very difficult, therefore, to interpret these '40 days' as clearly referring to a period connected to a pre-paschal 40-day Lent in Egypt.

Might they, however, be references to a unique and early Alexandrian custom and season? Talley certainly believed so and, after a detailed analysis of admittedly later Egyptian liturgical sources, concluded that this unique and early Alexandrian 40-day fast soon became a 40-day *pre-baptismal* fast for catechumens begun on the day after Epiphany (6 January), a feast which celebrated the baptism of Jesus. Following the chronology of the Gospel of Mark – the Gospel that Talley claimed was traditionally associated with the church of Alexandria – this fasting period concluded 40 days later with the solemn celebration of baptism and, in light of Canon 1 of Peter of Alexandria, perhaps with the reconciliation of penitents.

In conjunction with baptism, according to Talley, a passage may have been read from an alleged lost secret Gospel of Mark (the *Mar Saba Clementine Fragment*), which describes an 'initiation'(?) rite administered by Jesus himself. In this *Mar Saba Clementine Fragment*, a letter extant only in fragmentary form, Clement of Alexandria, its purported author, addresses a certain Theodore regarding a *mystikon evangelion* (a 'mystic' or 'secret' gospel), which contains certain additions to the Gospel of Mark, and which Mark himself allegedly added to his Gospel after coming to Alexandria from Rome.[7] These additions were to be read 'only to those who are being initiated into the great mysteries'.[8] Between the canonical Mark 10.32–34 and Mark 10.35–45 (where Jesus refers to the disciples sharing in his 'baptism' and drinking his 'cup') this 'Clementine' version of Mark inserts a narrative about Jesus 'initiating' a Lazarus-like figure he had raised from death six days earlier:

And they come to Bethany. And a certain woman whose brother had died was there. And, coming, she prostrated herself before Jesus and says to him, 'Son of David, have mercy on me.' But the disciples rebuked her. And Jesus, being angered, went off with her into the

---

7 This document was allegedly discovered by Morton Smith in Mar Saba (near Jerusalem) in 1958 and was subsequently analysed and edited by him, appearing as *Clement of Alexandria and a Secret Gospel of Mark* (Cambridge, MA: Harvard University Press 1973).
8 Smith, *Clement of Alexandria*, p. 446.

garden where the tomb was, and straightway a great cry was heard from the door of the tomb. And going near Jesus rolled away the stone from the door of the tomb. And straightway, going in where the youth was, he stretched forth his hand and raised him, seizing his hand. But the youth, looking upon him, loved him and began to beseech him that he might be with him. And going out of the tomb they came into the house of the youth, for he was rich. And after six days Jesus told him what to do and in the evening the youth comes to him, wearing a linen cloth over his naked body. And he remained with him that night, for Jesus taught him the mystery of the kingdom of God. And thence, arising, he returned to the other side of the Jordan.[9]

Later Coptic tradition preserves a memory that in the early Egyptian church baptisms were conferred on the sixth day of a six-week (or 40-day) fast, the day on which this tradition also claims that Jesus was to have baptized his disciples.[10] Because of this, Talley concluded that it was on this day that the above passage from Secret Mark would have been read to the candidates as part of their initiation. Similarly, 'The beginning of the Gospel of Jesus Christ, the Son of God' (Mark 1.1) through to his baptism by John (Mark 1.9–11) would have been read as the Gospel on 6 January, and then the 40-day or six-week fast, in strict imitation of Jesus' own post-baptismal fast in the wilderness (see Mark 1.12–13), would have begun immediately as a time for the pre-baptismal instruction of catechumens. This period, claimed Talley, would have been marked by the sequential Sunday readings of Mark's Gospel organized in such a way that the 'secret gospel' would have naturally occurred within the context of the rites of initiation themselves at the end of the 40 days.[11] While such an interpretation may seem rather speculative, Talley noted in support that in the later (tenth-century) lectionary of Constantinople, still used today in those churches

---

9 Smith, *Clement of Alexandria*, p. 447.
10 On this, in addition to Talley, *The Origins of the Liturgical Year*, pp. 194–214, see Paul F. Bradshaw, 'Baptismal Practice in the Alexandrian Tradition, Eastern or Western?' in Paul F. Bradshaw (ed.), *Essays in Early Eastern Initiation*, Alcuin/GROW Joint Liturgical Study 8 (Nottingham: Grove Books 1988), pp. 5–10; and most recently, Russo, 'The Origins of Lent', pp. 32–44.
11 For a shorter version of Talley's argument, see in Thomas J. Talley, *Worship: Reforming Tradition* (Washington, DC: The Pastoral Press 1990), 'The Origin of Lent at Alexandria'.

of the Byzantine Rite, the Gospel readings for the Sundays in Lent follow a sequential reading of Mark until the Saturday before Palm Sunday when, on this day called 'Lazarus Saturday', the Gospel reading (John 11.1–45) narrates Jesus' raising of Lazarus from the dead. Such a text, in Talley's opinion, was but the 'canonical equivalent' to the above story in the *Mar Saba Clementine Fragment*.[12] And in the next chapter in Markan sequence (Mark 11) is described Jesus' 'Palm Sunday' entrance into Jerusalem. If Talley was generally correct, the '40 days' of Lent ultimately have an Alexandrian origin. At the same time, he believed that this post-Epiphany practice at Alexandria would also explain the Constantinopolitan custom of baptism on Lazarus Saturday as well as the use there of Lazarus Saturday and Palm Sunday to distinguish and separate Lent from Great Week.

Talley's theory has come under serious criticism today. Indeed, it is based less on available early Alexandrian evidence and more on a hypothetical reconstruction of early Alexandrian practice discerned from the Markan sequence of Gospel readings for the Saturdays and Sundays of Lent in one of the later Byzantine Lenten lectionaries.[13] Even more importantly, the authenticity of the so-called *Mar Saba Clementine Fragment*, Talley's 'missing link', is strongly questioned, with several scholars now saying that it is nothing other than a forgery and a deliberate hoax, a scholarly trick played by Morton Smith, the 'discoverer' of the fragment, on the academic community.[14] While several others have

---

12 Talley, *The Origins of the Liturgical Year*, pp. 211–14.

13 See also the significant critique of Talley's overall theory provided by Harald Buchinger in the second edition of Hansjörg Auf der Maur, *Feiern im Rhythmus der Zeit. I: Herrenfeste in Woche und Jahr* (Regensburg: Pustet, forthcoming). It may well be that neither the 'standard theory', nor the more recent scholarly approach summarized in this chapter, is able to account accurately for the origins of Lent.

14 See Stephen Carlson, *The Gospel Hoax: Morton Smith's Invention of Secret Mark* (Baylor: Baylor University Press 2005). See also Larry W. Hurtado, *Lord Jesus Christ: Devotion to Jesus in Earliest Christianity* (Grand Rapids: Eerdmans 2003), pp. 433–4; and more recently, Peter Jeffery, *The Secret Gospel of Mark Unveiled: Imagined Rituals of Sex, Death, and Madness in a Biblical Forgery* (New Haven: Yale University Press 2007). That this 'secret Gospel' is a hoax, however, may not be the final answer to this puzzle. See Scott Brown, *Mark's Other Gospel: Rethinking Morton Smith's Controversial Discovery* (Waterloo, ON: Wilfrid Laurier University Press 2005), who argues that the ritual in question is not Christian baptism, nor intended to be. Similarly, Brown claims that this text is not only authentic Clement but even authentic Mark. See also Brown's critique of Jeffery, 'An Essay Review of Peter Jeffery, *The Secret Gospel of Mark Unveiled: Imagined Rituals of Sex, Death, and Madness in a Biblical Forgery*', *Review of Biblical Literature* <http://www.bookreviews.org> (2007).

questioned the authenticity of this document, it is Peter Jeffery who has concerned himself most directly with the liturgical implications of this reassessment. First, with regard to the origins of Lent, Jeffery notes that the so-called preference for the Gospel of Mark in the Alexandrian liturgical tradition is nowhere documented. What is documented in extant Coptic and Ethiopic lectionaries, in fact, does not show a system of *lectio continua* of any Gospel but rather a mixed use of all the Gospels during various seasons. This is also clear in the Epiphany and post-Epiphany cycles in Egypt, where the baptism of Jesus from Mark 1.9–11 does indeed occur, but already in the earliest Coptic lectionary source that we have (fifth century) it is part of a three-day celebration including the Matthean temptation account and the Johannine wedding at Cana.[15] Similarly, Gabriel Bertonière concluded some years ago that there is absolutely no evidence for a Markan sequence in Egypt such as Talley wanted to claim, and so there is no reason for seeing Constantinople's Markan Lenten sequence as having derived from Alexandria's post-Epiphany fast.[16] Indeed, even the raising of Lazarus (Talley's 'canonical equivalent' to Secret Mark) does not even appear in any extant Alexandrian lectionary cycle prior to the late ninth or early tenth century! On lectionary grounds, or on an assumed Markan sequence of Gospel pericopes, therefore, it is rather difficult to insert something like Secret Mark into either a post-Epiphany or Lenten fast.

Second, with regard to 'baptism' in Secret Mark, Jeffery claims that what 'baptismal' elements there may be in the text seem to be based on the sort of Anglican liturgical movement assumptions about early Christian baptism current at the time of its 'discovery', namely: a Romans 6 death and burial theology of baptism; initiation at a vigil; and the use of a baptismal garment (the *sindon*). For Jeffery, based on more recent scholarship on Christian initiation rites, none of this holds up. The theology of baptism for Egypt, he notes, is based more on John 3.5 and the baptism of Jesus, we know next to nothing about baptism taking place at a vigil in early Egypt, and the symbolic use of a baptismal garment is not documented until the late fourth century. Hence, while in the 1950s and even in the 1970s all of this may have been assumed for early church liturgy in general, more recent scholarship would put many of these developments no earlier than the fourth century.

---

15 Jeffery, *The Secret Gospel of Mark Unveiled*, p. 79.
16 Gabriel Bertonière, *The Sundays of Lent in the Triodion: The Sundays without a Commemoration*, OCA 253 (Rome: Pontifical Oriental Institute 1997), pp. 34ff.

In terms of lectionary evidence especially, Jeffery appears to be on solid ground about the question of the sequential reading of Mark in Alexandria and the so-called influence of that tradition on the Lenten sequence of the Byzantine lectionary. But, as Jeffery himself notes, early Egyptian lectionaries for Epiphany do suggest the beginnings of a 40-day fast at the time of Epiphany (including the reading of Mark 1.9–11), and later Lenten lectionaries do place a baptismal focus on either the Saturday of the sixth week of Lent or the sixth Sunday of Lent, a day which is even called the *Sunday of Baptizing*.[17]

The position that what became Lent ultimately derived from an earlier, pre-Nicene three-week period of baptismal preparation, either before Pascha or in general, has been challenged recently by Harald Buchinger. Following Alberto Camplani,[18] Buchinger argues that the evidence adduced in support of the primitive three-week pre-baptismal periods and the Egyptian post-Epiphany fast can be interpreted otherwise. Rather than providing a glimpse into pre-Nicene practices, Buchinger believes they more likely reflect much later (secondary) developments well posterior to the Council of Nicaea. As such, they tell us nothing about the emergence and early history of Lent. The safest course, he concludes, is to accept that 'the real origin of the Quadragesima lies in the dark'.[19] A recent article by Charles Renoux on the feast of the Annunciation must also be taken into account here. He critiques Talley's scholarship on Lent, claiming that an Alexandrian and Syrian fast at the beginning of the year started on 14 January and culminated on Palm Sunday, thus also encompassing the season of Lent, and had no relationship to either Epiphany or to Jesus' post-baptismal fast in the wilderness.[20] Renoux, however, does not refer to the earlier Alexandrian texts (e.g., Peter I of Alexandria and the *Canons of Hippolytus*), where, as we have seen, not only is the '40-day' fast mentioned but an association with Jesus' own fast is clearly made.

---

17 Jeffery, *The Secret Gospel of Mark Unveiled*, pp. 78–86.

18 Alberto Camplani, 'Sull' origine della Quaresima in Egitto' in David W. Johnson (ed.), *Acts of the Fifth International Congress of Coptic Studies, Washington, D.C., August 12th–15th, 1992* 2 (Rome: C.L.M. 1993), pp. 105–21.

19 Harald Buchinger, 'On the Early History of the Quadragesima: A New Look at an Old Problem and Some Proposed Solutions' in H. J. Feulner (ed.), *Liturgies in East and West: Ecumenical Relevance of Early Liturgical Development*, Österreichishe Studien zur Liturgiewissenschaft und Sakramententheologie 6 (Vienna: LIT-Verlag 2010).

20 Charles (Athanase) Renoux, 'L'Annonciation du rite arménien et l'Épiphanie', *OCP* 71 (2005), pp. 336–42.

Moreover, Russo has shown that the Egyptian sources, especially the canonical literature (*Canons of Hippolytus*, Athanasius, Basil, etc.), reveal that quadragesimal fasting regimens were a hallmark of that tradition. The ubiquity of that pattern and its use for varied circumstances (i.e., post-baptismal penance, catechesis, pre-baptismal purgation for those holding certain occupations, etc.) further suggests that it was likely to have been long established. Thus, if one is inclined to reject the historicity of the post-Epiphany fast and its subsequent transference – a tradition, it should be noted, that enjoyed wide currency in the Christian East – one must still account for the preponderance of 40-day fasts in fourth-century sources that are just as conservative of more ancient practices as they are innovative of new ones.[21] In other words, even now with the potential absence of Secret Mark as the 'missing link', one must still account for baptismal themes and terminology associated both with Epiphany and its 40-day fast.

Further, Russo notes,[22] the Egyptian theory about the origins of Lent does not rise and fall on the authenticity of Secret Mark. The fact that the tradition of an ancient post-Epiphany fast subsequently prefixed to Pascha circulated throughout the Christian East across geographic, liturgical and doctrinal divides (Egypt, Syria, Armenia) suggests that it has some basis in reality and is not merely a fabricated ritual aetiology. While agreeing with Camplani[23] that these medieval sources have constructed their past anachronistically through the liturgical lens of their present, Russo believes that beyond the confusion, contradictions and misnomers lies a historically accurate datum: some Egyptian Christians likely observed an annual fast in strict imitation of Jesus, that is, fasting for 40 days following the feast of Epiphany. Moreover, the prevalence of quadragesimal fasts in both canonical and extra-canonical sources establishes a sufficiently critical mass of scriptural warrants that it would be difficult to imagine that it took the Church over 300 years to seize upon the idea of fasting for 40 days.

In directing our attention to what he believes is a historically accurate datum with regard to the post-Epiphany fast, Russo also notes that F. C. Conybeare, as early as 1898, speculated that the post-Epiphany fast emerged first among early Jewish-Christian Quartodecimans. As evidence

---

21 See Russo, 'The Origins of Lent', pp. 389ff.
22 Russo, 'The Origins of Lent', pp. 126–49. See also Nicholas V. Russo, 'A Note on the Use of Secret Mark in the Search for the Origins of Lent', *SL* 37 (2007), pp. 181–97.
23 See above, n. 18.

of this, Conybeare pointed to the testimony of a certain Catholicos, Isaac, a twelfth-century pro-Byzantine Armenian prelate, who in criticizing certain Armenian heretics, says: 'Christ, after he was baptized, fasted forty days, and only [that]; *and for 120 years such was the tradition, which prevailed* [in the Church]. We, however, fast fifty days before [lit. near to] the Pascha.'[24] As Russo notes:

> Inexplicably, Isaac's independent witness to the post-Epiphany *quadragesima* was never brought to bear by Coquin or Talley. At first glance, his testimony amounts to nothing more than another among several late sources testifying to the custom. On closer inspection, however, Isaac seems to imply that he knows of heretics who still cling to this ancient fast, a fast superseded among the orthodox by the pre-paschal Lent. He also claims that this passé observance was the practice of the universal (?) Church for the first 120 years. While there is certainly no evidence for it in the apostolic period, his testimony further demonstrates how widespread the belief was that the post-Epiphany fast was *the* original *Quadragesima* of the Church. Isaac is especially trustworthy here since it is potentially embarrassing that the heretics are the ones adhering to the original practice of the Church; the orthodox, in this case, have departed from Tradition by adopting the pre-paschal Lent. Hypothetically, like Quartodecimans observing Pascha in strict imitation of the Jewish Pesach, certain adoptionist groups prone to literalist exegesis may have fasted a *quadragesima* in strict imitation of Jesus, i.e., after the annual commemoration of his baptism at Epiphany.[25]

If, then, a case can still be made for an Alexandrian origin to Lent, as Russo concludes, the question nevertheless remains: how does this Alexandrian 40-day post-Epiphany baptismal-preparation fast become the pre-paschal Lent? For this, there is no clear or easy answer. Coquin thought that Lent became a universal 40-day pre-paschal period as the result of the Council of Nicaea's determination of the calculation to be employed for the annual celebration of Easter throughout the churches.[26] The sudden post-Nicene near universal emergence of the 40

---

24 F. C. Conybeare, ed., *The Key of Truth* (Oxford: Clarendon Press 1898), p. lxxviii (emphasis added).

25 Russo, 'The Origins of Lent', p. 399.

26 Coquin, 'Une réforme liturgique du concile de Nicée (325)?'.

days of pre-paschal preparation for Easter and for baptism at Easter does suggest that the Nicene settlement included this preference for Easter baptism. This preference was now seemingly followed everywhere except at Alexandria, which, although shifting its traditional 40-day period to a pre-paschal location in order to conform generally to the rest of the churches, continued to celebrate baptism itself at the very end of this 40-day period, first on Good Friday, and second, because of the addition of another week of fasting later attached to the beginning of Lent, on the Friday before Holy Week. A vestige of this tradition continues in the Coptic Church today with baptisms not allowed between Palm Sunday and Pentecost.[27]

---

27 See Bradshaw, 'Baptismal Practice in the Alexandrian Tradition: Eastern or Western?'

Chapter 13

Calculating the forty days

When, after Nicaea, the 40 days of Lent became attached to pre-paschal preparation throughout the churches of the ancient world, different manners of calculating the actual duration of this season were employed. This resulted in both the differing lengths of Lent and the different fasting practices during Lent within the various churches which caused Socrates to express his surprise that all of them, nonetheless, used the terminology of '40 days' to refer to this period. In Rome, for example, the 40 days began on the sixth Sunday before Easter (called *Quadragesima*) and thus, including the traditional pre-paschal two-day fast on Good Friday and Holy Saturday, lasted for a total of 42 days. But, since Roman practice did not know fasting on Sundays, the total number of fast days was actually 36. Only much later, with the addition of four fast days beginning on the Wednesday before *Quadragesima* (later called Ash Wednesday because of the penitential practices which came to be associated with it), does Roman practice come to know an actual 40-day Lenten *fast* before Easter.[1]

Like Rome, Alexandria (as witnessed to by Athanasius' Festal Letters of 330 and 340[2]) also originally adopted a six-week Lenten period before Easter (including Holy Week). But, with no fasting on either Saturdays or Sundays in this tradition, there was a total of only 30 fast days before the fast of Holy Saturday. As indicated above, a week was added to the beginning of this period bringing the total to 35 days of fasting and, ultimately, even another week was added so that an actual

---

1 See Patrick Regan, 'The Three Days and the Forty Days' in Maxwell E. Johnson (ed.), *Between Memory and Hope: Readings on the Liturgical Year* (Collegeville: The Liturgical Press 2000), pp. 136–8.
2 *The Festal Epistles of S. Athanasius*, pp. 21, 100.

40-day fast, an eight-week inclusive Lent before Easter, became the result.[3]

While other liturgical sources for Jerusalem, Antioch and Constantinople suggest a six-week Lent with five fast days in each week concluding on the Friday before Lazarus Saturday and Palm Sunday, the pilgrim Egeria claims that Jerusalem knew a total eight-week pattern – a seven-week Lent and the six-day fast of Great Week – in the late fourth century.[4] Although her statement has often been dismissed as misinformation,[5] as 'an experiment that did not last',[6] or as reflecting the practice of an ascetical community in Jerusalem which began the Lenten fast one or two weeks before others did,[7] some comparative evidence has been provided by Frans van de Paverd, who in his study of John Chrysostom's *Homilies on the Statues* argues that fourth-century Antioch also knew a similar eight-week Lenten pattern.[8]

However Lent came to be calculated and organized in these various Christian traditions after Nicaea, it is clear that this '40 days' was understood eventually as a time for the final preparation of catechumens for Easter baptism, for the preparation of those undergoing public penance for reconciliation on or before Easter (on the morning of Holy Thursday in Roman practice), and for the pre-paschal preparation of the whole Christian community in general. Basing his comments primarily upon the mid-fifth-century Lenten sermons of Leo I, Patrick Regan summarizes this focus in the following manner:

> The purpose and character of Lent are entirely derived from the great festival for which it prepares. The Pasch is not only an annual celebration of the passion and passage of Christ, but it is for Christians of the fourth and fifth centuries the yearly reminder of their own incorporation into the paschal event through baptism. Consequently the approach of the Pasch renews in the memory of all the faithful their

---

3 See Thomas J. Talley, *The Origins of the Liturgical Year* (New York: Pueblo 1986; 2nd edn, Collegeville: The Liturgical Press 1991), p. 219.

4 Egeria, *Itinerarium* 46.1–4.

5 A. A. Stephenson, 'The Lenten Catechetical Syllabus in Fourth Century Jerusalem', *Theological Studies* 15 (1954), p. 116.

6 John Baldovin, *The Urban Character of Christian Worship*, OCA 228 (Rome: Pontifical Oriental Institute 1987) p. 92, n. 37.

7 See Talley, *The Origins of the Liturgical Year*, p. 174.

8 Frans van de Paverd, *St. John Chrysostom, The Homilies on the Statues*, OCA 239 (Rome: Pontifical Oriental Institute 1991), pp. XXIII, 210–16, 250–4, 358, 361.

commitment to live the new life of him who for their sake was crucified, buried, and raised. But it also accuses them of their failure to do so . . .[9]

Only in the late fifth century and beyond, when infant initiation comes to replace that of adult, thus effectively bringing about the extinction of the catechumenate, and when the system of public penance is replaced by the form of repeatable individual confession and absolution, do the 40 days then take on the sole character of preparation of the faithful for the events of Holy Week and the celebration of Easter. Such a focus, extremely penitential and 'Passion of Jesus' orientated in character and piety with little attention given to its baptismal origins, has tended to shape the interpretation and practice of the '40 days' of Lent until the present day.[10]

The season of Lent as it developed into a pre-paschal preparation period of '40 days' in length for catechumens, penitents and Christian faithful within the fourth-century post-Nicene context has multiple and complicated origins. While the development of the six-day pre-paschal fast may have played some role in its initial formation, what evidence there is suggests that this particular fast, although important for the origins of Holy Week, is separate and distinguished from that which came to be understood, properly speaking, as Lent. In other words, the traditional theory that the 40 days of Lent merely reflect the historically orientated backwards extension of the six-day pre-paschal fast in an attempt to assimilate those preparing for Easter baptism to Jesus' post-baptismal 40-day desert fast is highly questionable, if not clearly wrong. As we have seen, current scholarship argues that such historical assimilation of the 40 days to the fast of Jesus was already present before Nicaea within, at least, the Alexandrian liturgical tradition, although originally there it had no relationship either to Pascha or, possibly, to baptism at all. But as a fasting period already in place in this tradition it suitably became pre-baptismal in orientation because baptismal

---

9 Regan, 'The Three Days and the Forty Days', p. 129.
10 Among contemporary Roman Catholics and some Anglicans, for example, the devotional exercise of the Stations of the Cross is frequently held on the Fridays during Lent. And among Lutherans, in our experience, the Lenten tradition of mid-week worship often focuses on the medieval devotion of the so-called Seven Last Words of Jesus from the cross or includes each week a partial reading of the Passion narrative, often from sources that harmonize the four Gospel accounts. Both practices can tend to turn Lent into a 40-day Passion Sunday or Good Friday.

preparation necessarily included fasting as one of its major compo-
nents.[11] Then when paschal baptism, interpreted in the light of a
Romans 6 baptismal theology, became the normative *ideal* after Nicaea,
an ideal which does not seem to have been adopted even at Jerusalem
before 335,[12] this Alexandrian post-Epiphany pattern could become
eventually *the* pre-paschal Lenten pattern. It may be said, therefore, that
the sudden emergence of the 40-day Lenten season after Nicaea represents a harmonizing and standardizing combination of different,
primarily *initiatory*, practices in early, pre-Nicene Christianity. These
practices may have consisted of:

- an original 40-day post-Epiphany fast in the Alexandrian tradition
  already associated with Jesus' own post-baptismal fast in the desert,
  which, as a fasting period already in place, became the suitable time
  for the pre-baptismal preparation of catechumens;
- the three-week preparation of catechumens for Easter baptism in
  the Roman and North African traditions; and
- the three-week preparation of catechumens for baptism elsewhere
  either on a different liturgical feast or on no specified occasion
  whatsoever.

But after Nicaea – and probably as the result of Nicaea – these practices
all became 'paschalized' as the pre-Easter Lenten *Quadragesima*,
although in Alexandria this process, as we have seen, was only partially
successful and left the celebration of baptism itself separate from the
celebration of Easter.

If current scholarship on Lent, represented primarily now by Russo,
is correct, the origins of what becomes 'Lent' have very little to do with
Easter at all. Rather, those origins have to do both with early fasting

---

11 That those preparing for baptism, as well as the whole community, were expected to
fast as part of the immediate preparation for baptism is documented as early as *Didache*
7.4.
12 See Abraham Terian, *Macarius of Jerusalem, Letter to the Armenians, A.D. 335*,
AVANT: Treasures of the Armenian Christian Tradition 4 (Crestwood, NY: St Vladimir's
Seminary Press 2008), pp. 82–7, 121–6. According to the fifth-century historian
Sozomen (*Historia ecclesiastica* 2.26), 'initiation by baptism' was administered at
Jerusalem on the eight-day anniversary of the dedication of the holy places, which took
place on 13 September, 335. This appears to have left some trace in various Armenian
hymns of the cross. See M. Daniel Findikyan, 'Armenian Hymns of the Church and the
Cross', *St Nerses Theological Review* 11 (2006), pp. 63–105.

practices in general and with the final preparation of baptismal candidates for whenever their baptisms might be celebrated. Greater awareness of these origins, therefore, may serve today as a necessary corrective to the orientation, noted above, that frequently still tends to characterize and shape contemporary Christian Lenten observance.

Chapter 14

Holy Week in Jerusalem

Thanks to the 'historicism theory' of Gregory Dix in particular, the liturgical development of the days of Holy Week has often been explained as the result of post-Nicene preoccupation with Jerusalem, whose 'liturgically minded bishop', Cyril, was fixated on the liturgical commemoration of historical holy events at the very holy places where they once occurred.[1] From Jerusalem as a pilgrimage centre, then, these commemorations spread to the rest of the Church and tended to shape the way this week was celebrated elsewhere.

In fact, however, as early as the pre-Nicene *Didascalia Apostolorum*, the chronology of this week had already been assimilated to events in Jesus' last week. As Taft and Baldovin have demonstrated for Jerusalem,[2] the situation cannot be explained adequately as a simple interpretive shift from a pre-Nicene eschatological orientation to a fourth-century historical one. 'Eschatology' and 'history' are not mutually exclusive. Post-Nicene liturgical trends were evolutionary, not revolutionary, and were not suddenly instituted by individual influential figures (like Cyril) in response to the changed situation of the Church in the post-Constantinian world.[3]

Nonetheless, it is not surprising to find that it was at Jerusalem that specific liturgical rites commemorating the individual events assigned to the last week of Jesus' life in the Gospels first emerged and were subsequently imitated, at least partially, in other regions of the ancient world,

---

1 Gregory Dix, *The Shape of the Liturgy* (London: Dacre 1945), pp. 348–53.
2 Robert Taft, 'Historicism Revisited' in Robert Taft, *Beyond East and West: Problems in Liturgical Understanding* (2nd edn, Rome: Edizioni Orientala Christiana 1997); John Baldovin, *The Urban Character of Christian Worship*, OCA 228 (Rome: Pontifical Oriental Institute 1987), pp. 90–3.
3 See Paul F. Bradshaw, *The Search for the Origins of Christian Worship* (2nd edn, London: SPCK/New York: Oxford University Press 2002), pp. 65–7.

as pilgrims participated in them and carried news of them home. We have already described in Chapter 7 the fourth-century liturgical embellishments of the *triduum* at Jerusalem, and so all that remains to do here is to set out the similar developments in the earlier part of the week.

The celebrations began on the preceding Saturday. According to Egeria,[4] on this day the usual Saturday Lenten services took place in the morning, except that they were held on Sion and not at the Anastasis as in previous weeks, but in the afternoon there was a visit to Bethany ending at the Lazarium, the tomb of Lazarus, whom Jesus had raised from the dead (John 11). According to Talley, the liturgical commemoration of the raising of Lazarus at Jerusalem had suffered a turbulent history, going through at least four stages: (1) an original commemoration that took place on the fifth day of the Epiphany octave; (2) by the time of Egeria, a duplication of this on the Saturday before Holy Week, where there was a 'dramatic reenactment' of the raising of Lazarus, followed by a station at the Lazarium, during which John 11.55—12.11 was read; (3) by the early fifth century only the station with this reading, the 'dramatic reenactment' having been discontinued; (4) from the mid fifth century onwards, the disappearance of the commemoration during the Epiphany octave. This, he concluded, revealed that the Lazarus Saturday and Palm Sunday commemorations were not native to Jerusalem, but had been imported from elsewhere.[5]

Recently, however, Russo has challenged this reconstruction. He points out that what Egeria actually describes is not a 'dramatic re-enactment of the raising of Lazarus' at all but a re-enactment of Mary's meeting with Jesus as he approached Bethany prior to the raising of Lazarus (John 11.29), and that is why this element took place not at the Lazarium itself but at another church a half-mile away from the Lazarium – a church presumably built on the site to mark the precise location of the encounter – and why Egeria describes the reading as 'about Lazarus' sister Mary meeting the Lord'. Nor was the second station at the Lazarium apparently a commemoration of the raising of Lazarus, but of the visit by Jesus to Bethany that had taken place 'six days before the Passover', as the reading was John 11.55—12.11. Because, however, the New Testament reading from 1 Thessalonians 4

---

4 Egeria, *Itinerarium* 29.2–6.
5 Thomas J. Talley, *The Origins of the Liturgical Year* (New York: Pueblo 1986; 2nd edn, Collegeville: The Liturgical Press 1991), pp. 181–2.

and the psalms appointed for the day in the fifth-century Armenian Lectionary are identical to those for the post-Epiphany observance and evidently concerned with the theme of resurrection, Russo proposes that the development had been in the opposite direction from that suggested by Talley: the Saturday before Palm Sunday had been the original indigenous occasion for the commemoration of the raising of Lazarus established early in the fourth century, but that by the time of Egeria this commemoration had been duplicated in the post-Epiphany period, resulting in the related Gospel reading on the Saturday being excised and replaced with that concerning the subsequent visit of Jesus to Bethany, where Mary anointed his feet. By the early fifth century the commemoration of the meeting with Mary before the raising of Lazarus disappeared, and by the middle of the century the New Testament reading had also been replaced, while the Epiphany-octave commemoration too had been dropped, and John 11.1–46 was read instead on 7 September, a new commemoration of Lazarus altogether.[6]

In contrast to this, Palm Sunday seems not to present us with any critical difficulties. Once again according to Egeria, the Sunday services took place as normal in the morning, but in the afternoon the community gathered at the church on the Mount of Olives for a service of the word, followed by another at the Imbomon (the place from which Jesus was believed to have ascended), both composed of readings and psalms 'suitable to the place and the day', the second ending with the Matthean account of the entry into Jerusalem, after which they all processed down to the city carrying branches of palm or olive and singing psalms and the antiphon, 'Blessed is he who comes in the name of the Lord'. The day then ended with the usual Sunday evening service in the Anastasis.[7]

Similar celebrations of these two days are attested for other places in the East by the end of the fourth century and have seemingly been imitated from these Jerusalem originals. John Chrysostom refers to the observance of both days in a homily, although scholars have been uncertain whether this was delivered at Antioch or at Constantinople. What does seem clear from the homily, however, is that the Palm Sunday celebration did not yet include an actual procession with palms

---

6 Nicholas Russo, 'The Origins of Lent' (PhD dissertation, University of Notre Dame 2009), pp. 230–54.
7 Egeria, *Itinerarium* 30–1.

as at Jerusalem.[8] By contrast, however, Lazarus Saturday remained unknown in the West,[9] and Palm Sunday was slow to be adopted, the earliest reference to the name not occurring until around the year 600 in Spain and Gaul, and it is more than a century later before we have evidence of the blessing and carrying of branches of palm and other trees on that day. At Rome, on the other hand, it was known instead as Passion Sunday and involved the reading of the account of the Passion in Matthew's Gospel in preparation for the coming *triduum*, and it is not until the end of the eleventh century that we have a sure reference to the addition of a palm procession to the liturgy of the day there.[10]

From Monday to Wednesday the services at Jerusalem were as they had been throughout Lent, but with the addition of an extra afternoon service every day beginning at the ninth hour and lasting for four hours, during which Egeria says there were suitable readings. There was also an additional late evening service on Tuesday on the Mount of Olives, where there was a cave in which Jesus was believed to have taught his disciples, and where the bishop now read Matthew 24.1—26.2. On Wednesday a similar late evening service took place in the Anastasis, where a presbyter read the continuation of Matthew (26.3–16), the account of Judas agreeing to betray Jesus.[11]

Thursday, as might be expected, involved rather more activity. In addition to the usual weekday services, there was a celebration of the Eucharist in the Martyrium at the ninth hour, and then a second celebration 'Behind the Cross', at which Egeria notes that everyone received communion, and she says that this was the only day in the year when such a rite occurred in that location.[12] Why there should have been two eucharistic celebrations on this day is not immediately obvious, especially as neither of them took place where the Last Supper was believed to have occurred. It was only in the fifth century that a third celebration

---

8 John Chrysostom, *Expositiones in Ps.* 145. See Talley, *The Origins of the Liturgical Year*, pp. 186–7; Mark M. Morozowich, 'A Palm Sunday Procession in the Byzantine Tradition? A Study of the Jerusalem and Constantinopolitan Evidence', *OCP* 75 (2009), pp. 359–83.

9 The reference to the 'Saturday of Lazarus' in the later Ambrosian Rite (see *DBL*, pp. 187, 201) is to the last day of the week in which the Sunday Gospel had been the raising of Lazarus, and not to a day on which any special commemoration of the event was made.

10 See Pierre Jounel, 'The Year' in A.-G. Martimort *et al.* (eds), *The Church at Prayer* 4 (Collegeville: The Liturgical Press 1986), pp. 70–1.

11 Egeria, *Itinerarium* 32–4.

12 Egeria, *Itinerarium* 35.1–2.

was added on Sion for this purpose.[13] Pierre Jounel proposed that the first was the Eucharist that ended the Lenten fast and the second commemorated the institution of the Eucharist,[14] while Talley suggested that the two may have been intended for two quite different pilgrim communities that were following different chronologies of Holy Week,[15] but this is simply speculation. Augustine at the end of the fourth century certainly knew of the existence in some places of two celebrations on this day, one in the morning and the other in the evening, but it is impossible to say from this limited evidence whether the custom had been derived from Jerusalem or not. His own preference was for there to be only one celebration, before the customary meal at the ninth hour, so that communion could still be received fasting.[16]

All this did not complete the day's observance at Jerusalem, however. After returning home for a meal, the worshippers went once again to the cave on the Mount of Olives, where they kept a vigil of psalms and readings until about 11 p.m., when there was read Jesus' discourse in John 13.16—18.1, believed to have been given in that very spot. At midnight they went to the Imobomon for a further service of readings and psalms, and at cockcrow they moved on to a church believed to be the site where Jesus prayed during that night and Matthew 26.31–56 was read. Afterwards they continued on to Gethsemane for 'a reading from the Gospel about the Lord's arrest', and on into the city as dawn was breaking, ending at the Cross, where the account of Jesus before Pilate was read (John 18.28—19.16). The bishop then sent them home with words of encouragement for a short rest before the Good Friday observances began, though Egeria records that those with energy made an additional station on Sion 'to pray at the column where the Lord was scourged'.[17]

Although this long stational vigil was obviously intended to commemorate significant points in the Passion narrative in the very places where they were believed to have happened, it is to be noted that no attempt was made to replicate every detail of the story. The procession through the city did not seek to imitate exactly the route taken by Jesus,

13 See Baldovin, *The Urban Character of Christian Worship*, p. 87.

14 Jounel, 'The Year', p. 48.

15 Talley, *The Origins of the Liturgical Year*, pp. 44–5.

16 Augustine, *Ep.* 54.4–7. See also Mark Morozowich, 'Holy Thursday in Jerusalem and Constantinople: The Liturgical Celebrations from the Fourth to the Fourteenth Centuries' (PhD dissertation, Pontifical Oriental Institute, Rome 2002).

17 Egeria, *Itinerarium* 35.2–37.1.

with detours to the house of Caiaphas or Pilate, and there was no dramatic re-enactment of the events leading up to the crucifixion. It conforms, therefore, more to a liturgical style that Kenneth Stevenson many years ago labelled as 'rememorative', in which biblical events were celebrated but not directly re-enacted.[18] The visits to places and the readings helped to remind worshippers of the story and to bring it alive for them, but did not try to reproduce every detail in the manner that later medieval Passion plays would do, or the later observance of Palm Sunday, when a live donkey or a wooden reproduction of one would be brought into the scene. The primary element governing the choice of what to include and what to leave out on this route, however, and indeed for the special services in the rest of the week, seems to have been not the mention of them in the Gospel accounts so much as the prior existence on the pilgrim trail of specific places that were already associated with those particular events. In other words, it was geography, rather than history, that shaped the initial development of Holy Week rites.

---

18 See Kenneth Stevenson, *Jerusalem Revisited. The Liturgical Meaning of Holy Week* (Washington, DC: The Pastoral Press 1988), pp. 9f.

Christmas and Epiphany

Chapter 15

25 December: two competing theories

The earliest firm evidence for the Christian celebration of 25 December occurs in a document known as the Philocalian Calendar or Chronograph of 354, which contains a collection of both civil and religious chronologies, among them lists of consuls of the city of Rome up to 354, of Roman bishops from 255 to 352 arranged on an annual cycle in the order of the dates on which they died, and of the anniversaries of martyrs similarly organized.[1] The list of martyrs begins with the notation of the birth of Christ on 25 December, while the list of consuls includes not just this birth date, but that it was on a Friday, the fifteenth day of the new moon. Because the list of Roman bishops ends with the two most recent bishops out of sequence, it is generally agreed that this list was originally compiled in the year 336, prior to these additions, and therefore that the presumed date of Christ's birth was being celebrated as a festival in the city by that time.[2] But why was that particular date chosen?

The Chronograph could be thought to imply that the date had been arrived at by calculation, and, as we shall see later, for more than a century prior to this attempts had been made by individuals in various places to establish the precise date both of Jesus' death and of his birth – but there is no trace extant of anyone having previously suggested 25 December as a possible date for the birth, as the one apparent exception to this, a statement in the *Commentary on Daniel* by Hippolytus, is regularly held

---

1 For the Latin text, see Theodor Mommsen, 'Chronographus anni CCCLIIII' in *Monumenta Germaniae Historica, Auctorum Antiquissimorum* 9/1 (Berlin 1892 = Munich 1982), pp. 13–148. For the lists of martyrs and bishops, see below, pp. 176, 190.
2 See further Susan K. Roll, *Toward the Origins of Christmas*, Liturgia condenda 5 (Kampen, The Netherlands: Kok Pharos 1995), pp. 83–6.

by scholars to be a later interpolation into the work.[3] On the other hand, the Julian calendar observed throughout the Roman Empire decreed that 25 December was the date of the annual winter solstice prior to the year 325, when the Council of Nicaea adopted instead the true date, 21 December; and in the year 274 the Emperor Aurelian restored the cult of Sol Invictus, the Invincible Sun, proclaiming this divinity as the single official divine protector of the empire and of the emperor and establishing the yearly festival of the *Dies Solis Invicti* at the time of the winter solstice, to be observed with appropriate civic celebration, including 30 chariot races.[4] It is not surprising, therefore, that in searching for the reason for the celebration of Christmas on this same date Christian scholars have looked to this pagan feast as a possible influence.

Although some earlier scholars had hinted at this connection, the first to present a substantial case for it seems to have been Hermann Usener in 1889.[5] While some of his supporting arguments were seriously disputed by his critics, his basic thesis – that the Christian celebration of Christ's birth had been introduced in order to supplant the pagan festivities on that date – received approbation from a considerable number of later scholars.[6] The most significant contribution came from Bernard Botte in 1932, and his work continues to be cited as definitive down to the present day. Among the points that he made was a convincing argument that, contrary to what had generally been believed up till then, the celebration of 6 January had not existed at Rome prior to the adoption of 25 December but was a later addition there, as it did not appear anywhere in the Chronograph. He was also careful to say that the pagan feast had *influenced* the choice of date and not that Christians had adopted the feast, as some earlier writers had been inclined to do. On the contrary, it was intended as a counter-attraction to the pagan practice.[7]

This 'History of Religions' hypothesis (as it came to be known) did not, however, go unchallenged. Indeed, in the same year as Usener, Louis Duchesne published the first edition of his *Origines du culte*

---

3 Roll, *Toward the Origins of Christmas*, pp. 79–81.

4 Roll, *Toward the Origins of Christmas*, pp. 65, 113–14.

5 Hermann Usener, *Das Weihnachtsfest* (Bonn: Cohen 1889; 2nd edn 1911; 3rd edn 1969).

6 See Roll, *Toward the Origins of Christmas*, pp. 128–39.

7 Bernard Botte, *Les Origines de la Noël et de l'Épiphanie*, Textes et Études liturgiques 1 (Louvain: Abbaye de Mont César 1932), esp. pp. 54, 62.

chrétien, in which he claimed that the theory failed to account for the existence of a feast on 6 January, whereas his own explanation (later termed the Calculation or Computation hypothesis) accounted for both dates. He cited several ancient authors who alleged that 25 March had been the date of Christ's death, and so he asserted, though without supporting evidence, that Christ must have been thought to have lived for a whole number of years, because symbolic number systems do not allow the imperfection of fractions, and therefore the annunciation must have been thought also to have occurred on 25 March and the nativity nine months later on 25 December.[8] As we shall see in the next chapter, he made a similar claim for 6 January in relation to those who dated Christ's death on 6 April.[9] However, he was forced to admit that

> this explanation would be the more readily received if we could find it fully stated in some author. Unfortunately we know of no text containing it, and we are therefore compelled to put it forth as an hypothesis, but it is an hypothesis which falls in with what we may call the recognized methods in such matters.[10]

While his theory found some favour with some, it never succeeded in converting the majority of scholars away from the History of Religions hypothesis.

An attempt to revive Duchesne's hypothesis was made by Hieronymus Engberding in 1952. Perhaps his most significant contribution to the debate was to find support for it in a Latin tractate, *De solstitiis et aequinoctis*, a critical edition of which had already been appended to Botte's seminal work.[11] Once believed to have been a sermon by John Chrysostom, it is now generally thought to have originated in the early fourth century and in places shows signs of both African and Syriac influence. Because it noted that the conception and birth of Christ and the conception and birth of John the Baptist had taken place at the four cardinal points of the year, it had been cited by Botte as supportive of the History of Religions hypothesis, and he dismissed the fact that it also remarked upon the coincidence of the conception and the death of

---

8 Louis Duchesne, *Origines du culte chrétien* (Paris: Thorin 1889), pp. 247–54.

9 See below, pp. 135–6.

10 ET (from the third French edition): *Christian Worship: Its Origins and Evolution* (London: SPCK 1903), pp. 263–4.

11 Botte, *Les Origines de la Noël et de l'Épiphanie*, pp. 88–105.

Christ on 25 March as being not pivotal to its argument.[12] Engberding thought otherwise, and claimed that the dates assigned to these events were independent of and preceded any liturgical observance of them.[13] In a review of his article, Botte rejected this argument as very weak.[14] Some years later August Strobel attempted to strengthen the Calculation hypothesis by pointing to rabbinic belief that the patriarchs had lived for an exact number of years[15] – but this still failed to provide any more evidence as why the dates of death and *conception* rather than birth might have been thought to have been identical in the case of Christ.

It was Talley who in his 1986 book did most to try to breathe new life into Duchesne's theory. He added the Talmud tractate *Rosh Hashanah* to the testimony already adduced by Strobel with regard to rabbinic belief about the lives of the patriarchs, and he cited *De solstitiis* as giving 'full substantiation to Duchesne's hypothesis'.[16] Moreover, drawing on an observation made many years earlier by Gottfried Brunner and others,[17] he pointed out that Augustine, in one of his sermons, alluded to the fact that the Donatists in North Africa, unlike the Catholics, had not adopted the celebration of the feast of the Epiphany on 6 January, which seemed to imply that they did celebrate 25 December. This in turn suggested that Christmas must already have existed prior to the Donatist schism in 311, and hence at a date when it would have been unlikely that the Christians would have wanted any 'accommodation to less than friendly imperial religious sentiment'.[18] He also noted that Leonard Fendt and others had consequently raised the possibility that the celebration of Christmas may have appeared first in North Africa rather than at Rome, and he tentatively supported the idea, but he did not address Fendt's concern about the reliance that could be placed on what was essentially an argument from silence with regard to the

---

12 Botte, *Les Origines de la Noël et de l'Épiphanie*, p. 92.

13 Hieronymus Engberding, 'Der 25. Dezember als Tag der Feier der Geburt des Herrn', *ALW* 2 (1952), pp. 25–43, here at p. 34.

14 *Bulletin de théologie ancienne et médiévale* 7 (1955), pp. 198–9.

15 August Strobel, 'Jahrespunkt-Spekulation und frühchristliches Festjahr', *Theologische Literaturzeitung* 87 (1962), pp. 183–94, here at p. 193; August Strobel, *Ursprung und Geschichte des frühchristlichen Osterkalendars*, Texte und Untersuchungen 121 (Berlin: Akademie-Verlag 1977), pp. 128–33.

16 Thomas J. Talley, *The Origins of the Liturgical Year* (New York: Pueblo 1986; 2nd edn, Collegeville: The Liturgical Press 1991), pp. 81–3, 91–5.

17 Gottfried Brunner, 'Arnobius ein Zeuge gegen das Weihnachtsfest?', *Jahrbuch für Liturgiewissenschaft* 13 (1933), pp. 178–81.

18 Talley, *The Origins of the Liturgical Year*, pp. 86–7, 89–90.

Donatist observance of 25 December – a concern that others too have echoed[19] – nor did he manage to produce any new evidence for the alleged identification among early Christians of the dates of Christ's conception and death, which is perhaps the weakest point in the Calculation hypothesis.

The case thus remains unproven one way or the other. As Susan Roll has observed, Germanic and Romance language scholars have on the whole tended to lean in the direction of the History of Religions hypothesis, with Anglo-Saxon writers tending to favour the Calculation theory instead.[20] Yet whatever their preference, they have traditionally assumed that the feasts on 25 December and 6 January must have developed in parallel, and that whatever was the cause of the emergence of the one must also have been responsible for the development of the other. But there seems no reason why this should necessarily have been so, especially as that on 6 January appears to have begun to be celebrated in other places a considerable period of time before we hear of 25 December being adopted at Rome. Could it perhaps have been that it was the absence at Rome of any feast comparable to that being kept elsewhere on 6 January that led to the emergence of Christmas there in the fourth century, with the date being chosen as a counter-attraction to the pagan festivities taking place then, regardless of whatever may have been the original motivation behind the choice of 6 January elsewhere?

Subsequently, of course, Christmas did spread from its root in Rome to other parts of the ancient world, but when that began to happen is a subject that has provoked nearly as much controversy as that surrounding the origins of the feast. First, there is the question of when it began to be celebrated in other parts of the West. Whatever weight may be given to Talley's argument from silence concerning the Donatist

---

19 Talley, *The Origins of the Liturgical Year*, pp. 87, 103; Leonard Fendt, 'Der heutige Stand der Forschung über das Geburtsfest Jesu am 25.12 und über Epiphanie', *Theologische Literaturzeitung* 78 (1953), columns 1–10, here at 4, picking up a point expressed by Hieronymus Frank, 'Frühgeschichte und Ursprung des Römischen Weihnachtsfestes im Lichte neuerer Forschung', *ALW* 2 (1952), pp. 1–24, here at pp. 14–15; Martin F. Connell, 'Did Ambrose's Sister become a Virgin on December 25 or January 6? The Earliest Western Evidence for Christmas and Epiphany outside Rome', *SL* 29 (1999), pp. 145–58, here at pp. 153–5.

20 Roll, *Toward the Origins of Christmas*, pp. 96, 147–8. A recent exception to that general trend is Hans Förster, *Die Feier der Geburt Christi in der Alten Kirche*, Studien und Texte zu Antike und Christentum 4 (Tübingen: Mohr Siebeck 2000); Hans Förster, *Die Anfänge von Weihnachten und Epiphanias*, Studien und Texte zu Antike und Christentum 46 (Tübingen: Mohr Siebeck 2007).

observance of Christmas prior to 311, the earliest unquestionable testimony to its celebration outside Rome comes from a sermon delivered at the feast by Optatus, Bishop of Milevis in North Africa, probably around 361–3.[21] This speaks of the nativity of Christ as being a *sacramentum*, thus bestowing on it a greater status than Augustine will grant to it at the end of the century, when he distinguishes Christmas as a mere commemoration (*memoria*) from Easter as a *sacramentum*: 'A celebration of something is a sacrament only when the commemoration of the event becomes such that it is understood also to signify something that is to be received as sacred.'[22] On the other hand, Optatus' vocabulary is in line with that of Leo the Great at Rome in the fifth century.[23]

As for northern Italy, to which one might have expected the celebration of 25 December also to have migrated quite quickly, the evidence for its early adoption is much less firm. In the course of the history of the controversy over the origin of Christmas, considerable use was made of a passage in Ambrose of Milan's *De virginitate*, written in 378, in which he recalled the occasion over 20 years earlier (in 353 or 354) on which his sister Marcellina dedicated herself to virginity before Liberius, Bishop of Rome. Ambrose had said that 'you marked your profession by a change of clothing in the Church of St Peter on the birthday of the Saviour', and then claimed to be citing an extract from the sermon delivered by Liberius on that day which referred to the miracles at the wedding at Cana and at the feeding of the multitude.[24] This had been seized upon by those scholars who had argued that Epiphany had been celebrated at Rome as the birth of Christ prior to the adoption of Christmas, because the biblical events mentioned in the sermon were Epiphany themes. In 1923 Thomas Michels had put forward an alternative explanation – that Ambrose's supposed recollection was actually shaped by the practice with which he was familiar in Milan in his own day, where the birth of Christ was still being celebrated on 6 January and not 25 December[25] – an explanation also advanced more recently by Martin Connell, who supports his claim by noting that Christmas is never mentioned in Ambrose's commentary on the Gospel of Luke but

---

21 See Roll, *Toward the Origins of Christmas*, pp. 195–6.
22 Augustine, *Ep.* 55.2.
23 Leo, *Sermones* 26.1, 4; 27.6. See also Roll, *Toward the Origins of Christmas*, pp. 212–14.
24 Ambrose of Milan, *De virginitate* 3.1.1.
25 Thomas Michels, 'Noch einmal die Ansprache des Papstes Liberius bei Ambrosius, de virg. III 1,1ff', *Jahrbuch für Liturgiewissenschaft* 3 (1923), pp. 105–8.

surprisingly the Magi from Matthew's Gospel feature prominently.[26] He thus argues that the earliest sure testimony to the celebration of 25 December anywhere in northern Italy comes instead from a contemporary of Ambrose, Filastrius, in Brescia around 383,[27] although Roll still maintains that several of the hymns composed by Ambrose point to the existence of the Christmas feast at Milan in his day, and especially *Intende qui regis Israel*, which was cited by Pope Celestine in 430 as having been ordered to be sung at Christmas by Ambrose.[28] Connell also rightly challenges as inconclusive sources that have been cited in order to demonstrate the existence of Christmas in Spain in the 380s.[29]

If we turn to the emergence of the 25 December feast in the East, several sermons preached by John Chrysostom in the year 386 seem to indicate that its adoption in Antioch was a relatively recent development, but just how recent has been the subject of some debate by scholars. In one of the sermons, Chrysostom attempts to promote the feast's observance, mentioning that the date of Christ's birth has been known for less than ten years. Some would conclude from this that the feast had already been in existence for that length of time, but others argue that because his Pentecost sermon in the same year had mentioned only three festivals – Theophany (Epiphany), Pascha and Pentecost – and describes the first of these as being the one on which 'God has appeared on earth and lived with men', Christmas can only have been celebrated there for the very first time at the end of that year.[30] Whatever the case at Antioch, however, sermons by Gregory of Nazianzus preached at Constantinople in 380–1 indicate that 25 December was already being observed there at that time, but whether the feast had been newly introduced by Gregory or had existed for some years before has again been disputed by scholars.[31] It all depends on

---

26 Connell, 'Did Ambrose's Sister become a Virgin on December 25 or January 6?', pp. 146–9.

27 Connell, 'Did Ambrose's Sister become a Virgin on December 25 or January 6?', pp. 151–2.

28 Roll, *Toward the Origins of Christmas*, pp. 200–3.

29 Connell, 'Did Ambrose's Sister become a Virgin on December 25 or January 6?', pp. 155–7.

30 For further details, see Talley, *The Origins of the Liturgical Year*, pp. 135–7; Förster, *Die Anfänge von Weihnachten und Epiphanias*, pp. 166–79; J. N. D. Kelly, *Golden Mouth: The Story of John Chrysostom – Ascetic, Preacher, Bishop* (London: Duckworth/Ithaca, NY: Cornell 1995), p. 70.

31 Talley, *The Origins of the Liturgical Year*, pp. 137–8; Förster, *Die Anfänge von Weihnachten und Epiphanias*, pp. 182–98.

whether Gregory's designation of himself as ἐξαρχός of Christmas in Constantinople means 'originator' of the feast here or simply the one who presided over it. While its appearance in Cappadocia also seems to belong to the same time period, it remained unknown both in Jerusalem and in Egypt until the fifth century, and was not adopted at all in Armenia.[32]

Thus, the claim often made that the observance of Christmas spread with extraordinary rapidity to nearly all parts of the ancient Christian world appears not to be strongly supported by the evidence. On the contrary, there seems to have been a gap of at least 40 years between the earliest witness to its adoption in Rome and the very first signs of its challenge to the dominance of 6 January in other churches that were already keeping that feast day. Similarly, the common assertion that the speed of its appropriation was due at least in part to the value that a celebration of the divine incarnation would have had to the Nicene party against their Arian opponents is also open to question. In her survey of the relevant literature Roll has pointed out the essential Christological ambiguity of the feast, and Connell has gone further and suggested that the apparent delay in and resistance to its widespread adoption may have been precisely because the narrative of the vulnerable infant in a manger would not have helped promote the high Christology of the Son as 'one in being with the Father' but rather have been more congenial to the Arian cause.[33] Whatever may be the truth of that, it is perhaps worth noting that the liturgical readings in later Roman sources encompass not just a commemoration of the event of Christ's nativity but a celebration of his Incarnation, with John 1 being just as deeply embedded as the Lucan account of the nativity.[34]

32 Talley, *The Origins of the Liturgical Year*, pp. 138–41.

33 Roll, *Toward the Origins of Christmas*, pp.168–89, esp. pp. 174–7; Martin F. Connell, *Eternity Today: On the Liturgical Year* 1 (New York/London: Continuum 2006), pp. 101–3.

34 See Lester Ruth, 'The Early Roman Christmas Gospel. Magi, Manger, or Verbum Factum?', *SL* 24 (1994), pp. 214–21.

Chapter 16

6 January in the East

The 6 January feast of the Epiphany (Theophany), long associated in the West with the visit of the Magi (Matt. 2.1–12) and often occurring today in Roman Catholic communities on the Sunday between 2 and 8 January, commemorates in the East the event of Jesus' baptism in the Jordan by John, an event that is celebrated today on the Sunday *after* the Epiphany in Western liturgical calendars. Together with Jesus' baptism in the Jordan and the visit of the Magi, other epiphanies, manifestations or revelations of Jesus' identity, such as the wedding at Cana and his transfiguration on Mount Tabor, have also been included as part of the feast's several themes as well. As noted in the previous chapter, scholarly approaches to the origins of this feast have been divided also between the more traditional *Religionsgeschichte* (History of Religions) hypothesis and the Calculation hypothesis.

According to the History of Religions approach, Epiphany, like Christmas, was but a Christian replacement feast for, or Christianization of, various pagan festivals celebrated on or near 6 January, especially in ancient Egypt. The pagan festivals in question are the Egyptian celebration in honour of the birth of the god Aion, born of the virgin Kore on 11 Tybi (= 6 January), and another, called *Pater Liber*, in honour of Dionysius on 5 January. Our principal source for the correlation of Epiphany and a celebration of the birth of the god Aion comes from the *Panarion*, or *Refutation of All Heresies*, of Epiphanius of Salamis (315–403).

The Saviour was born in the 42nd year of Augustus, emperor of the Romans, in the Consulate of the same Octavius Augustus for the 13th time and of Silanos as the consulator of the Romans show. For in those this is found: in the consulate of these, that is, of Ocatavius for the 13th time and of Silanos the Christ was born on 8 before the Ides of January, 13 days after the winter solstice and the increasing of the day and of the

131

light. This day is celebrated by the Hellenes, i.e., by the idolaters, on 8 before the Kalends of January, called among the Romans 'Saturnalia,' among the Egyptians 'Kronia,' among the Alexandrians 'Kikellia.' This is the day on which the change takes place, i.e., the solstice, and the day begins to grow, the light receiving an increase. There are accomplished the number of 13 days until 8 before the Ides of January, until the day of the birth of Christ, the thirtieth of an hour being added to each day. As also the wise Ephrem testified to the Syrians in his commentary, saying that 'thus was established the parousia of our Lord, his birth according to the flesh, that is his perfect incarnation which is called Epiphany, at 13 days interval from the augmentation of the light. That must be the type of the number of our Lord and his twelve disciples, which accomplishes the number of 13 days from the increasing of the light.' Many other things sustain and testify to this fact; I speak of the birth of the Christ, that he has come and he comes.

For also the leaders of the worship of idols are constrained to recognize a part of the truth, and being shrewd, to deceive the idolaters persuaded by them, they make in many places a very great feast in this same night of the Epiphany, so that those who believe in error may not see the truth. First of all, at Alexandria, in the so-called Koreion – it is a very large temple that is the sanctuary of Kore. They watch all night, celebrating their idol with chants and the sound of flutes and, the vigil ended, after cockcrow, they descend, carrying torches, into a subterranean chapel and they bring back a wooden statue, seated nude upon a litter, having a mark of a cross of gold on the forehead, and on the hands two other such marks and on the two knees two others, the five marks being similarly of gold. And they carry the statue seven times in a circle around the temple with flute playing and kettledrums and hymns, and having revelled they carry it back again to the underground place. And asked what this mystery is, they answer and say: today, at this hour, Kore (that is, the virgin) has given birth to the Aion. And this is done also in Petra, the metropolis of Arabia which is written Edom in the scriptures, and they hymn the virgin in the Arabic dialect, calling her in Arabic 'Chaamou,' that is, Kore or virgin, and the one born from her 'Dousares,' that is, only begotten of the Master. And this happens also in the city of Eleusis throughout that night, as in Petra and in Alexandria.[1]

---

1 Epiphanius, *Panarion* 51.22.3–11; ET from Thomas J. Talley, *The Origins of the Liturgical Year* (New York: Pueblo 1986; 2nd edn, Collegeville: The Liturgical Press 1991), pp. 104–6.

Because Epiphanius refers here to a celebration of the birth of Christ as the content of Epiphany in relationship to the winter solstice (e.g., the *Saturnalia*), traditional scholarship concluded that, like Christmas supposedly, the feast of Epiphany, the Eastern feast of Christ's 'Nativity', was instituted precisely to counteract the popularity of pagan solstice celebrations in Egypt, Petra and Arabia. Such an approach includes, logically, viewing this as a deliberate attempt to replace a celebration of the virgin Kore giving birth to Aion with the Virgin Mary giving birth to Christ.[2] In fact, based on Epiphanius' incorrect dating of the Roman *Saturnalia* to '8 before the Kalends of January' (= 25 December) and the birth of Christ 13 days after the winter solstice, that is, '8 before the Ides of January' (6 January), a distinction known also to Ephrem the Syrian,[3] some scholars, especially Botte,[4] argued that the original date of the solstice in Egypt was 6 January. Owing to calendar errors over the centuries, however, the solstice migrated to 25 December with the end result that there were two Egyptian solstice festivals, 25 December and 6 January.

Further, in the earliest extant lectionary evidence we have for Egypt, a fifth-century parchment palimpsest,[5] the pericope of the wedding at Cana (John 2.1–7) is already assigned to the third of the three days (or the second of two days) of Epiphany, together with the baptism of Jesus (Mark 1.9–10) and the temptation of Jesus (Matt. 4.2) on 6 January itself. Again it is Epiphanius who draws attention to possible parallel pagan feasts on this day:

> Therefore, in many places up to our own day there is reproduced that divine prodigy which took place then in testimony to the unbelieving; thus they testify in many places to springs and rivers changed to wine. Thus the spring of the Cibyra in the city of Cari, at the hour when the servants drew out and he said, 'give to the ruler of the feast.' And the spring in Gersa of Arabia gives the same witness. We have

2 See Bernard Botte, *Les Origines de la Noël et de l'Épiphanie*, Textes et Études liturgiques 1 (Louvain: Abbaye de Mont César 1932), pp. 68–78.
3 See Ephrem, *Hymns on the Nativity* 5.13. Talley speculates here that both Epiphanius and Ephrem may well be displaying resistance to the Western 25 December date of Christmas by their comments: *The Origins of the Liturgical Year*, p. 105.
4 See Botte, *Les Origines de la Noël et de l'Épiphanie*, p. 66.
5 Mario Geymonat, 'Un antico lezionario della chiesa di Alessandria' in *Laurea Corona: Studies in Honour of Edward Coleiro*, ed. Anthony Bonanno and H. C. R. Vella (Amsterdam: Grüner 1987), pp. 186–96.

drunk from the spring of Cibyra, and our brothers from the spring, which is in the martyrium in Gerasa. And many in Egypt testify the same of the Nile. Therefore on the eleventh of Tybi according to the Egyptians all draw water and set it aside in Egypt itself and in many countries.[6]

Because other Christian and pagan sources refer either to the Nile's own inundation process, to festal drawing water out of rivers, to the Alexandrian custom of bathing in water and blessing boats on 6 January, or even to water turning into wine for great feasts (Dionysius),[7] scholars have again argued that pre-Christian myths and celebrations in Egypt associated with the waters of the Nile were influential in the adoption of the Cana story as well.

As attractive as the History of Religions approach may be to the origins of Epiphany, including the Cana pericope, Talley's work has made it very difficult to accept that approach to the subject any longer. At least two reasons may be given for this. First, with regard to the dating of the pre-Christian Egyptian feasts on the supposed two solstice celebrations in Egypt, Talley demonstrated that there is absolutely no reliable correspondence between them and the Christian celebration of Epiphany.[8] J. Neil Alexander offers a concise summary of Talley's conclusions on this issue:

One of the principal explanations of the connection between Christmas on December 25 and Epiphany on January 6 has been sought by means of reconciling the calendrical inconsistencies caused by the quarter days of the annual solar cycle. The most valiant effort in this regard proposed that way back in 1996 B.C.E., during the reign of Amenemhet I, the winter solstice took place on a date that when transferred to the Julian calendrical system yielded January 6. According to this theory, an error in the calendar of one day in every 128 years pushes the date of the winter solstice to December 25 by the fourth century B.C.E. . . . . [H]owever . . . the originator of this widely accepted hypothesis allowed one error in the sources to slip his otherwise precise calculations. The error is that whatever

---

6 Epiphanius, *Panarion* 51.30.8–1–3; ET from Talley, *The Origins of the Liturgical Year*, pp. 112–13.
7 For texts, see Talley, *The Origins of the Liturgical Year*, pp. 112–17.
8 Talley, *The Origins of the Liturgical Year*, pp. 103–17.

calendars may have been in use in Egypt, the Julian calendar dates only to 45 B.C.E. and any reconciliation of dates with it before that time, are historically meaningless, no matter how precise their calculation . . . A close reading of the sources that lie behind these suggestions [therefore] fails to substantiate . . . a close relationship between any pagan festivals and the Christian feast of Epiphany. The relationship between pagans and Christians at Rome, a relationship that shared a rich repertoire of solar metaphors and images does not have a clear parallel in the development of Epiphany.[9]

Second, although in the light of the fifth-century palimpsest parchment lectionary the addition of the Cana miracle was incorporated earlier into the immediate Epiphany context in Egypt than Talley assumed, he is certainly correct in noting that the several references to various water rites, including especially Christian blessings of the font on Epiphany in the East and drawing water, appear to be Christian in origin. And, significantly, water rites associated with pagan festivals, with the exception of, at least, one of the four annual feasts of the god Dionysius occurring on 5 January (*Pater Liber*), do not provide the sort of foundation from which to project a Christian feast. Talley wrote:

> When all is said and done . . . from all the evidence we have considered for a pagan background to Epiphany nothing points definitely to a widespread festival on January 6. Even if we accept Epiphanius' account of the Aion festival, we are left with severe problems. That festival seems to be distinguished from disquietingly similar observances on December 25 because the Aion feast is the distinctive local observance of the guardian of Alexandria, and thus not a widespread observance.[10]

As we saw in the previous chapter regarding the origins of Christmas, the alternative to the History of Religions hypothesis is the Calculation hypothesis, that hypothesis advanced originally by Duchesne in 1889, defended further by Engberding in the early 1950s, and reinvigorated by Talley. As with the date of Christmas occurring nine months after 25 March (= 14 Nisan, the traditional date of Jesus' death

---

9 J. Neil Alexander, *Waiting for the Coming: The Liturgical Meaning of Advent, Christmas, Epiphany* (Washington, DC: The Pastoral Press 1993), pp. 70–1.
10 Talley, *The Origins of the Liturgical Year,* p. 117.

and, presumably, his conception, in the West, according to this theory), so Duchesne, Engberding and Talley claimed that for Christians in Asia Minor 6 April (14 Artemisios) was chosen as the solar equivalent to 14 Nisan, the date of the Quartodeciman Pascha in the East, with the result that exactly nine months later 6 January occurs as the date of Jesus' birth.[11] Again, as Alexander summarizes,

> once April 6 is established as the eastern date of the death (and conception) of Jesus, the date of his birth, a perfect nine months later, is easily calculated to be January 6. It would appear, once again, that the possibility of the date of Jesus' birth, having been established on the basis of the acceptance of a particular date for his death, accurate or not, commends itself as the basis of January 6, at least as strongly as any similarity between pagan and Christian festivities.[12]

The modern appeal of the Calculation hypothesis for both Christmas and Epiphany is due, undoubtedly, to the theologically inviting paschal connotations of the dating, whereby the modern fascination with the 'paschal mystery' naturally commends itself even as somehow the origin for these two feasts. That is, it is theologically appealing to say that it is Christ's death and resurrection, as the root metaphor for Christian life, which even determines and sheds light on the feasts of Jesus' beginnings (i.e., Pascha + nine months = Epiphany or Christmas). This squares nicely with the approach of Raymond Brown's excellent work on the infancy narratives (Matt. 1—2 and Luke 1—2) in both his *The Birth of the Messiah* (New York: Doubleday 1977) and his more popular version, *An Adult Christ at Christmas* (Collegeville, MN: The Liturgical Press 1978).

One problem with this, however, as Engberding noted for Christmas, is that the calculation of a date does not necessarily mean that a celebration on that date appeared at the same time in history,[13] and, hence, the eventual celebration of a feast on a particular date can be related to several factors, cultural, socio-political, as well as theological. Another problem, certainly, is the same as that noted for 25 March in the previous chapter, namely, unlike the birth parallels that proponents of this hypothesis have advocated, the fact remains that for

---

11 Talley, *The Origins of the Liturgical Year*, pp. 8ff., 93.
12 Alexander, *Waiting for the Coming*, p. 72.
13 See above, p. 126.

Christmas and Epiphany either 25 March or 6 April become Jesus' *conception* day and not the day of his birth. While, then, the Calculation hypothesis may still have much to commend it, perhaps even more for 6 January than for 25 December, based on the rather questionable existence of pagan parallels for 6 January, it does not provide, unfortunately, the definitive answer for the establishment of either Christmas or Epiphany.

Whether or not the History of Religions or the Calculation hypothesis (or some combination thereof) is the correct approach to the origins of Epiphany, one thing is absolutely certain. We know that already in the late second or early third century the date of 6 January was associated in Egypt both with Christ's birth and with his baptism in the Jordan, and that among some, at least, it was already a liturgical celebration with a vigil. Our source for this is the *Stromateis* of Clement of Alexandria (150–215), his treatise that focuses primarily on the relationship between Christian faith and classic philosophy:

> From Julius Caesar, therefore, to the death of Commodus, are two hundred and thirty-six years, six months. And the whole from Romulus, who founded Rome, till the death of Commodus, amounts to nine hundred and fifty-three years, six months. And our Lord was born in the twenty-eighth year, when first the census was ordered to be taken in the reign of Augustus. And to prove that this is true, it is written in the Gospel by Luke as follows: 'And in the fifteenth year, in the reign of Tiberius Caesar, the word of the Lord came to John, the son of Zacharias.' And again in the same book: 'And Jesus was coming to His baptism, being about thirty years old,' and so on . . . From the birth of Christ, therefore, to the death of Commodus are, in all, a hundred and ninety-four years, one month, thirteen days. And there are those who have determined not only the year of our Lord's birth, but also the day; and they say that it took place in the twenty-eighth year of Augustus, and in the twenty-fifth day of Pachon. And the followers of Basilides hold the day of his baptism as a festival, spending the night before in readings.
>
> And they say that it was the fifteenth year of Tiberius Caesar, the fifteenth day of the month Tubi; and some that it was the eleventh of the same month, And treating of His passion, with very great accuracy, some say that it took place in the sixteenth year of Tiberius, on the twenty-fifth of Phamenoth; and others the twenty-fifth of Pharmuthi and others say that on the nineteenth of Pharmuthi the

Saviour suffered. Further, others say that He was born on the twenty-
fourth or twenty-fifth of Pharmuthi.[14]

It was Roland Bainton who subjected Clement's calculations to close
scrutiny, with the outcome that the calendrical information given in the
Stromateis results in the date of Jesus' birth being assigned in Egypt to
6 January in 2 BCE.[15]

If 6 January was thought of as the date of Jesus' birth, however,
it was also the day, at least for the heretical (Gnostic) Basilidians, for
celebrating Jesus' baptism in the Jordan, though the date wavers
between 10 January (15 of Tybi) and 6 January (11 of Tybi). Whether
Clement's community at Alexandria already celebrated the baptism of
Jesus at Epiphany or not, it is abundantly clear that Clement's own
theology of baptism would have been highly consistent with such a
celebration. He writes:

But do not find fault with me for claiming that I have such
knowledge of God. This claim was rightfully made by the Word, and
he is outspoken. *When the Lord was baptized, a voice loudly sounded
from heaven, as a witness to him who was beloved: 'You are my beloved
Son; this day have I begotten you.'*

This is what happens with us, whose model the Lord made
himself. When we are baptized, we are *enlightened*; being *enlightened*,
we become *adopted sons* [see Gal 4:5]; becoming *adopted sons*, we are
made perfect; and becoming perfect, we are made divine. 'I have
said,' it is written, 'you are gods and all the sons of the Most High'
[Ps 81:6]. This ceremony is often called 'free gift' [Rom 5:2, 15;
7:24], 'enlightenment' [Heb 6:4; 10:32], 'perfection' [Jas 1:7; Heb
7:11], and 'cleansing' [Titus 3:5; Eph 5:26] – 'cleansing,' because
through it we are completely purified of our sins; 'free gift,' because
by it punishments due to our sins are remitted; *'enlightenment,'* since
by it we behold the wonderful holy light of salvation, that is, it
enables us to see God clearly; finally, we call it 'perfection' as needing

---

14 *Stromateis* 1.21; ET from *ANF* 2, pp. 332–3.
15 See Roland H. Bainton, 'Basilidian Chronology and New Testament Interpretation',
Journal of Biblical Literature 42 (1923), pp. 81–134; Roland H. Bainton, 'The Origins of
Epiphany' in his *Early and Medieval Christianity* (Boston: Beacon Press 1962), pp.
22–38.

nothing further, for what more does he need who possesses the knowledge of God?[16]

That Jesus' own baptism by John in the Jordan is Clement's primary model for interpreting Christian baptism is further expressed by his use of the Old Testament typology of the Israelites crossing the Jordan under Joshua (= Jesus) into the promised land (see Josh. 3—5),[17] a major theme also in Origen's own treatment of baptism in the middle of the third century.[18] And what many have suggested is a fragment of an early Epiphany homily in *The Letter to Diognetus* 11.3–5 points theologically in the same direction as well:

> For which reason he sent the Word, that he might be manifested to the world; and he, being despised by the people [of the Jews], was, when preached by the Apostles, believed on by the Gentiles. This is he who was from the beginning, who appeared as if new, and was found old, and yet who is ever born afresh in the hearts of the saints. *This is he who, being from everlasting, is today called the Son*; through whom the Church is enriched, and grace, widely spread, increases in the saints, furnishing understanding, revealing mysteries, announcing times, rejoicing over the faithful, giving to those that seek, by whom the limits of faith are not broken through, nor the boundaries set by the fathers passed over.[19]

Whatever the situation may have been for Clement and Origen, liturgically it is Jesus' baptism on 6 January, not his birth in Bethlehem, which will remain or become the primary content of Epiphany in the Christian East, with the exception of Jerusalem.[20] In addition to the

---

16 *Paedagogus* 6.25–6; ET from Thomas M. Finn (ed.), *Early Christian Baptism and the Catechumenate: Italy, North Africa, and Egypt*, Message of the Fathers of the Church 6 (Collegeville: The Liturgical Press 1992), p. 186 (emphasis added).

17 *Eclogae propheticae* 5–6.

18 See Jean Laporte, 'Models from Philo in Origen's Teaching on Original Sin' in Maxwell E. Johnson (ed.), *Living Water, Sealing Spirit: Essays on Christian Initiation* (Collegeville: The Liturgical Press 1995), pp. 113–15. For more on Origen's baptismal theology, see also C. Blanc, 'Le baptême d'après Origène', *SP* 11 (1972), pp. 113–24; H. Crouzel, 'Origène et la structure du sacrement', *Bulletin de littérature ecclésiastique* 2 (1962), pp. 81–92; Jean Daniélou, *The Bible and the Liturgy* (Notre Dame: University of Notre Dame Press 1956), pp. 99–113; Jean Daniélou, *Origen* (New York: Sheed and Ward 1955), pp. 52–61; Everett Ferguson, 'Baptism according to Origen', *Evangelical Quarterly* 78 (2006), pp. 117–35.

19 ET from *ANF* 1, p. 29 (emphasis added).

20 See below, pp. 146–8.

fifth-century parchment palimpsest lectionary, which, as we have seen, clearly assigns Jesus' baptism (Mark 1.10–11) to 6 January, the so-called *Canons of Athanasius* from, at least, the second half of the fourth century in Egypt also witnesses to the connection between Epiphany and Jesus' baptism. The relevant portion of Canon 16 reads:

> [A]t the feast of the Lord's Epiphany, which was in [the month] Tûbah, that is the [feast of] Baptism, they shall rejoice with them. The bishop shall gather all the widows and orphans and shall rejoice with them, with prayers and hymns, and shall give unto each according to his needs; for it is a day of blessing; in it was the Lord baptised of John . . . The last of all fruits is the olive, which is gathered in that day; wherefore by the Egyptians this is called the feast of the beginning of the year. As with the Hebrews New Year's Day was at the Pascha, which is the first of Barmûdah. So again in the month of Tûbah did our Saviour appear as God, when, by a wondrous miracle, He made the water wine.[21]

John Cassian (d. 435) testifies to the same connection and, in passing, also indicates that Egypt had not yet accepted the 25 December date for Christ's nativity in the early fifth century:

> In the country of Egypt this custom is by ancient tradition observed that – when Epiphany is past, which the priests of that province regard as the time, both of our Lord's baptism and also of His birth in the flesh, and so celebrate the commemoration of either mystery not separately as in the Western provinces but on the single festival of this day – letters are sent from the Bishop of Alexandria through all the Churches of Egypt, by which the beginning of Lent, and the day of Easter are pointed out not only in all the cities but also in all the monasteries.[22]

Based especially on the *Canons of Athanasius*, Talley was certainly correct in noting that just as the Chronograph of 354 indicates that at

21 W. Riedel and W. E. Crum, *The Canons of Athanasius of Alexandria* (London: Williams & Norgate 1904), pp. 26–7. See also Talley, *The Origins of the Liturgical Year*, p. 122.
22 John Cassian, *Conferences* 10.2; ET from *NPNF* 2nd Series 11, p. 401.

Rome the liturgical year began with Christmas,[23] so the evidence for Egypt indicates that it began there with Epiphany.[24] And, just as the miracle at Cana is clearly connected to Jesus' baptism already in the *Canons of Athanasius*, so John Cassian connects Jesus' birth in the flesh and baptism in his *Conferences*. Talley himself, however, tried to argue that the reason why the *Canons of Athanasius* make no reference to Jesus' birth in connection with Epiphany, unlike both Epiphanius and Cassian, and, presumably, Clement, is because of the overall influence of Mark's Gospel in the Alexandrian tradition. But, as we saw in our chapter on Lent, Talley's theory that particular Gospels shaped the liturgical calendars of particular churches (e.g., the Gospel of Mark in Egypt) is no longer defensible in light of contemporary challenges to that hypothesis.[25]

What seems more likely to be the case, we would suggest, is that Jesus' 'birth' and baptism in Egypt were seen together early on as essentially one event, namely, his baptism, in spite of what may legitimately be called Adoptionist overtones, and this was also the event of his being 'begotten' by God the Father at his baptism in the Jordan, as the textual variant of Luke 3.22 makes clear: 'Thou art my beloved Son; today I have begotten thee.' Such is the theology of Clement and Origen for Egypt, a theology highly consonant in associating birth and baptism together, and one that is particularly strong in the early Syrian tradition to which we turn in the next section of this chapter. Whether that indicates that the Gospel of Mark was influential in shaping the entire Egyptian lectionary is not clear, since it is the Lucan variant that is the most suggestive here. Nevertheless, it is Mark 1.10–11 that is read on Epiphany in Egypt and, of course, it is in the first chapter of Mark where the Gospel writer claims to be presenting 'the *beginning* of the gospel' (Mark 1.1, emphasis added). And, the fact that the Cana pericope would be attached to this celebration should not be all that surprising since, as Peter Jeffery has noted, 'the baptismal interpretation of the Cana story has long-standing importance in Christian Egypt'.[26]

---

23 See above, p. 123.
24 Talley, *The Origins of the Liturgical Year*, p. 123.
25 See above, pp. 102–4.
26 Peter Jeffery, *The Secret Gospel of Mark Unveiled: Imagined Rituals of Sex, Death, and Madness in a Biblical Forgery* (New Haven: Yale University Press 2007), p. 78.

SYRIA

In her monumental essay, 'Die Licht-Erscheinung bei der Taufe Jesu und der Ursprung des Epiphanie-festes',[27] Gabriele Winkler not only underscores the overall Eastern origins of Epiphany, arguing for a date within the earliest stratum of Christian history, but, by means of a detailed and exhaustive analysis of early Syrian and Armenian sources, claims precisely that the earliest layer of celebration had to do with Jesus' pneumatic 'birth' in the Jordan, where, according to these texts, the Holy Spirit comes to 'rest' on him and the divine voice and fire or shining light reveal the moment of his 'birth'. She writes:

> It must be stressed here with all clarity that in the original under-standing of the baptism of Jesus, the issue was first of all his divine conception and birth, not a rebirth, and not a revelation of his deity at the Jordan, as Usener has already indicated. An impartial examina-tion of the material clearly shows that Jesus was born as the Son of God at his baptism – whether that material be the account of the baptism in Mark's Gospel which, as is well known, combines the beginning of Jesus with his baptism in the Jordan and stresses that the Holy Spirit descended '*into him*,' or Luke's Gospel with the well attested variant to the voice from heaven: 'You are my Son, this day have I begotten you,' both of which are in striking harmony with the Jewish-Christian Gospels. Traces of this archaic conception can still be detected in Syrian and Armenian sources. Furthermore, it makes one stop and think when one realizes that the Syrian and, in connec-tion with that, the Armenian baptismal rites were originally based on John 3:3–5 and thematize exclusively the birth of the baptizand from the maternal womb of the Spirit (later the raising from the maternal womb of the water) and at the same time stress that the prototype of Christian baptism is the baptism of Jesus. That is to say nothing else than that the baptism of Jesus was understood as a birth.[28]

---

27 *Oriens Christianus* 78 (1994), pp. 177–229; ET = 'The Appearance of the Light at the Baptism of Jesus and the Origins of the Feast of Epiphany' in Maxwell E. Johnson (ed.), *Between Memory and Hope: Readings on the Liturgical Year* (Collegeville: The Litur-gical Press 2000), pp. 291–348, from where it will be cited in this chapter.
28 Johnson, *Between Memory and Hope*, p. 330.

At Antioch in the late 380s John Chrysostom, in one of his Epiphany homilies, similarly notes that the content of the feast is the baptism of Jesus, including a rite for the sanctification of waters, and in another he indicates that the 25 December date for Christ's birth had only been known there for about ten years.[29] Within the hymns of Ephrem as well, Winkler concludes that while several themes were connected with the single feast of Jesus' beginnings on 6 January in Syria, above all it was the birth and baptism of Jesus that emerge as the primary foci. Connell also draws attention to the hymns of Ephrem, noting the important juxtaposition of Incarnation, birth and baptism. In Hymn 23, for example, Ephrem says:

> Blessed is Your birth that stirred up the universe! . . .
> [Too] small for You is the earth's lap,
> but large enough for You is Mary's lap. He dwelt in a lap,
>   and He healed by the hem [of his garment].
> He was wrapped [in] swaddling clothes in baseness, but they
>   offered Him gifts.
> He put on the garments of you, and helps emerged from them.
> *He put on the water of baptism, and rays flashed out from it.*
> With His humiliations [came] His exaltations. Blessed is He
>   who joins His glory to His suffering! . . .
> Great One Who became a baby, by Your birth again You begot me.
> Pure One Who was baptized, let Your washing wash us of impurity.
> Living One Who was embalmed, let us obtain life by Your death.[30]

Indeed, for Winkler, it is precisely the shining light at Jesus' baptism in the Jordan (translated above as 'rays flashed out from it'), according also to the ancient *Gospel of the Ebionites* and reflected even in the name for Epiphany in the Syrian East (*Denha*, 'Dawn of the Light'), that ultimately gave rise to the association of the light at Jesus' birth (Luke 2.8–9) and even within the Synoptic accounts of Jesus' transfiguration

---

29 See Martin F. Connell, *Eternity Today: On the Liturgical Year* 1 (New York/London: Continuum 2006), p. 167. In his Epiphany homily in 387 Chrysostom refers to people drawing out sanctified water on 6 January and taking it home with them for use; for ET, see Talley, *The Origins of the Liturgical Year*, pp. 114–15. Such blessing of water for home use is a practice still done in the Byzantine tradition and elsewhere in the Christian East today.

30 *Ephrem the Syrian: Hymns*, trans. and intro. Kathleen E. McVey (New York: Paulist Press 1989), pp. 189–90 (emphasis added).

on Mount Tabor, another part of the Epiphany themes in some communities. This Syrian focus Winkler sees reflected already in Clement of Alexandria's assertion about the date of Epiphany in Egypt.

> [I]t is especially interesting that the oldest attestation of the Feast of Epiphany derives from Basilides and his followers who, like Tatian, come from Syria. They too assign the greatest significance to the light . . . The followers of Basilides celebrated the baptism of Jesus in Egypt on the 11th or the 15th of the Month of Tybi, as Clement of Alexandria is able to report . . . The 15th of Tybi corresponds with the 10th of January. One should not be dissuaded from this since the selection of the 15th of Tybi is connected with the dating based on the course of the moon, as Usener has already pointed out: The 15th of the month was looked upon in the religious imagination as a day of the full moon and a day of light.[31]

Further, Winkler summarizes the later development of Epiphany as the separation of Jesus' birth and baptism:

> Just as one may discern in the sources a shift from the shining light at the baptism of Jesus to his equally Spirit-wrought birth in Bethlehem, so also a shift has taken place in the accent of the leitmotivs connected with Epiphany. First, the baptism of Jesus, apparently understood *as birth*, was most solemnly celebrated. This made room for a shift in emphasis to his birth in Bethlehem. At first, however, his baptism in the Jordan still remained attached to his birth. The witness of Ephrem, for example, shows this. The initial oscillation between the birth and baptism of Jesus as the *emphasis* of the leitmotivs for the Feast of Epiphany further contrasted the two themes. This oscillation is nothing other than precursor for the separation, whose way was prepared in the fourth century, of the most important contents of Epiphany: the 6th of January established itself as the feast of the baptism of Jesus, and a new separate feast was introduced, *i.e.*, the celebration of the birth of Jesus on December 25.[32]

---

31 Winkler, 'The Appearance of the Light', p. 345.
32 Winkler, 'The Appearance of the Light', p. 345.

One of the major reasons for such a shift is the further development of orthodox Christology, representing a move away from the potential Adoptionist overtones of Jesus' 'birth' in the Jordan. Russo has recently drawn attention to the fact that F. C. Conybeare in 1898 had already noted that Epiphany was *the* feast of Adoptionist Christianity; that is, the spiritual birth of Christ in the Jordan, the moment at which Jesus became the Father's only-begotten Son (cf. Ps. 2.7), was the centre of salvation history and the model for humanity's adoption unto divine sonship.[33] Conybeare had also noted that Christ's baptism was an integral component of early creedal formulae in Syria and Armenia, an understanding that Winkler herself has surveyed in detail within the Syrian and Armenian sources.[34] The lack of any mention of it in the Nicene Creed, therefore, is almost certainly deliberate.

This Christological shift Winkler sees further documented especially in the Greek terminology associated with the feast. From the Syriac *Denha* ('The Dawn of the Light') and possibly the Greek τὰ φῶτα ('The Lights') as the title for the feast in Cappadocia,[35] other terminology used as equivalents for both 6 January and 25 December elsewhere in the East, that is, either ἡ ἐπιφάνεια (plural, τὰ ἐπιφάνια) and even ἡ θεοφάνεια, all underscore the sense of the revelation or manifestation of Jesus' *divine identity* in the Bethlehem manger or at the Jordan.[36] Such terminology used for the feasts of both Christmas and Epiphany has moved considerably away from viewing Jesus' baptism in the Jordan as his 'birth'.

Several years ago Georg Kretschmar, in his study of the baptismal liturgy in Egypt, claimed that Egypt and Syria shared a common 'root relationship' in both rite and theology.[37] Winkler's work now suggests that this commonality certainly extended also to the origins and celebration of Epiphany.

---

33 Nicholas Russo, 'The Origins of Lent' (PhD dissertation, University of Notre Dame 2009), p. 393. The reference to Conybeare is to *The Key of Truth*, p. xcviii, n. 2.

34 See Gabriele Winkler, *Über die Entwicklungsgeschichte des armenischen Symbolums. Ein Vergleich mit dem syrischen u. griechischen Formelgut unter Einbezug der relevanten georgischen u. äthiopischen Quellen*, OCA 262 (Rome: Pontifical Oriental Institute 2000).

35 On Epiphany in Cappadocia see below, pp. 149–50.

36 Winkler, 'The Appearance of the Light', pp. 346–7.

37 Georg Kretschmar, 'Beiträge zur Geschichte der Liturgie, inbesondere der Taufliturgie, in Ägypten', *Jahrbuch für Liturgik und Hymnologie* 8 (1963), pp. 47–8.

JERUSALEM

According to the fifth-century Armenian Lectionary, the church at Jerusalem celebrated Christ's nativity on 6 January, reading Matthew 2.1–11 (the adoration of the Magi), which was prefaced the day before in Bethlehem at 4.00 p.m. by a short station at the Shepherds' Field, with the reading of Luke 2.8–10 assigned, and by an all-night vigil.[38] Unfortunately, the manuscript of Egeria's pilgrimage diary, our principal source for the feasts and seasons of Jerusalem in the late fourth century, has a lacuna, an entire missing leaf, at the very point when she is beginning to describe Epiphany. In fact, all we learn from her is that at both Jerusalem and Bethlehem the feast is celebrated for eight days, the decorations 'really are too marvellous for words', and the bishop has to be in Jerusalem to celebrate the feast.[39] Presumably, what Egeria is alluding to in her description is what the Armenian Lectionary contains, and it is the return procession from the vigil at Bethlehem where the manuscript begins. That is, Epiphany at Jerusalem celebrated the nativity of Christ on 6 January. Indeed, we know from Jerome in 411 that the 25 December Christmas still had not yet been accepted in Jerusalem, though Jerome makes the interesting point that 6 January was the day in the Christian East that celebrated Christ's 'baptism, at which the heavens opened for Christ . . .'[40]

Most recently, Terian's critical edition and commentary on *The Letter of Macarius I to the Armenians* provides evidence that in 335, almost 50 years earlier than Egeria's visit, the Jerusalem church was celebrating baptism on Easter, Pentecost *and* Epiphany, giving us the earliest date after Clement and, possibly, the *Letter to Diognetus*, for connecting Epiphany and the conferral of baptism on that day in the Christian East.[41] If it is the case, however, that Jerusalem was already celebrating baptisms in conjunction with the 'Epiphany of the Nativity' on 6 January, neither Egeria nor the author of the *Mystagogical Catecheses* demonstrates any knowledge of this. Nevertheless, it is important to note with Kilian McDonnell that even with the strong Romans 6 theology of

---

38 Charles (Athanase) Renoux, *Le Codex arménien Jérusalem 121* 2, Patrologia Orientalis 36 (Turnhout: Brepols 1971), pp. 211–21.
39 Egeria, *Itinerarium* 25.8–12.
40 Jerome, *Commentary on Ezekiel* (*PL* 25:18).
41 Abraham Terian, *Macarius of Jerusalem, Letter to the Armenians, A.D. 335*, AVANT: Treasures of the Armenian Christian Tradition 4 (Crestwood, NY: St Vladimir's Seminary Press 2008), pp. 83–5.

the *Mystagogical Catecheses* during the time in which paschal baptism is becoming the theoretical initiatory 'norm',[42] the interpretation of the post-baptismal anointing with chrism demonstrates that 'there is no retreating from the Jordan event as being normative for the sacrament of initiation'.[43] Combined with this, a clear focus on Jesus' baptism as paradigmatic for Christian baptism in Cyril of Jerusalem's *Baptismal Catecheses*[44] suggests that the Epiphany correlation with baptism documented in Macarius' *Letter to the Armenians* may still be playing some role, at least theologically, in the Jerusalem rites of the late fourth century.

Further, the lacuna at this location in Egeria becomes quite interesting since, because of it, we really have no idea what was actually being celebrated as Epiphany on 6 January in Jerusalem during her visit. If we take, naturally, the contents of the Armenian Lectionary as representing the late-fourth-century Jerusalem celebration of Epiphany and its octave, one could only conclude, as we have seen, that it is Christ's birth, including the visit of the Magi (Matt. 2.1–12), that was the focus. Alexander, for example, takes this as a given, arguing that an initial three-day celebration of Epiphany in Jerusalem during Egeria's visit was structured according to a course reading of the Gospel of Matthew at the beginning of the liturgical year, a principle we have seen before as indicative of Thomas Talley's approach to the liturgical year in general, where a single Gospel was read sequentially, thus giving shape to the calendar itself. According to Alexander, the list of Matthean Gospel readings for the first three days of the feast originally would have been Matthew 1.18–25 (6 January), Matthew 2.1–12 (7 January) and Matthew 2.13–23 (8 January). By the time of the Armenian Lectionary, however, the Matthew 2.1–12 reading had shifted from 7 January to 5 January, where it became the Gospel reading of the Epiphany vigil at Bethlehem.[45] But Alexander's hypothesis is challenged by the assigned readings for the newly established 25 December feast of Christmas in the Georgian Lectionary, with Matthew 1.18–25 assigned to the 24 December vigil and Matthew 2.1–23 to the liturgy on 25 December itself.[46] And what is of great interest is that the next text in Matthean

---

42 See above, pp. 81–6.
43 Kilian McDonnell, *The Baptism of Jesus in the Jordan: The Trinitarian and Cosmic Order of Salvation* (Collegeville: Glazier 1996), p. 225.
44 See McDonnell, *The Baptism of Jesus in the Jordan*, pp. 218–20.
45 Alexander, *Waiting for the Coming*, pp. 80–90.
46 Michel Tarchnischvili, *Le Grand Lectionnaire de l'Église de Jérusalem (Ve–VIIIe siècles)*, Corpus Scriptorum Christianorum Orientalium 188 (Louvain 1959), pp. 19–20.

sequence, Matthew 3.1–17, the baptism of Jesus, appearing nowhere in the Armenian Lectionary, is assigned in the Georgian Lectionary to 6 January at the Martyrium, complete with a preliminary baptismal-oriented vigil, including a blessing of water.[47]

It is well known, of course, that the Armenian Church never accepted the 'new' 25 December date for Christ's nativity and, instead, has maintained the 6 January date until the present day. But what is celebrated by the Armenians on 6 January is both the birth of Christ, with Matthew 1.18–25 (not Matt. 2.1–12) being read at the *Badarak* (eucharistic liturgy), and a concluding rite focused on the baptism of Jesus, including a blessing of the waters with Matthew 3.1–17 assigned as the Gospel text. Scholars, such as Renoux and Talley, have argued that this Armenian connection between birth and baptism on 6 January represents a later synthesis based upon 'Monophysite' doctrinal concerns and polemics against a focus on a separate 'bodily' nativity celebration.[48] Winkler, however, has challenged this argument, seeing the Armenian connection of these feasts as reflecting a very early stage in the development of Epiphany:

> The further development of the celebration of Epiphany in the fourth century and the introduction of the feast of Christmas at this time in several regions of the East has to be tied . . . to the evolution and change in the christological debates. The initial tension between the baptism of Jesus and his birth in Bethlehem, which lay behind the Gospels and also seems most closely to affect the feast of Epiphany at its beginnings, is thereby gradually resolved: from the one feast on Epiphany, which in its oldest eastern form apparently understood the baptism of Jesus as his birth, there first developed a celebration on January 6 which linked Jesus' baptism with his birth in Bethlehem (as, for example, in Syria, Armenia, and Egypt). Then, the emphasis shifted either to Jesus' birth in Bethlehem (as was the case above all in Jerusalem for a considerable length of time), or else a new feast was introduced . . .[49]

---

47 Tarchnischvili, *Le Grand Lectionnaire*, pp. 19–20. See also John Baldovin, *The Urban Character of Christian Worship*, OCA 228 (Rome: Pontifical Oriental Institute 1987), pp. 74–5.

48 See Charles (Athanase) Renoux, 'L'Épiphanie à Jérusalem au IVe et au Ve siècle d'après le Lectionnaire arménien de Jérusalem', *Revue des études arméniennes* 2 (1965), pp. 343–59; Talley, *The Origins of the Liturgical Year*, pp. 139–40.

49 Winkler, 'The Appearance of the Light', pp. 294–5.

Both the *Letter of Macarius to the Armenians* and current Armenian liturgical practice on Epiphany would support strongly Winkler's hypothesis.

CAPPADOCIA (AND CONSTANTINOPLE)

Prior to Terian's restoration of the *Letter of Macarius* as an early-fourth-century document, the earliest undisputed testimony to the baptism of converts on the feast of Epiphany was Gregory of Nazianzus' *Homily 40 On Holy Baptism*, preached in Constantinople on 6 January 380. Here, in his attempt to convince people not to wait until one of the major feasts to be baptized, Gregory demonstrates that, as at Jerusalem around 335, so also at Constantinople, and most likely Cappadocia, Epiphany, Easter and Pentecost had existed for some time as the three major occasions for conferring baptism.[50]

Regarding the origins of Epiphany itself in Cappadocia, however, we do not have evidence of it until Christmas on 25 December had already been established as well.[51] Similarly, traditional scholarship sought to unpack the various names associated with both of these feasts in Cappadocia – τὰ φῶτα, ἡ ἐπιφάνεια, τὰ θεοφάνια, and τὰ Γενέθλια – claiming that after the establishment of Christmas in 380 the terms Theophany (Θεοφάνια) and Nativity or Birth (τὰ Γενέθλια) were reserved exclusively for 25 December, and the title 'The Lights' (τὰ φῶτα) was a new term essentially replacing Epiphany as the designation for the 6 January feast now celebrating exclusively Jesus' baptism in the Jordan.[52] Talley, however, took a rather different approach to the

---

50 Gregory of Nazianzus, *Oratio* 40.24. For understanding the origins and development of the 6 January feast among the Cappadocians, the work of Jill Burnett Comings is indispensable, and she is largely dependent on her in this section: *Aspects of the Liturgical Year in Cappadocia (325–430)*, Patristic Studies 7 (New York: Lang 2005), pp. 61–94. See also Everett Ferguson, *Baptism in the Early Church: History, Theology, and Liturgy in the First Five Centuries* (Grand Rapids: Eerdmans 2009), pp. 582–616; Nancy E. Johnson, 'Living Death: Baptism and the Christian Life in the Works of Basil of Caesarea, Gregory of Nazianzus, and Gregory of Nyssa' (PhD dissertation, University of Notre Dame 2008). For a study and translation of the homilies and other writings of Gregory of Nazianzus, see the recent work of Brian E. Daley, *Gregory of Nazianzus* (London/New York: Routledge 2006).

51 See above, p. 130.

52 See Christine Mohrmann, 'Epiphania', *Revue des sciences philosophiques et théologiques* 37 (1953), pp. 655ff.; Botte, *Les Origines de la Noël et de l'Épiphanie*, pp. 78ff.; Justin Mossay, *Les Fêtes de Noël et de l'Épiphanie d'après les sources cappadociennes du IVe siècle* (Louvain: Abbaye du Mont César 1965), pp. 214ff.

question of terminology for the feast. Claiming that Basil of Caesarea already knew the 25 December feast of Christmas in Cappadocia, according to a homily of Basil's, *In sanctam Christi generationem*, which both Botte and Talley assigned to 25 December during Basil's episcopate (363–79), Talley noted that τὰ Γενέθλια became the term of choice in the Christian East for 25 December, with both Theophany and the Feast of Lights for 6 January.[53] It should also be recalled here that Winkler suggested, however tentatively, that the use of τὰ φῶτα for 6 January, together with the Syriac *Denha*, may well be among the earliest designations for the feast, before an emphasis on the revelation of Jesus' divine identity became the focus.[54]

Further, at the end of our previous chapter we expressed some doubt about the traditional scholarly approach to the origins of Christmas, which claims that the adoption of the 25 December feast was a deliberate anti-Arian move focusing on the pre-existence and Incarnation of the Logos. But there can be no question that in Cappadocia, according to the sermons studied by Jill Burnett Comings, Nicene and Constantinopolitan orthodox Trinitarian and Christological concerns played a strong role in the celebration of both 25 December and 6 January.[55] While this does not mean necessarily that the adoption of Christmas and Epiphany came about for doctrinal reasons, it does underscore the use of the content of these feasts for promoting and defending orthodox dogma.

The real dogmatic concerns with Epiphany and Christmas in the East, however, have to do with the separation of Jesus' birth and baptism on 6 January. That is, contemporary scholarship on Epiphany in the East, viewing 6 January, like 25 December in the West, as a feast of Jesus' 'beginnings' at the head of the year, has enabled us to see that Christological issues are part of the mix with 6 January from the start. At the same time that the separation of Jesus' birth and baptism into distinct feasts is taking place, both now concerned with the revelation of his divine identity, not only are we in the midst of the great Trinitarian and Christological debates but we are precisely in that moment of history when, shortly after the Council of Nicaea, baptism at Easter is becoming the theoretical, but certainly not the practical, norm in both

---

53 Talley, *The Origins of the Liturgical Year*, p. 138.
54 See Winkler, 'The Appearance of the Light', pp. 346–7.
55 Burnett Comings, *Aspects of the Liturgical Year in Cappadocia (325–430)*, pp. 87–90.

East and West.[56] Therefore, as a result of later Christological development in the Church, together with the eventual acceptance of the 25 December Christmas in the East, the apparent Adoptionist overtones of the earlier theology of Jesus' pneumatic 'birth' in the Jordan were suppressed, overtones that would have appealed greatly to the Arian theological position, and a reinterpretation of Epiphany not as the 'birth' of Christ in the Jordan but as a commemoration of his baptism alone resulted.

---

56 See above, pp. 81–6.

Chapter 17

6 January in the West

The standard theory on the development of Epiphany in the West has been that in the second half of the fourth century East and West simply exchanged their 'Nativity' feasts of Jesus. The Eastern Churches now placed Jesus' birth, together with the visit of the Magi, on 25 December, with the baptism of Jesus and the wedding at Cana on 6 January. Similarly, the Western Churches celebrated Jesus' birth on 25 December, but now with the Magi, the wedding at Cana, and, in some places, at least, the baptism of Jesus on 6 January.[1] The problem with this theory, however, thanks especially to the work of Connell, is that, as in the East, evidence for the feast of 6 January in the West outside Rome and North Africa actually pre-dates the acceptance and celebration of the 25 December Christmas in several different churches.[2] And the themes of Epiphany celebrations outside of Rome and North Africa, as we shall see, included the baptism of Jesus, as well as the wedding at Cana, the transfiguration of Jesus on Mount Tabor, and even the feeding miracle of the multiplication of loaves and fish.

Although Christmas may have already been established at Rome in 334, according to the Chronograph of 354, our first Western witness to Epiphany is in Gaul and refers to an event in Paris in 361, where the emperor, Julian the Apostate, according to the journals of Ammianus Marcellinus, entered a Christian church to worship the Christian god on Epiphany in the month of January. The twelfth-century Christian historian Zonaras narrates the same event, noting that what Epiphany

---

1 See, for example, Adolph Adam, *The Liturgical Year: Its History and Meaning after the Reform of the Liturgy* (New York: Pueblo 1981), pp. 184ff.
2 Martin F. Connell, *Eternity Today: On the Liturgical Year* 1 (New York/London: Continuum 2006), pp. 168–79, upon which this section of our chapter is dependent. See also Thomas J. Talley, *The Origins of the Liturgical Year* (New York: Pueblo 1986; 2nd edn, Collegeville: The Liturgical Press 1991), pp. 141–7.

celebrated then was the 'birthday' (*Genethlia*) of the Saviour. Hence, Connell is certainly correct in claiming that, in 361, 25 December had not yet been embraced in Gaul.[3] Later Gallican evidence tends to support this hypothesis, since in the fifth century, after Christmas had surely been adopted, 6 January in Gaul included the visit of the Magi, the baptism of Jesus, and the wedding at Cana. In fact, various prayers assigned to Epiphany in the extant Gallican Missals of the eighth century, most notably the *Missale Gallican vetus*[4] and the *Missale Gothicum*,[5] contain abundant references to what will come to be called the *tria miracula*, the 'three miracles' of the Magi, Jesus' baptism and his changing of water into wine at Cana. But, what is more, these same documents demonstrate that Epiphany itself either still was or had been a day for the conferral of baptism in Gaul,[6] something possibly the case at one time also in Spain.[7] And, as we shall see in the next chapter, preparation for baptism on Epiphany in the West may still be related to the origins and evolution of the Advent season.

In northern Italy as well, the themes of Epiphany are varied and it is clearly the case in some places that it is an older feast than Christmas. While some elements in the writings of Ambrose of Milan may suggest an early acquaintance with a 25 December Christmas, Connell has made a compelling argument based on Ambrose's hymns and biblical commentaries that Christmas itself was not yet celebrated in Milan in his time. In particular, Connell draws our attention to the classic Ambrosian hymn, *Illuminans altissimus*, which many have taken to be a Christmas hymn but which Connell argues is an Epiphany composition, since all of the narratives employed therein are related to Epiphany.[8]

Not only does this hymn place Jesus' baptism first in the sequence of Epiphany themes, but, as we saw above,[9] Ambrose also witnessed to the

---

3 Connell, *Eternity Today* 1, p. 169.
4 Leo Cunibert Mohlberg (ed.), *Missale Gallicanum vetus*, Rerum Ecclesiasticorum Documenta 3 (Rome: Herder 1958).
5 Leo Cunibert Mohlberg (ed.), *Missale Gothicum*, Rerum Ecclesiasticorum Documenta 5 (Rome: Herder 1961).
6 See Joseph Levesque, 'The Theology of the Postbaptismal Rites in the Seventh and Eighth Century Gallican Church' in Maxwell E. Johnson (ed.), *Living Water, Sealing Spirit: Essays on Christian Initiation* (Collegeville: The Liturgical Press 1995), pp. 159–201.
7 See below, pp. 161–3.
8 Connell, *Eternity Today* 1, pp. 171–2.
9 See above, p. 81.

enrolment on 6 January of candidates for baptism at Easter, thus under-scoring the baptismal connotations of the feast, even if, by now, paschal baptism had come to dominate liturgically and theologically. What is of equal interest in this baptismal context is that the earliest Latin Epiphany sermon we have comes from Chromatius of Aquileia (338–407) and the focus of this sermon was specifically the baptism of Jesus by John in the Jordan, including references to Christian baptism, which may indicate that baptisms were conferred on this day. But at the same time in Turin, Maximus preached on both Jesus' baptism and the wedding at Cana. And, like Ambrose, Maximus knew of the enrolment of baptismal candidates on Epiphany, rather than the conferral of baptism itself, which may have been the case also in Aquileia.[10]

Elsewhere in northern Italy the situation is somewhat similar with regard to a diversity of themes. So, for example, Peter Chrysologus in fifth-century Ravenna (380–450) refers to the threefold theme of Magi, baptism and Cana on Epiphany. Earlier at Brescia, in the late fourth century, Filastrius (385–91) refers only to the visit of the Magi as the theme of Epiphany in his church, while noting that 'some', by which he means 'heretics', celebrate the 'Epiphanies' of the Lord, namely, Jesus' baptism and his transfiguration on the mount. But Filastrius here is deliberately downplaying Epiphany itself as a festival lesser in import than Christmas and it may well be that he is already reflecting the influence of Roman festal practice.[11] Of course, in the light of the Christological disputes we encountered above in our analysis of Epiphany in the Christian East, it is tantalizing to speculate on the potential anti-Arian sentiments directed here against the 'heretics' who celebrate either Jesus' baptism or transfiguration on 6 January, two events where the divine voice from heaven signals Jesus' sonship!

Our other evidence for Epiphany in the West comes to us from North Africa and Rome, usually dated during the pontificate of Damasus (366–84), and where, as at Brescia, the focus of the feast on 6 January is the adoration of the Magi, thus making Epiphany almost a doublet of Christmas. Even at Rome, however, according to the earliest lectionary evidence, the Johannine version of Jesus' 'baptism' (John 1.29–34) is assigned to the third day after 'Theophany' (*Feria III post theophania*), and the wedding at Cana is assigned to the second Sunday

---

10 For references, see Connell, *Eternity Today* 1, pp. 173–6.
11 See Talley, *The Origins of the Liturgical Year*, pp. 144–5.

after 'Theophany'.[12] While it is certainly true that it was only in 1960 (!) that the baptism of Jesus was given its own feast in the Roman calendar on the Octave Day of Epiphany (i.e., 13 January), and moved to the Sunday after Epiphany in 1969,[13] the fact remains that the *tria miracula* of Magi, baptism and Cana made up the themes of Epiphany at Rome as well, even if the adoration of the Magi was to become the dominant focus on 6 January itself. Scholars have traditionally either ignored or not noticed this reference to the Johannine account of Jesus' baptism so close to 6 January in the Roman liturgy and have instead focused on the relative uniqueness of Rome in limiting Epiphany to the adoration of the Magi. Hence, the question has often been raised as to why Rome receives an Epiphany that is focused on the Magi rather than on the baptism of Jesus, but the lectionary evidence suggests that, while the adoration of the Magi is the focus for 6 January itself, the baptism of Jesus is clearly not that far behind.

Nevertheless, it is the adoration of the Magi, complete with giving them names eventually (Caspar, Balthazar and Melchior) and venerating their relics (at Cologne), that will capture the Christian imagination about Epiphany throughout the West up to and including the present day. And theologically as well, it is the identity of the Magi as *Gentiles* that will come to dominate the meaning of the revelation or manifestation of Jesus' identity on this day. Already in Augustine's homilies on Epiphany this approach is clear:

> On the day of his birth, our Lord was manifested to the shepherds aroused by an angel, and on that day, too, through the appearance of a star he was announced to magi in the distant East, but it was on this day that he was adored by the magi. Therefore, the whole church of the Gentiles has adopted this day as a feast worthy of most devout celebration, for who were the magi but the first-fruits of the Gentiles?[14]

---

12 See Theodor Klauser (ed.), *Das römische Capitulare evangeliorum: Texte und Untersuchungen zu seiner ältesten Geschichte* 1, Liturgiegeschichtliche Quellen und Forschungen 28 (Münster: Aschendorff 1935), p. 14.

13 See Adam, *The Liturgical Year*, p. 148.

14 Sermon 199, *On the Epiphany of the Lord*; ET from *Saint Augustine: Sermons on the Liturgical Seasons*, trans. Mary Muldowney (New York: Fathers of the Church 1959), p. 71.

The same approach is emphasized in the Epiphany sermons of Pope Leo the Great, whose Sermon 3 on Epiphany is still read in Vigils (or Office of Readings) in the current Roman Liturgy of the Hours on 6 January:

> Now the Gentiles in their multitudes enter the household of our father and, as children of the promise, receive that blessing which Abraham's fleshly children rejected. All the peoples of the earth, in the persons of the three wise men, adore their Maker, and God is known not only in Judea but throughout the world so that 'his name might be great in Israel' everywhere.
>
> Now that these mysteries of God's gracious favor are made known to us, let us rejoice on this day of our birth and of the world's vocation; let us celebrate and thank our merciful God, 'who has made us worthy to share the lot of the saints in light; who has rescued us from the power of darkness and brought us into the kingdom of his beloved Son.' This is the day, which Abraham rejoiced to see, when the children of his faith would be blessed in his offspring, Christ. This is the day of which David sang: 'All the nations shall come and adore you, Lord.' All these prophecies began to be fulfilled when the star led the three magi from their distant land that they might recognize and adore the King of heaven and earth. Their example urges us to be servants, as best we can, of the grace that invites all people to Christ.[15]

We might say, then, that it is the Canticle of Simeon (Luke 2.29–32), the Nunc dimittis, with its reference to Christ's birth as 'light for revelation to the Gentiles, and for glory to [God's] people Israel', that supplies the hermeneutical key for Epiphany at Rome, and from Rome eventually throughout Western Christianity.

From a unitary feast celebrating both Jesus' birth and baptism, or his baptism as his 'birth' in the Jordan, in both Egypt and Syria, the 6 January feast of Epiphany or Theophany will become universally the feast of the revelation of Jesus' identity through the use of differing narratives associated in the Gospels with Jesus' 'beginnings'. In the East, after the establishment of the 25 December Christmas, the focus of the Epiphany revelation will continue to be primarily on Jesus' baptism in the Jordan on 6 January, with the birth narratives themselves moving to

---

15 *Sermon 3, On the Epiphany*; ET from Maxwell E. Johnson (ed.), *Benedictine Daily Prayer: A Short Breviary* (Collegeville: The Liturgical Press 2005), pp. 91–2.

25 December. In the West, while the adoration of the Magi, thanks to Rome, will become the dominant focus of the 6 January feast, other meanings of Epiphany, including Jesus' baptism, are clearly part of the overall themes of the feast, especially in Gaul and northern Italy, where either the baptism of Jesus or some sort of baptismal connections (e.g., the enrolment of baptismal candidates on Epiphany in Milan and Turin) are clearly present. But even at Rome, as we have seen, the baptism of Jesus is still lurking in the background, though assigned to the third day after Epiphany itself, where it remained until the modern period.

Together with recent scholarship, then, we see every reason to agree with the original assessment of Talley on Epiphany:

> In the light of the theological struggles prior to and just following the victory over Arianism in 381, the exclusion at Rome and in Africa of the baptism of Jesus from the themes of what had been the oriental *epiphania*, the celebration of the incarnation, is not difficult to understand. In Cappadocia, similar considerations led to the transfer of that title for the celebration of the new December nativity date, while at Alexandria we find that the old celebration of the baptism of Jesus on January 6 now came to celebrate the nativity as well. In the closing decades of the fourth century, theological development engendered a measure of embarrassment with the baptism of Jesus as the beginning of the gospel . . . Indeed, what seems to have been the oldest gospel assignment for the celebration of the nativity at Rome, the prologue of the fourth gospel, may also have been read at Ephesus in the beginnings of what would become the feast of the Epiphany. There we encounter the *Grundtext* of orthodox teaching on the incarnation, *kai ho logos sarx egeneto*, but the context of that declaration is the witness of a man sent from God, whose name was John.[16]

The only thing we would add is that at Rome the baptism of Jesus was not excluded from the mix, just relegated to a much lesser role within the Epiphany octave.

---

16 Talley, *The Origins of the Liturgical Year*, pp. 146–7.

Chapter 18

Advent

The season of Advent (from the Latin *adventus*, 'coming', and a translation of the Greek παρουσία and/or ἐπιφάνεια), as a liturgical season with that specific title, is a purely Western Christian phenomenon and comes into existence as a time associated with what Connell calls scriptural, ascetic and/or eschatological[1] preparation for Christmas, of course, only after Christmas itself came to be established on 25 December. And it is not until the reign of Pope Gregory I (590–604) that the four-Sunday Advent season with its strong eschatological orientation clearly makes its appearance under Gregory's own leadership.

This is not to say, however, that such a season of preparation was and is only Western or, as we shall see, that it is only related to Christmas in its origins. In the Byzantine Rite, for example, beginning with the 21 November feast of the Presentation of Mary in the Temple, multiple Marian images associated with the 'Ark of the Covenant', the 'Tabernacle', and even as the 'heavenly Temple' appear in the various *troparia* and prayers throughout the season.[2] And, two Sundays before Christmas, the Byzantine Rite commemorates 'The Holy Ancestors of Christ', culminating in Mary, and on the Sunday before Christmas is celebrated 'all the Fathers who down the centuries have been pleasing to God, from Adam to Joseph, husband of the Most Holy Mother of God'.[3] Among the Syrian Christian traditions, both West Syrian (i.e., Syrian and/or

---

1 Martin Connell, 'The Origins and Evolution of Advent in the West' in Maxwell E. Johnson (ed.), *Between Memory and Hope: Readings on the Liturgical Year* (Collegeville: The Liturgical Press 2000), pp. 349–71. See also Martin Connell, *Eternity Today: On the Liturgical Year* 1 (New York/London: Continuum 2006), pp. 59–74.
2 See Mother Mary and Archimandrite Kallistos Ware, *The Festal Menaion* (London/Boston: Faber and Faber 1969), pp. 164–98.
3 Pierre Jounel, 'The Year' in A. G. Martimort *et al.* (eds), *The Church at Prayer* 4 (Collegeville: The Liturgical Press 1986), p. 93.

Antiochene Orthodox and Maronite) and East Syrian (i.e., Church of the East, Chaldean and Syro-Malabar), the assigned Gospel readings on the Sundays for the season of Christmas preparation, called 'Weeks of Annunciations', include, in order, the annunciation to Zechariah, the annunciation to Mary, the visitation, the nativity of John the Baptist, and, finally, the annunciation to Joseph. Indeed, for these reasons, what Western Christians refer to as 'Advent' is often thought of as a 'Marian' season in the Christian East.

Further, this Eastern approach to the season of preparation for Christmas has some resonance in the West as well. While the precise origins of the 25 March celebration of the Annunciation of Our Lord are obscure,[4] the feast on this date was celebrated already in the East by the beginning of the sixth century. Before that shift to a calendrical date, the Annunciation appears to have been celebrated on the Sunday before Christmas. Interestingly enough, the location of the feast of the Annunciation actually varied as to date in the calendars of other Western liturgical traditions throughout the Middle Ages. In Spain it was celebrated on 18 December, where even today in the Mozarabic Rite 18 December has remained a solemnity of Mary called, simply, *Sancta Maria*.[5] At Milan the Annunciation was and still is celebrated by the Ambrosian Rite on the last of the *six* Sundays of Advent. Even in the liturgical tradition of Rome, a similar correlation between, at least, Annunciation and Christmas became also true of *Roman* Advent itself, although Rome had clearly accepted the 25 March date of the feast by the time of Pope Sergius I (687–701). Prior to the post-Vatican II liturgical reform of the calendar, in fact, the Gospel pericopes of both the annunciation and the visitation were read, respectively, on the Wednesday and Friday of the third week of Advent, formerly known as the Advent 'Ember Days', one of four annual 'seasons' of special prayer and fasting throughout the liturgical year.[6] Hence, even with the acceptance of the 25 March date for the feast in the West, a close proximity between the celebration of the Annunciation (and the Visitation) and Christmas remained a traditional characteristic of Western liturgical history in general.

---

4 See below, p. 210.
5 Conferencia Episcopal Española, *Missale Hispano-Mozarabicum* (Barcelona 1994), pp. 34, 136–42.
6 On Ember Days, see Thomas J. Talley, 'The Origins of the Ember Days: An Inconclusive Postscript' in Paul De Clerck and Eric Palazzo (eds), *Rituels: Mélanges offerts à Pierre-Marie Gy, OP* (Paris: Cerf 1990).

What became the pre-Christmas Advent season in the West may have had its origins, outside of Rome, in a period of ascetical preparation for baptisms celebrated on Epiphany, understood in part, as we saw in the previous chapter, as the celebration of Jesus' baptism itself. Prior to the work of Talley, in fact, it was generally accepted that our earliest references to 'Advent' in the West were those presumably concerned with a three-week period of such preparation. The first is that of Hilary of Poitiers (d. 367), who, in an excerpt from his alleged *Liber Officiorum*, points to a three-week period before Epiphany, a 'three-week Lent',[7] and the second is Canon 4 of the Spanish Council of Saragossa (380), which directs that 'for twenty-one days in a row, from December 17 until the day of Epiphany, which is January 6, for continuous days no one should be absent from church or stay hidden at home or escape to the country or to the mountains or run around in bare feet, but all should come together in church'.[8]

Contemporary scholarship on Advent, however, represented primarily by Talley, has tended to discount this theory.[9] The authorship of the text attributed to Hilary, for example, has been seriously questioned, with no consensus among scholars yet reached;[10] and Talley believed that Christmas was already being celebrated in Spain by 380 and so considered it as having been included within these 21 days.[11] Alexander takes Talley's approach a step further, suggesting that:

> every day of this three-week period was, or soon came to be, a day of special observance, December 25 included among them, and that it was the intention of the bishops to commend the keeping of these days to the faithful. It might be suggested since the first week of this period, December 17–23, was the time of the pagan saturnalia, that part of the motivation for the observance of those days was to place quite intentionally a Christian festival period over against the pagan.

---

7   A. Wilmart, 'Le prétendu *Liber Officiorum* de St. Hilaire et l'Avent liturgique', *Revue Bénédictine* 27 (1910), pp. 500–13.
8   ET from Connell, 'The Origins and Evolution of Advent in the West', p. 363.
9   See Thomas J. Talley, *The Origins of the Liturgical Year* (New York: Pueblo 1986; 2nd edn, Collegeville: The Liturgical Press 1991), pp. 147ff.; J. Neil Alexander, *Waiting for the Coming: The Liturgical Meaning of Advent, Christmas, Epiphany* (Washington, DC: The Pastoral Press 1993), pp. 8–23.
10   See J. P. Brisson, *Hilaire de Poitiers, Traité des mystères*, Sources chrétiennes 19 (Paris: Cerf 1947), pp. 64–8, 164; Jounel, 'The Year', p. 91.
11   Talley, *The Origins of the Liturgical Year*, p. 150.

Although this is possible, another explanation could be that the
annual observance of saturnalia was followed by a seasonal cessation
from work, a sort of mid-winter recess, and it is entirely possible that
the bishops of the council were calling their people to the faithful
observance of the holy days that overlapped with their vacation. In
other words, the canon has less to do with the shape of a particular
liturgical observance than it does with a reminder to the faithful not
to forget their obligation to the church while on holiday.[12]

Alexander's comments seem overly speculative. If there is nothing
explicit in this canon about Epiphany baptism or about this three-week
period having anything to do with pre-baptismal catechesis, there is
certainly nothing about this time period being a post-*Saturnalia*
vacation period. And it becomes difficult to know what this period was
about at all.

It is here where Connell's critique of Talley's position must be taken
into serious account.[13] Connell notes, in particular, that outside of
Rome and North Africa in 380 there is no evidence *anywhere* in the
West for the celebration of Christmas. Further, the period between
17 December and 6 January is described as one of continuous activity,
possibly ascetic in nature, with no room for a festive break on 25 December but culminating on Epiphany, the only festival designated. He
also points to a parallel possibility of a Spanish ascetic, identified by
Gabriel Morin in 1928, whose writing refers both to a three-week fast
and to the feast of Epiphany, though, as Connell notes, it could have
come from almost any of the Latin churches outside of Rome, where
Christmas had not yet made its appearance. As we saw earlier in our
chapter on Lent,[14] a three-week period of baptismal preparation in early
Christianity appears to have existed in a wide variety of distinct
churches: that is, Rome, Jerusalem, North Africa, Naples, Constantinople and Spain. That such a three-week pattern would have been in
existence for baptism on Epiphany as well seems perfectly reasonable.
For Spain, in particular, as we saw, the three-week 'Lenten' period not
only appears to be confirmed by the first canon of the Second Council
of Braga (572) but actually uses similar language to Saragossa in
reference to the time span, while directing that bishops 'shall teach that

12 Alexander, *Waiting for the Coming*, pp. 10–11.
13 Connell, *Eternity Today* 1, pp. 67–9.
14 See above, pp. 92–8.

catechumens (as the ancient canons command) shall come for the cleansing of exorcism twenty days before baptism, in which twenty days they shall especially be taught the Creed, which is: I believe in God the Father Almighty . . .'[15] It would be difficult to see both of these Spanish references to three weeks of time (21 days or 20 days) as not having some baptismal connotations.

The strongest argument against viewing this three-week period in early Spain as one of preparation for baptism on Epiphany with any degree of certainty comes from Alexander. He correctly draws our attention to the fact that in 385 Pope Siricius wrote a letter to Himerius, Bishop of Tarragona, in which it is documented, a mere five years after the Council of Saragossa, that baptisms took place in Spain on Easter, Pentecost, Epiphany, various saints' days, and, most telling, now on Christmas as well.[16] Such evidence, notes Alexander, makes it 'unlikely that the period could be preparation for Epiphany baptism if another major baptismal day, December 25 . . . took place on intervening days'.[17] At the same time, nowhere does this document indicate exactly where it is in Spain that baptisms were being conferred on Epiphany, saints' days and Christmas, since Himerius himself claims to know only Easter and Pentecost baptism as the practice of his church at Tarragona. In other words, if this letter is a witness to the celebration of Christmas on 25 December in Spain in 385, it does not tell where it first makes its appearance in Spain, nor does it tell us necessarily anything about the practice of Saragossa five years earlier. And Alexander himself adds:

> The possibility exists, of course, that the three-week period before Epiphany was a vestige of an earlier time before the bifurcation of that unitive festival into the separate feasts of Christmas and Epiphany, a possibility in light of the influence of the eastern rites on much of the early liturgy of Gaul and Spain . . . [I]t is difficult to assess . . . the exact intent of the bishops convened at Saragossa. It is impossible at this stage to dismiss completely the possibility that this three-week period before Epiphany had some measurable impact on the formation of Advent, but the weight of the evidence presently available makes it equally impossible to see anything more than a very small, ill-formed piece of a larger puzzle, certainly not the secure roots of western Advent.[18]

---

15 *DBL*, p. 158.
16 *Ep. Ad Himerium* (*PL* 13:1154–5).
17 Alexander, *Waiting for the Coming*, p. 11.
18 Alexander, *Waiting for the Coming*, pp. 11–12.

However, while we may have to settle for this particular conciliar reference to three weeks before Epiphany in Spain as only a *possibility* in pointing to a nascent Advent, the mere fact that both the baptism of Jesus and Christian baptisms were celebrated in various Western Churches on Epiphany would undoubtedly necessitate some kind of period of preparation for baptism and, as we saw in our chapter on Lent, a three-week period is a strong candidate for this. Since Himerius claims to know that some churches in Spain celebrated baptism on the new 25 December Christmas, is it not reasonable to suspect that some kind of similar preparation period for Christmas baptism must also have been in existence? Is it possible that the three-week period specified by the Council of Saragossa was used for both occasions? In either case, such a period of three weeks of preparation before baptism here would square with our suggestion above in the chapter on Lent that three weeks of baptismal preparation may well have been a rather free-floating period of preparation tied to whenever baptisms occurred in the life of a church.

Some scholars have suggested that there are additional references to an Advent-type of preparation period oriented towards Epiphany in other non-Roman Western liturgical sources. In Sicily in the middle of the fifth century we have evidence from a letter of Pope Leo I that Epiphany was a regular occasion for baptism there, a custom he tried to discourage in favour of Easter and/or Pentecost, but, unfortunately, he makes no reference to any kind of preparation period.[19] More importantly, in late-fifth-century Gaul Bishop Perpetuus of Tours (d. 490) legislated that from the feast day of his predecessor, St Martin of Tours (11 November), until Christmas, a period of seven weeks or 40 days, fasting was to take place on three days each week.[20] Josef Jungmann argued that this legislation was based on an earlier 'St Martin's Lent', a 40-day period of preparation for Epiphany baptism, with five days of fasting each week from St Martin's day until Epiphany, resulting in exactly 40 fasting days. Such, he believed, was designed to provide a parallel to the season of Lent before Easter baptism.[21] But while this may have been the case, there is really no hard evidence in support of it,

---

19 *Ep.* 16 (*PL* 54:699–702).
20 See Connell, *Eternity Today* 1, pp. 70–1.
21 Josef Jungmann, 'Advent und Voradvent; Überreste des gallischen Advents in der römischen Liturgie' in Josef Jungmann, *Gewordene Liturgie: Studien und Durchblicke* (Innsbruck: Rauch 1941), pp. 237–49.

and what we see instead in later Gallican sources, such as Gregory of Tours' *History of the Franks* and the Council of Mâcon (582), is that the parallel to a pre-paschal Lent, that is, this 40-day season, strongly ascetic in character, culminates at Christmas and not at Epiphany.[22]

If a three-week or 40-day preparation for Epiphany baptism may have played some role in what ultimately became the Western season of Advent, another tradition more directly related to the nativity theme must be taken into account. Here, in particular, the evidence adduced by Connell for Advent in northern Italian sources is paramount.[23] As we saw in the previous chapter, Epiphany as celebrating the nativity of Christ in Bethlehem, together with other themes, appears to be the earlier tradition in northern Italy, and there may be vestiges of this in the continued enrolment of candidates for baptism on Epiphany in Milan and Turin. But the 25 December Christmas itself is not clearly known in northern Italy until the late fourth century in Brescia, where Bishop Filastrius (d. 391) in his *Diversarum hereseon liber* notes that there are four fasts the Church celebrates during the year: at Jesus' birth, Easter, Ascension and Pentecost.[24] Since Christmas was apparently a new feast in northern Italy, Connell suggests, we cannot know if the fast at Jesus' birth was a practice that had merely shifted from before Epiphany to before Christmas or if it was a newly established fast altogether. In roughly the same time period, that is, the end of the fourth century, Maximus of Turin witnesses to what may have been two Sundays of preparation for Christmas, a practice confirmed in mid-fifth-century Ravenna, where the evidence suggests that Peter Chrysologus preached on the annunciation to Zechariah (Luke 1.5–25) two Sundays before Christmas and the annunciation to Mary (Luke 1.26–38) on the Sunday before Christmas, a practice highly consistent with various Eastern Christian pre-Christmas traditions. While the precise length of 'Advent' cannot be known from these sources, it is well known that eventually at Milan, in what is called the Ambrosian Rite, as well as in Spain in the Mozarabic Rite, Advent will become a period of six weeks before Christmas, hence, similar in length to the Gallican 40-day period of 'St Martin's Lent', which also lasted into the Middle Ages in Gaul. Theologically as well, if Spain and Gaul contributed to the emerging Advent what might be called an ascetic or more

---

22 Connell, *Eternity Today* 1, p. 71.
23 Connell, 'The Origins and Evolution of Advent', pp. 353–63; Connell, *Eternity Today* 1, pp. 59–66.
24 See Connell, *Eternity Today* 1, p. 60.

penitential (baptismal preparation?) character, the northern Italian sources suggested a more scriptural or incarnational focus.

A six-week Advent was also practised at Rome, although our evidence for this comes only from those liturgical sources for Rome known to be pre-Gregory I (590–604) in content, that is, the Würzburg Capitulary and the old Gelasian Sacramentary. As with Lent at Rome, it is again the work of Chavasse, based on these sources, that shows us that in the six weeks before Christmas, the first five Sundays were explicitly now called *de adventu*, while the Sunday immediately before Christmas was designated *Dominica vacat*, owing to the fact that the previous Wednesday through the Saturday vigil Mass were part of what were called the Ember Days, a purely Roman phenomenon.[25] It has been suggested that the fast of the tenth month (the other quarterly or *quat-tember* fasts being in summer, autumn and spring) may have had something to do with the origins of Advent at Rome, especially when it is recalled that the annunciation to Mary (Luke 1.26–39) and the visita-tion of Mary to Elizabeth (Luke 1.39–47) appear as the Gospel readings for the Wednesday and Friday of this week in the sources.[26]

What happens at Rome at the end of the sixth century is that the six-week Advent received by Gregory I is shortened by him to four weeks in length. Connell suggests that the reason for this is that Gregory did not know the baptismal and/or Epiphany imagery associated elsewhere in the West with a six-week or 40-day period,[27] though this cannot be known with any degree of certainty. At the same time, Alexander draws attention to the fact that in the pertinent liturgical sources for Advent at Rome, the liturgical year *begins* with the vigil Mass of Christmas, but ends with what comes to be known as Advent. That the year would begin with Epiphany or with Christmas is surely no surprise, given what we have seen in the previous chapters of this section. Hence, if in Spain and Gaul, the pre-Christmas season comes to have an ascetic or peniten-tial focus, perhaps, as suggested by Adolf Adam, under the influence of Irish monasticism especially in Gaul,[28] and if in northern Italy it is the

25 Antoine Chavasse, 'L'Avent romain du VIe au VIIIe siècle', *Ephemerides Liturgicae* 67 (1953), pp. 37–52. On Ember Days, see further above, p. 159.

26 Theodor Klauser (ed.), *Das Romische Capitulare evangeliorum: Texte und Unter-suchungen zu seiner altesten Geschichte*, Liturgiegeschichtliche Quellen und Forschungen 28 (Münster: Aschendorff 1935), 1, p. 127.

27 Connell, *Eternity Today* 1, pp. 73–4.

28 Adolph Adam, *The Liturgical Year: Its History and Meaning after the Reform of the Liturgy* (New York: Pueblo 1981), p. 132.

coming nativity of Christ, announced by the Scripture readings preceding it, the very location of 'Advent' at Rome as the *final* period of the year, together with the Gospel pericopes focusing on the *parousia* or Second Coming of Christ, suggest an eschatological orientation to the season. Alexander explains this as indicating that 'Advent at Rome may have first been conceived of as a period *before Christmas* in its integrity, rather than as a *pre-Christmas* fast or season of ascetically focused preparation for the celebration of the Nativity.'[29]

What will happen is that the Roman Advent will eventually become imported elsewhere into Western Christianity, ultimately replacing the various local traditions, although the Ambrosian and Mozarabic Rites will retain, even today, their customary six-week practice. And Advent itself will become in time a mixture of the various biblical, ascetic and eschatological orientations we have noticed. Focused as it is, somewhat ambiguously, on the 'Advent' or coming of Christ, without specifying which 'coming' is intended, Bernard of Clairvaux (d. 1153) well summarizes the theology of the final form of the Roman four-week Advent as orientated to the three comings of Christ: past, present and future:

> We know that there are three comings of the Lord. The third lies between the other two. It is invisible, while the other two are visible. In the first coming he was seen on earth, dwelling among men; he himself testifies that they saw him and hated him. In the final coming all flesh will see the salvation of our God, and they will look on him whom they pierced. The intermediate coming is a hidden one; in it only the elect see the Lord within their own selves, and they are saved. In his first coming our Lord came in our flesh and in our weakness; in this middle coming he comes in spirit and in power; in the final coming he will be seen in glory and majesty . . . Because this [middle] coming lies between the other two, it is like a road on which we travel from the first coming to the last. In the first, Christ was our redemption; in the last, he will appear as our life; in this middle coming, he is our rest and consolation.[30]

Regarding its origins, however, we can do no better than the following words of Connell:

---

29 Alexander, *Waiting for the Coming*, p. 21.
30 Bernard of Clairvaux, *Sermo* 5, *In Adventu Domini* 1–3; ET from *The Liturgy of the Hours* 1 (New York: Catholic Book Publishing House 1975), p. 169.

[W]e do know that the Epiphany was being celebrated in Gaul, in Spain, in Northern Italy, and in the East long before Christmas was received in those places. And we know that in most . . . of those non-Roman western churches the nativity and baptism of Jesus were among the epiphanies marked in the celebration . . . We also know that the enrollment of catechumens was celebrated on Epiphany in Milan (and perhaps elsewhere), and . . . we read Leo the Great's advice against baptisms on Epiphany when he wrote to the bishop of Sicily. So surely some of those southern Italian communities were initiating on January 6. Might it be, then, that the forty-day span prominent later on in Gaul carried a remnant of the baptismal span preceding Epiphany in earlier times? . . . Might the forty days have been linked not to Easter as is commonly assumed in liturgical scholarship, but to baptism whenever this took place? Perhaps only later did the introduction of Christmas, broadly coincident with the decline of the catechumenate, join with the forty-day span to become a preparatory period no longer for baptism but for the relatively new date in the calendar, December 25.[31]

If Connell is correct here, an earlier understanding and orientation may still appear as traces or remnants in the extant sources and, as such, may help in the assessment that outside of Rome it was especially a pre-Epiphany baptismal preparation period that functioned as a kind of nascent Advent. As with Lent, then, it is possible that 'Advent' also owes its origins, in part at least, to various baptismal preparation periods. What this also means is that the Roman Advent as it develops is somewhat of an anomaly in comparison with the other liturgical traditions, but an anomaly that would be consistent with other liturgical traditions indigenous to Rome, though sometimes copied elsewhere (e.g., the development of the sacrament of confirmation, and the unique structure and contents of the Roman eucharistic prayer or *canon missae*). And since at Rome the origins of Advent are rather late and deliberately, it seems, shortened in relationship to what other churches are doing, it becomes difficult to understand its meaning and function vis-à-vis the 25 December Christmas at all. Hence, we cannot but agree also with Alexander that the strong eschatological character of Roman Advent and its actual location within the classic Roman liturgical books at the end of the year has more to do with the *conclusion* of the year than

31 Connell, 'The Origins and Evolution of Advent', pp. 369–70.

with its annual beginning, contrary to our current liturgical reckoning. Historically, its proximity to Christmas, therefore, would have been more accidental than deliberate in Rome. Of course, if Christmas itself is perceived not as the celebration of Jesus' nativity *in illo tempore*, that is, as a commemoration of a historical event or as Baby Jesus' birthday, but as itself a celebration of his *parousia*, his Advent, his coming again in glory, then an eschatologically oriented Advent season makes perfect sense.

Martyrs and other saints

Chapter 19

The first martyrs and saints

No study of the origins of feasts, fasts and seasons in early Christianity would be complete without attention to one of the most significant early developments in Christian liturgical celebration, namely, the cult of martyrs and, later, of other saints, combining to make up eventually a *sanctorale*, or sanctoral cycle, in the liturgical calendars, a cycle of saints' feasts to be distinguished from the temporal cycle, to which this book has been dedicated up until now. It has often been the case among liturgical scholars, with some notable exceptions,[1] that the *sanctorale* was treated as but an appendage or extended footnote to what was perceived to be the more important focus of the major feasts and seasons. For example, Talley in *The Origins of the Liturgical Year* did not deal with the origins and development of the *sanctorale* at all. Indeed, part of the reason the sanctoral cycle has not always received the attention that it should, we suspect, is that theologians, historians and, perhaps especially, liturgiologists have tended to denigrate or even dismiss, albeit unconsciously, what is often (even pejoratively) called 'popular religion' as but 'superstition', vestiges of 'paganism', or as reflecting somehow a 'lower' form of belief and practice among the 'unenlightened' than the 'official religion' of the elite, and it is certainly the case that the cult of martyrs and saints, on one level at least, is part and parcel of what may be called 'popular religion'.

More recent scholarship, however, has been willing to embrace a much broader view of the whole, including the religious lives and practices of the poor, women and others as theological and liturgical 'sources'. For our purposes here, Peter Brown's important 1981 work,

1 Adolph Adam, *The Liturgical Year: Its History and Meaning after the Reform of the Liturgy* (New York: Pueblo 1981), pp. 199–272; Pierre Jounel, 'The Year' in A. G. Martimort *et al.* (eds), *The Church at Prayer* 4 (Collegeville: The Liturgical Press 1986), pp. 108–29.

The Cult of the Saints, represents a significant scholarly shift in this context. Here, in particular, Brown argues convincingly that the *real* history of the early Church is to be read, precisely, in the development of the 'popular' practices and beliefs associated with the cult of the martyrs and later saints at their shrines in the overall shaping of late antique culture, religion and society, practices shared by both the intellectually elite and others in the Church, in spite of their differing intellectual facilities. That is, such practices must be seen as a basic, rather than peripheral, expression of Christian faith and piety in general within this period.[2]

On a similar note, Robert Taft has written of the turn in this direction that his own work has taken, saying:

> In so doing I have, in a sense, been responding to my own appeal, made years ago, that we 'integrate into our work the methods of the relatively recent *pietà popolare* or *annales* schools of Christian history in Europe' and study liturgy not just from the top down, i.e., in its official or semi-official texts, but also from the bottom up, 'as something real people did'.[3]

And Ramsay MacMullen has argued in his 2009 study, *The Second Church*, based largely on archaeological evidence, that of the Christian populations in ancient urban centres, perhaps 5 per cent of that population (the elite) participated regularly in the Church's official worship, while the other 95 per cent constituted the 'second church', whose Christian identity and practice was shaped by and focused on the cult of the martyrs in cemeteries and tombs.[4] So important and formative was this martyr cult in antiquity, according to Candida Moss, that, based on various written Acts of the martyrs,[5] which present the martyr(s) as

2 Peter Brown, *The Cult of the Saints: Its Rise and Function in Latin Christianity* (Chicago: University of Chicago Press 1981), pp. 12ff. See also Dennis Trout, 'Saints, Identity, and the City', and Kimberly Bowes, 'Personal Devotions and Private Chapels', in Virginia Burrus (ed.), *Late Ancient Christianity* (Minneapolis: Fortress Press 2005), pp. 165–87, 188–210.
3 Robert F. Taft, 'The Order and Place of Lay Communion in the Late-Antique and Byzantine East' in M. E. Johnson and L. E. Phillips (eds), *Studia Liturgica Diversa: Essays in Honor of Paul F. Bradshaw* (Portland: The Pastoral Press 2004), pp. 129–49, here at p. 130.
4 Ramsay MacMullen, *The Second Church: Popular Christianity A.D. 200–400* (Atlanta: Society of Biblical Literature 2009).
5 The standard collection of these Acts in Greek and Latin with English translation remains Herbert Musurillo, *The Acts of the Christian Martyrs* (Oxford: Clarendon Press 1972).

another Christ in his Passion, the Acts themselves functioned, along with canonical sources, in the development of popular Christology, even to the point at times with the martyrs threatening to replace Christ, an issue with which certainly Augustine will deal in North Africa. Moss argues further that, in the first three centuries at least, Christian discipleship, especially as a literal 'imitation of Christ', was conceived of primarily as martyrdom.[6] Robin Darling Young, too, offers an excellent overview of the early role of the cult of the martyrs:

> Of all early Christian practices, the veneration of the martyr-saints was the most popular and accessible. With a unanimity that eluded them in other matters of belief, Christians repeatedly gave three reasons for honouring these men and women as the most admirable and intensely exemplary of believers. First, the imitation of Christ enjoined on all believers appeared most visibly in their triumphant deaths. Second, in reward for their faithfulness, the martyrs now in heaven possessed special powers. And third, when Christians praised and supplicated them, the martyrs would return the favor of visible assistance. This complex rationale appears either implicitly or explicitly in numerous forms of literature attesting to early Christian martyrdom.[7]

Given the importance that the cult of the saints was to have in the development of Christianity in both East and West, it is disappointing to find minimal written documentary evidence from within the time frame of the first three centuries. What evidence we do have, however, underscores that the cult of the martyrs was local and associated directly with the martyrs' burial places. What most scholars refer to as our earliest evidence is the account of the martyrdom of Polycarp of Smyrna, traditionally dated to 23 February 155/6, with the account itself, actually a letter from the church at Smyrna, traditionally dated to the year following the event. The relevant portion of this account reads:

> Accordingly, we afterwards took up his bones, as being more precious than the most exquisite jewels, and more purified than gold, and deposited them in a fitting place, whither, being gathered together, as

---

6 Candida Moss, *The Other Christs: Imitating Jesus in Ancient Christian Ideologies of Martyrdom* (New York/London: Oxford University Press 2010), *passim*.
7 Robin Darling Young, 'Martyrdom as Exaltation' in Burrus, *Late Ancient Christianity*, pp. 70–92, here at pp. 74–5.

opportunity is allowed us, with joy and rejoicing, the Lord shall grant us to celebrate the anniversary of his martyrdom, both in memory of those who have already finished their course, and for the exercising and preparation of those yet to walk in their steps.[8]

While this account may still reflect a mid-second-century date, Moss has challenged this assumption, arguing that its 'sophisticated and nuanced view on martyrdom', as well as the fact that it appears to have had no literary impact before the second half of the third century, makes it difficult to date before the third century.[9] But whether mid second century or third, this account still provides us with a picture of what such martyr anniversary celebrations contained before the time of Constantine, namely, a local gathering of the Christian community at the martyr's tomb on the anniversary of his or her death, the date now viewed as the martyr's *natale*, or heavenly birthday, with the reading of the martyr's Acts (account of martyrdom), and, consistent with their pagan neighbours, the sharing of a meal, the *refrigerium* (refreshment), which in a Christian context would come to include the Eucharist. At the same time, MacMullen has shown, based again on archaeological evidence of tombs, including that of St Peter in Rome and St Paul in Ostia, such *refrigeria* seem also to have included the pouring of a libation of wine into prepared holes with tubes in the actual tomb of the deceased as a way of communing with them as part of the celebration.[10] Such funerary practices seem to be behind the 22 February Roman feast called the *Cathedra Petri*, the Chair of Peter. In pre-Christian Rome 13–22 February was a time for commemorating deceased friends and family members and at these gatherings an empty *cathedra* would be placed for particular departed ones. By the middle of the fourth century, at least, 22 February became the *natale* of St Peter and, in time, the *cathedra* associated with the feast was to become reinterpreted as the very *cathedra* on which Peter sat as Bishop of Rome.[11]

Clear evidence that within the third century, at least, Christian communities were keeping local lists of martyrs and celebrating the Eucharist at their tombs on their anniversary days is provided by Cyprian of Carthage in two of his letters. In one he notes:

---

8 *The Martyrdom of Polycarp* 18; ET from *ANF* 1, p. 43.
9 Moss, *The Other Christs*, pp. 196–7.
10 MacMullen, *The Second Church*, pp. 77ff.
11 Adam, *The Liturgical Year*, p. 241.

His [Celerinus'] grandmother, Celerina, was some time since crowned with martyrdom. Moreover, his paternal and maternal uncles, Laurentius and Egnatius, who themselves also were once warring in the camps of the world, but were true and spiritual soldiers of God, casting down the devil by the confession of Christ, merited palms and crowns from the Lord by their illustrious passion. *We always offer sacrifices for them, as you remember, as often as we celebrate the passions and days of the martyrs in the annual commemoration.*[12]

In the other, while exhorting the clergy to attend to the needs of confessors in prisons, he adds:

Finally, also, *take note of their days on which they depart, that we may celebrate their commemoration among the memorials of the martyrs,* although Tertullus, our most faithful and devoted brother, who, in addition to the other solicitude and care which he shows to the brethren in all service of labour, is not wanting besides in that respect in any care of their bodies, has written, and does write and intimate to me the days, in which our blessed brethren in prison pass by the gate of a glorious death to their immortality; and *there are celebrated here by us oblations and sacrifices for their commemorations,* which things, with the Lord's protection, we shall soon celebrate with you.[13]

This local connection between the martyrs, their places of burial and the Christian community's annual celebration of their *natale* is reflected at fourth-century Rome in the *depositio martyrum* within the Chronograph of 354, a document so important, as we have seen, in relationship to the origins of Christmas.[14] Not only does this *depositio martyrum* list the dates of the anniversaries (see Table 19.1 overleaf) but it provides the location for those anniversary celebrations in the various cemeteries within Rome.

Theologically as well, it is important to attend to the eucharistic imagery and connotations of martyrdom not only with regard to the celebration of the Eucharist on the martyrs' *natale* but within the descriptions and interpretations of the act of martyrdom itself. In the martyrdom of Polycarp, for example, the text shows us Polycarp offering

---

12 Cyprian, *Ep.* 33.3; ET from *ANF* 5, p. 312 (emphasis added).
13 Cyprian, *Ep.* 36.2; ET from *ANF* 5, p. 315 (emphasis added).
14 See above, p. 123.

Table 19.1: *Depositio Martyrum*

25 December	Christ born in Bethlehem of Judaea
20 January	Fabian (in Callixtus)
	Sebastian (in cemetery called Catacumbas)
21 January	Agnes (on the Via Nomentana)
22 February	Chair of Peter
7 March	Perpetua and Felicity (Africans)
19 May	Parthenius and Calocerus (in San Callixtus), in the Ninth Year of Diocletian and the Eighth Year of Maximianus [304]
29 June	Peter (Catacumbas) and Paul (Ostia), moved during the consulate of Tuscus and Bassus [258]
10 July	Felician and Filippa (in Priscilla), Vitalis and Alexander (in Iordanorum Martialis), Silanus and Novatus (in Maximus), and Januarius (Prætextatus)
30 July	Abdon and Sennen (Cemetery of Pontianus)
6 August	Sixtus (in Callixtus), Felicissimus, and Agapitus (in Prætextatus)
8 August	Secundus, Carpophorus, Victor, and Severus (in Albano); Cyriacus, Largus, Crescentianus, Memmia, Juliana, and Smaragdus (in Ostia at the seventh milestone)
9 August	Laurence (on the Via Tiburtina)
13 August	Hippolytus (on the Via Tiburtina) and Pontian (in Callixtus)
22 August	Timothy (Ostia)
29 August	Hermes (in Basilla on the Old Via Salaria)
5 September	Acontus (on the Via Portunensis), Nonnus, and Herculanus and Taurinus
9 September	Gorgonius (on the Via Labicana)
11 September	Protus and Jacintus (in Basilla)
14 September	Cyprian (African) (celebrated in Rome at Callixtus)
22 September	Basilla (on the Old Via Salaria), in the Ninth Year of Diocletian and the Eighth Year of Maximianus [304]
14 October	Callixtus (on the Via Aurelia at the third milestone)
9 November	Clement, Sempronianus, Claudius, and Nicostratus, companions
29 November	Saturninus (in Trasonis)[15]

---

15 Latin text in Theodore Mommsen, 'Chronographus anni CCCLIIII' in *Monumenta Germaniae Historica, Auctorum Antiquissimorum* 9/1 (Berlin 1892 = Munich 1982), pp. 71–2.

a eucharistic-type prayer in which, clearly more consistent with a mid-third-century date in both theology and prayer structure than the second, he offers *himself* in sacrifice rather than the bread and cup as the eucharistic oblation:

> They did not nail him [Polycarp] then, but simply bound him. And he, placing his hands behind him, and being bound like a distinguished ram [taken] out of a great flock for sacrifice, and prepared to be an acceptable burnt-offering unto God, looked up to heaven, and said, 'O Lord God Almighty, the Father of thy beloved and blessed Son Jesus Christ, by whom we have received the knowledge of thee, the God of angels and powers, and of every creature, and of the whole race of the righteous who live before thee, I give thee thanks that thou hast counted me, worthy of this day and this hour, that I should have a part in the number of thy martyrs, in the cup of thy Christ, to the resurrection of eternal life, both of soul and body, through the incorruption [imparted] by the Holy Ghost. Among whom may I be accepted this day before thee as a fat and acceptable sacrifice, according as thou, the ever-truthful God, hast foreordained, hast revealed beforehand to me, and now hast fulfilled. Wherefore also I praise thee for all things, I bless thee, I glorify thee, along with the everlasting and heavenly Jesus Christ, thy beloved Son, with whom, to thee, and the Holy Ghost, be glory both now and to all coming ages. Amen.'

Following this prayer the eucharistic symbolism of 'bread baking' is unmistakable in describing Polycarp's execution:

> When he had pronounced this *amen*, and so finished his prayer, those who were appointed for the purpose kindled the fire. And as the flame blazed forth in great fury, we, to whom it was given to witness it, beheld a great miracle, and have been preserved that we might report to others what then took place. For the fire, shaping itself into the form of an arch, like the sail of a ship when filled with the wind, encompassed as by a circle the body of the martyr. And he appeared within not like flesh which is burnt, but as bread that is baked, or as gold and silver glowing in a furnace. Moreover, we perceived such a sweet odour [coming from the pile], as if frankincense or some such precious spices had been smoking there.[16]

---

16 *Martyrdom of Polycarp* 14–15; ET from *ANF* 1, p. 42.

Similar eucharistic symbolism is already present in the late-first- or early-second-century letters of Ignatius of Antioch, especially in his letter to the Romans, as he tries to convince the Roman Christians not to interfere in his forthcoming martyrdom:

> For if ye are silent concerning me, I shall become God's; but if you show your love to my flesh, I shall again have to run my race. Pray, then, do not seek to confer any greater favour upon me than that I be sacrificed to God while the altar is still prepared; that, being gathered together in love, ye may sing praise to the Father, through Christ Jesus, that God has deemed me, the bishop of Syria, worthy to be sent for from the east unto the west. It is good to set from the world unto God, that I may rise again to him.[17]

> Suffer me to become food for the wild beasts, through whose instrumentality it will be granted me to attain to God. I am the wheat of God, and let me be ground by the teeth of the wild beasts, that I may be found the pure bread of Christ. Rather entice the wild beasts, that they may become my tomb, and may leave nothing of my body; so that when I have fallen asleep [in death], I may be no trouble to any one. Then shall I truly be a disciple of Christ, when the world shall not see so much as my body. Entreat Christ for me, that by these instruments I may be found a sacrifice.[18]

> I have no delight in corruptible food, nor in the pleasures of this life. I desire the bread of God, the heavenly bread, the bread of life, which is the flesh of Jesus Christ, the Son of God, who became afterwards of the seed of David and Abraham; and I desire the drink of God, namely his blood, which is incorruptible love and eternal life.[19]

Such language of Eucharist, sacrifice and libation (e.g., Ignatius' request that he be 'poured out to God') on the part of the martyrs leads Robin Darling Young to view martyrdom, in the words of Origen's *Exhortation to Martyrdom*, as a going 'in procession before the world', a public ritual and liturgy in antiquity. Martyrdom, she writes,

---

17 Ignatius, *Romans* 2.2; ET from *ANF* 1, p. 74.
18 Ignatius, *Romans* 4.1–2 (*ANF* 1, p. 75).
19 Ignatius, *Romans* 7.3 (*ANF* 1, p. 77).

functioned as a public liturgical sacrifice in which the word of Jesus and his kingdom was confessed and acted out, and an offering made that repeated his own. If the Eucharist of the early Christians was a kind of substitute sacrifice, then the martyrs' was an imitative one. When the Eucharist was still private, not open to non-Christian view, the martyrs' sacrifice was public and dramatic . . . Martyrdom was also a ritual, in all likelihood imagined ahead of time and understood as both a repetition of baptism or a substitute for it, and a sacrifice parallel and similar to Christ's passion and the Eucharist, that is to say, as a redemptive sacrifice. It was the instantiation of the Temple's new presence among Christians, who saw themselves as true Israel and spiritual temples. Inasmuch as it generated a priesthood and spiritual gifts, it occasioned the desire of Christians to conduct and regulate its benefits; this was the commerce that authority and orthodoxy, especially episcopal orthodoxy, could bring about. Not only the point of encounter between the church and the world, and furthermore between heaven and earth, martyrdom was also the locus of an economic exchange between these last two; an offering went up, and upon acceptance, benefits came down. To put it crudely, martyrdom was a bargain for Christian communities. One member of the community died faithfully and many investors were rewarded.[20]

So strong is this connection between the martyr and the Eucharist that the bodies – or other remains (relics) – of the martyrs would become viewed and venerated as 'eucharistized', consecrated or holy (bones 'more valuable than gold'), with which and with whom some form of communion at their tombs would be sought.[21]

The martyrs were not only commemorated at their tombs on their anniversaries, but as those who had already been exalted to heaven with Christ they were appealed to increasingly by prayer and supplication. In an article some years ago, Cyrille Vogel noted that up until the middle of the second century ancient burial inscriptions reveal that Christians

20 Robin Darling Young, *In Procession before the World: Martyrdom as Public Liturgy in Early Christianity*, The Père Marquette Lecture in Theology, 2001 (Milwaukee: Marquette University Press 2001), pp. 11–12. For a similar approach, but focused on the letters of Ignatius of Antioch, see Frederick C. Klawiter, 'The Eucharist and Sacramental Realism in the thought of St. Ignatius of Antioch', *SL* 37 (2007), pp. 129–63.
21 See Albertus G. A. Horsting, 'Transfiguration of Flesh: Literary and Theological Connections between Martyrdom Accounts and Eucharistic Prayers' in Maxwell E. Johnson (ed.), *Issues in Eucharistic Praying* (Collegeville: The Liturgical Press, forthcoming).

prayed both *for* and *to* deceased Christians, whether they were martyrs or not, a point underscored by Taft in a more recent essay as well.[22] Such prayer *for* deceased baptized Christians as part of the *communio sanctorum*, of course, is highly consistent with some of the classic eucharistic prayers of antiquity. In the Anaphora of St John Chrysostom, for example, prayer is made even *for* (ὑπέρ) the *Theotokos* and the saints,[23] and in the Armenian version of the Anaphora of St Basil the *Theotokos* and the saints are simply *commemorated* at the Eucharist.[24] Also of note is that the Roman *canon missae* is rather striking in this regard since in its *Communicantes* the assembly merely prays in 'communion' with and 'venerating the memory' (*et memoriam venerantes*) of Mary, the twelve apostles and sainted martyrs and bishops, and the *Nobis quoque peccatoribus* merely asks for our admission into the company of the apostles and martyrs, with a list of Roman and North African martyrs provided.[25]

By the end of the second century, however, prayer to deceased Christians, or, at least, asking the martyrs in particular for their intercession, even with regard to exercising the office of the keys, was becoming a rather common Christian practice. So, for example, the famous late-second- or early-third-century North African *Passion of St Perpetua and Felicitas* describes a vision of the martyr Saturus, who sees Perpetua and himself after their martyrdoms being appealed to by his bishop Optatus and a presbyter Aspasius. This vision is well summarized by Frederick Klawiter:

> In a vision Saturus saw himself and the other martyrs transported to paradise after death. They were carried by angels to a place whose walls were made of light. Upon entering they heard voices chanting endlessly in unison, making but one sound: 'Holy, holy, holy.' As the martyrs stood before a throne, angels lifted them up to kiss an aged

22 Cyrille Vogel, 'Prière ou intercession? Une ambiguïté dans le culte paléochrétien des martyrs', in *Communio Sanctorum: Mélanges offerts à J.J. von Allmen* (Geneva: Labor et Fides 1982), pp. 284–9; Robert Taft, 'Prayer to or for the Saints? A Note on the Sanctoral Intercessions/Commemorations in the Anaphora' in *Ab Oriente et Occidente (Mt 8, 11): Kirche aus Ost und West: Gedankschrift für Wilhelm Nyssen* (St Ottilien: Eos Verlag 1996), pp. 439–55. See also Michael Kunzler, 'Insbesondere für unsere allheilige Herrin . . .' in A. Heinz and H. Rennings (eds), *Gratias Agamus: Studien zum eucharistischen Hochgebet* (Freiburg/Basel/Vienna: Herder 1992), pp. 227–40.
23 For text, see R. C. D. Jasper and G. J. Cuming (eds), *Prayers of the Eucharist: Early and Reformed* (3rd edn, New York: Pueblo 1987), pp. 133–4.
24 See Gabriele Winkler, *Die Basilius-Anaphora*, Anaphorae Orientales 2: Anaphoricae Armeniacae 2 (Rome: Pontifical Oriental Institute 2005), pp. 250–1.
25 For text, see Jasper and Cuming, *Prayers of the Eucharist*, pp. 164–6.

man of youthful countenance, who touched their faces with his hand. Then they were commanded to go and play. They went out before the gates and saw their bishop Optatus and the presbyter Aspasius approaching them. Optatus and Aspasius were apart from one another and very sad. Throwing themselves at the feet of Perpetua and Saturus, they said: 'Make peace between us, for you departed and left us thus.' Perpetua and Saturus embraced them and began to talk to them; however, they were interrupted by angels who scolded the bishop and presbyter, instructing them to settle their own quarrels and advising the bishop about shepherding his flock. The angels thought that Perpetua and Saturus should be allowed to rest (*refrigerare*), and, in addition, it was time to close the gates (*claudere portas*).[26]

While this vision may be interpreted as offering a statement against the invocation of martyrs that they might exercise the office of the keys after death, Klawiter is certainly correct in noting that the text says that 'Saturus and Perpetua "were very moved and embraced" (*moti et conplexi sunt*) the bishop and presbyter. Evidently, they were not displeased that the two had come to them for a resolution.'[27] He adds: 'The reasonable view is that Perpetua and Saturus had departed by death before Aspasius and Optatus were able to approach them in order to receive peace. Thus, this situation compelled the bishop and presbyter to approach them *through prayer* after Perpetua and Saturus had died.'[28] Similarly, in his *De oratione* Origen himself not only witnesses to but actually advocates prayer to the saints, saying:

> [I]t is not foolish to offer supplication, intercession, and thanksgiving also to the saints. Moreover, two of them, I mean intercession and thanksgiving, may be addressed not only to the saints but also to other people, while supplication may be addressed only to the saints if someone is found to be a Paul or a Peter so as to help us by making us worthy of receiving the authority given them to forgive sins.[29]

---

26 Frederick C. Klawiter, 'The Role of Martyrdom and Persecution in Developing the Priestly Authority of Women in Early Christianity: A Case Study of Montanism', *Church History* 49 (1980), pp. 258–9. The text in question is *Passio SS. Perpetuae et Felicitatis* 12–13.

27 Klawiter, 'The Role of Martyrdom and Persecution', p. 259.

28 Klawiter, 'The Role of Martyrdom and Persecution', p. 259, n. 29 (emphasis added).

29 Origen, *De oratione* 14.6; ET from *The Classics of Western Spirituality* (New York: Paulist Press 1979), pp. 111–12.

Similarly, the fragmentary prayer called the Strasbourg Papyrus, quite possibly a eucharistic prayer, sometimes dated as early as second-century Egypt, already contains the following invocation: '. . . grant us to have a part and lot with the fair . . . of your holy prophets, apostles, and martyrs. Receive(?) [through] their entreaties [these prayers].'[30]

Whatever the extent of such invocation and supplication to the martyrs in the first three centuries, there is no question but that from after the Peace of Constantine (312) onwards, such devotion will be a major characteristic of Christian piety. On the one hand, anniversary celebrations at the martyrs' tombs became more elaborate and buildings known as *martyria* began to be erected over the tombs to house the bodies of the saints inside. But it would be a mistake to think that what went on in these places was simply or only some kind of official public liturgical worship. Dennis Trout provides a tantalizing description of what took place in the late-fourth-century shrine of St Felix of Nola, Italy (14 January), based on the poems of its famous bishop Paulinus:

> Paulinus' writings suggest, even if indirectly, many of the aims and expectations of the visitors, petitioners, and fairgoers who came to venerate Felix at his Nolan tomb and, in some cases, to see Paulinus as well. Aristocratic friends and travellers, such as the family of Melania the Elder of Nicetas, bishop of distant Remesiana, might stop for a time at Nola, and Paulinus' public verses often praised their faith and ascetic virtues. Yet the anonymous characters who populate Paulinus' *natalicia* better represent the Shrine's role in regional society, just as they also foreshadow later accounts of the activity that swirled around the grave of a renowned saint. For such humbler folk, the holy tomb appears as a place of comfort and protection where holy power becomes manifest in awe-inspiring ways. Here the sick and insane are healed or cleansed of their demons. They return home with holy oil charged with curative power through contact with Felix's coffin. They appeal to Felix for the protection of their fields and herds and well-being of their families. At the fair associated with Felix's midwinter festival, peasants present the saint with gifts of pigs and cattle. Echoing old patterns of behavior, they fulfil vows by butchering their livestock and, at Paulinus' urging, sharing the meat with the poor who have gathered at the shrine. Such practices Paulinus encouraged, while simultaneously working to reform those

---

30 ET from Jasper and Cuming, *Prayers of the Eucharist*, p. 54.

'rustics' who came to Nola looking simply to fill their bellies with food and late-night wine.[31]

On the other hand, if *martyria* were being erected in cemeteries over the tombs of the martyrs, it is also the case that the bodies of martyrs were increasingly being removed from cemeteries into church buildings elsewhere, a process known either as *translatio*, the re-burial or re-housing of remains, or even of *dismemberatio*, that is, dividing up the remains into various fragments and distributing them to multiple churches and individuals at the same time.[32] So begins the great spread of the cult of the saints beyond their local celebrations as churches – and individuals – will increasingly trade such 'relics' back and forth, including the feast days themselves, thus contributing to a universalizing of various martyrs. It may well have been the case that *translatio* and *dismemberatio* were more common practices in the Christian East since Roman law, at least until the seventh century, forbade the opening or re-siting of a grave, in order to protect the peace of the dead. Thus, for example, in 365–6 at Constantinople the Emperor Constantius ordered the relics of Timothy, the apostle Andrew, and the evangelist Luke to be brought to Constantinople, an event accomplished with great solemnity. In the West generally, secondary relics, or 'contact relics', were more common and included items such as linen cloths (*brandea* or *palliola*), which had been touched to the saints' body or grave, as well as clothing, oil, instruments of the martyrs' torture, or even scrapings from the tomb or the locale around it. According to G. J. C. Snoek, 'these types of relics – and occasionally corporeal relics – were, like the Eucharistic bread, kept at home to provide protection, were worn around the neck as a substitute for the pagan amulet and taken into the grave in the hopes of resurrection with the martyr in question'.[33] Here, as well, might be noted the practice of burial *ad sanctos*,[34] that is, burial near the graves of the martyrs and later in

---

31 Trout, 'Saints, Identity, and the City', p. 169.
32 This section is dependent upon G. J. C. Snoek, *Medieval Piety from Relics to the Eucharist* (Leiden: Brill 1995), pp. 9–16. See also John Crook, *The Architectural Setting of the Cult of the Saints in the Early Christian West* (New York/London: Oxford University Press 2000); Victor Saxer, *Morts, martyrs, reliques en Afrique chrétienne aux premiers siècles*, Théologie Historique 55 (Paris: Beauchesne 1980).
33 Snoek, *Medieval Piety from Relics to the Eucharist*, p. 9.
34 See MacMullen, *The Second Church*, pp 28, 42–4; Crook, *The Architectural Setting of the Cult of the Saints in the Early Christian West*, pp. 14ff.

churches near to their tombs and/or relics, as well as the practice called 'incubation', that is, sleeping in martyrs' tombs or sanctuaries in supplication for particular needs.[35]

It should not be assumed uncritically, however, that Christians in the West, unlike their Eastern counterparts in the first seven centuries, did not from time to time also practise *translatio* and *dismemberatio* of the martyrs. If *dismemberatio* was widely discouraged, the welcome acceptance of such dismembered saints' relics from the East into the West was, nonetheless, certainly known. And there is plenty of evidence in the West for the *translatio* of saints' remains, though it is true that it only becomes common at Rome itself from the early seventh century onwards, where on 13 May 609, for the dedication of the Pantheon as a Christian church, renamed as *Santa Maria ad martyres*, Pope Boniface IV had 28 wagonloads of the bones of the martyrs brought to this basilica from the various cemeteries,[36] with 13 May becoming, as a result, one of the earliest dates for the Western celebration of what eventually will become the feast of All Saints.[37]

One of our earliest witnesses in the West to the practice of *translatio* is Ambrose of Milan and the *translatio* of the popular saints Gervasius and Protasius into Ambrose's cathedral of Milan. While Ambrose had been critical of Monica's North African cemetery rituals in Milan,[38] he certainly cherished having these particular relics. Writing to his sister, Ambrose describes the discovery of their intact bodies, their translation to his basilica, and what he said to the church at Milan on this occasion:

> 2. Why should I use many words? God favoured us, for even the clergy were afraid who were bidden to clear away the earth from the spot before the chancel screen of SS. Felix and Nabor. I found the fitting signs, and on bringing in some on whom hands were to be laid, the power of the holy martyrs became so manifest, that even whilst I was still silent, one was seized and thrown prostrate at the holy burial-place. We found two men of marvellous stature, such as those of ancient days. All the bones were perfect, and there was much

35 See Johan Leemans, Wendy Mayer, Pauline Allen and Boudewijn Dehandschutter, *'Let Us Die That We May Live': Greek Homilies on Christian Martyrs from Asia Minor, Palestine and Syria (c. AD 350-AD 450)* (New York: Routledge 2003).

36 Adam, *The Liturgical Year*, p. 229.

37 See Thomas Talley, 'The Feasts of All Saints' in Thomas Talley, *Worship: Reforming Tradition* (Washington, DC: The Pastoral Press 1990), pp. 113–23.

38 Augustine, *Confessions* 6.2.

blood. During the whole of those two days there was an enormous concourse of people. Briefly we arranged the whole in order, and as evening was now coming on transferred them to the basilica of Fausta, where watch was kept during the night, and some received the laying on of hands. On the following day we translated the relics to the basilica called Ambrosian. During the translation a blind man was healed . . .

9. . . . Not without reason do many call this the resurrection of the martyrs. I do not say whether they have risen for themselves, for us certainly the martyrs have risen. You know – nay, you have yourselves seen – that many are cleansed from evil spirits, that very many also, having touched with their hands the robe of the saints, are freed from those ailments which oppressed them; you see that the miracles of old time are renewed, when through the coming of the Lord Jesus grace was more largely shed forth upon the earth, and that many bodies are healed as it were by the shadow of the holy bodies. How many napkins are passed about! how many garments, laid upon the holy relics and endowed with healing power, are claimed! All are glad to touch even the outside thread, and whosoever touches will be made whole . . .

12. The glorious relics are taken out of an ignoble burying-place, the trophies are displayed under heaven. The tomb is wet with blood. The marks of the bloody triumph are present, the relics are found undisturbed in their order, the head separated from the body . . .

13. Let these triumphant victims be brought to the place where Christ is the victim. But He upon the altar, Who suffered for all; they beneath the altar, who were redeemed by His Passion. I had destined this place for myself, for it is fitting that the priest should rest there where he has been wont to offer, but I yield the right hand portion to the sacred victims; that place was due to the martyrs. Let us, then, deposit the sacred relics, and lay them up in a worthy resting-place, and let us celebrate the whole day with faithful devotion.[39]

Augustine of Hippo himself, who was, incidentally, in attendance at the above event narrated by Ambrose,[40] was generally critical of the popular celebrations accompanying the martyr cult in North Africa, criticizing not only the raucous behaviour of people at such events, including

---

39 Ambrose of Milan, *Ep.* 22; ET from *NPNF* 2nd Series 10, pp. 437–8.
40 See Augustine, *City of God* 8.

drinking and dancing, but beyond this, his fear of superstition as well as perceived competition and popular confusion on the part of the faithful between the martyrs and Christ.[41] After 415, at which point Hippo acquired some prestigious relics of St Stephen the Protomartyr, Augustine developed a different view and became, like Ambrose, a staunch defender of the martyrs and the miracles associated with their cult and relics. In his *City of God*, Augustine writes of several miracles at the shrines of martyrs in North Africa. What follows are his comments related to healings in proximity to the relics of St Stephen:

> It is not yet two years since these relics were first brought to Hippo-regius, and though many of the miracles which have been wrought by it have not, as I have the most certain means of knowing, been recorded, those which have been published amount to almost seventy at the hour at which I write . . .
>
> One miracle was wrought among ourselves, which, though no greater than those I have mentioned, was yet so signal and conspicuous, that I suppose there is no inhabitant of Hippo who did not either see or hear of it, none who could possibly forget it. There were seven brothers and three sisters of a noble family of the Cappadocian Cæsarea, who were cursed by their mother, a new-made widow, on account of some wrong they had done her, and which she bitterly resented, and who were visited with so severe a punishment from Heaven, that all of them were seized with a hideous shaking in all their limbs. Unable, while presenting this loathsome appearance, to endure the eyes of their fellow-citizens, they wandered over almost the whole Roman world, each following his own direction. Two of them came to Hippo, a brother and a sister, Paulus and Palladia, already known in many other places by the fame of their wretched lot. Now it was about fifteen days before Easter when they came, and they came daily to church, and specially to the relics of the most glorious Stephen, praying that God might now be appeased, and restore their former health. There, and wherever they went, they attracted the attention of every one. Some who had seen them elsewhere, and knew the cause of their trembling, told others as occasion offered. Easter arrived, and on the Lord's day, in the morning, when there was now a large crowd present, and the young

---

41 On this, see Moss, *The Other Christs*, pp. 166–9; MacMullen, *The Second Church*, pp. 58–9, 108–9.

man was holding the bars of the holy place where the relics were, and praying, suddenly he fell down, and lay precisely as if asleep, but not trembling as he was wont to do even in sleep. All present were astonished. Some were alarmed, some were moved with pity; and while some were for lifting him up, others prevented them, and said they should rather wait and see what would result. And behold! he rose up, and trembled no more, for he was healed, and stood quite well, scanning those who were scanning him. Who then refrained himself from praising God? The whole church was filled with the voices of those who were shouting and congratulating him. Then they came running to me, where I was sitting ready to come into the church. One after another they throng in, the last comer telling me as news what the first had told me already; and while I rejoiced and inwardly gave God thanks, the young man himself also enters, with a number of others, falls at my knees, is raised up to receive my kiss. We go in to the congregation: the church was full, and ringing with the shouts of joy, 'Thanks to God! Praised be God!' every one joining and shouting on all sides, 'I have healed the people,' and then with still louder voice shouting again. Silence being at last obtained, the customary lessons of the divine Scriptures were read. And when I came to my sermon, I made a few remarks suitable to the occasion and the happy and joyful feeling, not desiring them to listen to me, but rather to consider the eloquence of God in this divine work. The man dined with us, and gave us a careful account of his own, his mother's, and his family's calamity. Accordingly, on the following day, after delivering my sermon, I promised that next day I would read his narrative to the people. And when I did so, the third day after Easter Sunday, I made the brother and sister both stand on the steps of the raised place from which I used to speak; and while they stood there their pamphlet was read. The whole congregation, men and women alike, saw the one standing without any unnatural movement, the other trembling in all her limbs; so that those who had not before seen the man himself saw in his sister what the divine compassion had removed from him. In him they saw matter of congratulation, in her subject for prayer. Meanwhile, their pamphlet being finished, I instructed them to withdraw from the gaze of the people; and I had begun to discuss the whole matter somewhat more carefully, when lo! as I was proceeding, other voices are heard from the tomb of the martyr, shouting new congratulations. My audience turned round, and began to run to the tomb. The young woman, when she had come down from the steps where she had been standing, went to pray at the holy relics, and no sooner had she touched the bars than she, in the same way as her brother, collapsed, as if falling asleep, and rose up cured. While, then, we were asking what had happened, and what occasioned this noise of joy, they came into the basilica where we were, leading her from the martyr's tomb in perfect health. Then, indeed, such a shout of wonder rose from men and women together, that the exclamations and the tears seemed like never to come to an end. She was led to the place where she had a little before stood trembling. They now rejoiced that she was like her brother, as before they had mourned that she remained unlike him; and as they had not yet uttered their prayers in her behalf, they perceived that their intention of doing so had been speedily heard. They shouted God's praises without words, but with such a noise that our ears could scarcely bear it. What was there in the hearts of these exultant people but the faith of Christ, for which Stephen had shed his blood?[42]

As Peter Brown has noted with regard to the discovery and *translatio* of martyrs' relics in the ancient Christian world:

> The discovery of a relic . . . was far more than an act of pious archae-ology, and its transfer far more than a strange new form of Christian connoisseurship: both actions made plain, at a particular time and place, the immensity of God's mercy. They announced moments of amnesty. They brought a sense of deliverance and pardon into the present . . . A sense of the mercy of God lies at the root of the discovery, translation, and installation of relics. In such a mood, the relic itself may not have been as important as the invisible gesture of God's forgiveness that had made it available in the first place; and so its power in the community was very much the condensation of the determination of that community to believe that it had been judged by God to have deserved the *praesentia* of the saint.[43]

Together with the saint's *praesentia* via his or her relics comes the healing availability of the saint's *potentia* at that very place and in that very basilica or shrine.[44]

---

42 Augustine, *City of God* 22.8; ET from *NPNF* 1st Series 2, pp. 489–91.
43 Brown, *The Cult of the Saints*, p. 92.
44 See Brown, *The Cult of the Saints*, chs 5 and 6.

It is during the fourth century that other categories of 'saint' will become added to the Church's annual anniversary celebrations, and so begins what Lawrence Cunningham refers to as the 'age of the ascetics and monks'.[45] But even before them came the category of 'confessors', that is, those who had confessed the faith and been imprisoned and tortured and so given their 'witness', but had not become martyrs in the strict sense that the word had now come to mean. Nevertheless, as the addition of names like the non-martyrs but confessors Pontian and Hippolytus (whose names appear above on 13 August in the Chronograph of 354) and others were made to local lists of commemorations, the same liturgical and popular honours accorded to the martyrs themselves will now be given to them.[46] In a sense, confessors become incorporated into the cult of saints as 'martyrs by extension'.

The same is true of the ascetics and monks. That the theology of martyrdom still controlled the development of whom to commemorate is made clear by the fact that the ascetics themselves were viewed as embracing a new form of martyrdom, the martyrdom of mortification and self-denial. Philippe Rouillard summarizes this transition:

> Since persecutions had ended, one could no longer be a martyr by shedding one's blood, but one could be a martyr by practicing asceticism. Monks succeeded martyrs in their renunciation of the world, their resolve to follow Christ, and their battle against the powers of evil. They also succeeded martyrs in popular devotion. At the time of his death, St. Antony of Egypt ordered his disciples to hide his burial place to prevent the construction of a *martyrium*. A few bishops who had spent long years in monastic life were also part of this group; they owed their renown more to their asceticism than to their episcopal function. Such was the case with St Basil of Caesarea (✝ 375) and his brother St Peter of Sebaste (✝ 391), both venerated before 395, and in the West, St Martin of Tours (✝ ca. 397), who became the object of cult immediately after his death.[47]

---

45 Lawrence Cunningham, *A Brief History of Saints* (Oxford: Blackwell 2005), p. 19.
46 See Jounel, 'The Year', p. 111.
47 Philippe Rouillard, 'The Cult of the Saints in the East and the West' in Anscar Chupungco (ed.), *Handbook for Liturgical Studies* 5 (Collegeville: The Liturgical Press 2000), p. 302.

Within early Christianity, still within the fourth century, the same honours will be accorded to the various illustrious bishops and other leaders, intimately associated either with the apostolic foundations or the continued growth of various churches or with the fame of those churches and leaders throughout the world. And like the cult of the martyrs, so also the cult of these local bishops, along with their relics, will spread. As Rouillard notes, 'about 380, Constantinople celebrated St Athanasius of Alexandria and St Cyprian of Carthage. Similarly, the anniversary of the deacon and martyr Vincent of Saragossa (304) was celebrated in the whole world.'[48]

Together with the *depositio martyrum* in the Chronograph of 354, our earliest calendars, which reflect the late fourth century, already show the development we have just noted with regard to confessors, ascetics and bishops. In fact, the Chronograph of 354 also includes a *depositio episcoporum* with death date, anniversary date, and burial location (see Table 19.2).

Given this parallel construction with the *depositio martyrum*, even though these bishops are non-martyrs, Pierre Jounel is certainly correct here in suggesting 'the difference between these two types of anniversaries must have been rather vague in practice'.[49]

Table 19.2: *Depositio episcoporum*

26 December	Dionysius (in Callixtus)	(d. 268)
30 December	Felix (in Callixtus)	(d. 274)
31 December	Sylvester (in Priscilla)	(d. 335)
10 January	Miltiades (in Callixtus)	(d. 314)
15 January	Marcellinus (in Priscilla)	(d. 304)
4 March	Lucius (in Callixtus)	(d. 254)
22 April	Gaius (in Callixtus)	(d. 296)
2 August	Stephen (in Callixtus)	(d. 257)
21 October	Eusebius (in Callixtus)	(d. 310/311)
7 December	Eutychian (in Callixtus)	(d. 283)
7 October	Mark (in Balbina)	(d. 336)
12 April	Julius (on Via Aurelia, at the third milestone, in Callixtus)	(d. 352)[50]

48 Rouillard, 'The Cult of the Saints in the East and the West', p. 303.
49 Jounel, 'The Year', p. 113.
50 Latin text in Mommsen, 'Chronographus anni CCCLIIII', p. 70.

Two other lists from roughly this time period need brief consideration. First, the fifth-century Armenian Lectionary, which we have encountered before in this study, provides us with an overview of a rudimentary sanctoral cycle for fourth-century Jerusalem (see Table 19.3), though

Table 19.3: *Armenian Lectionary sanctoral cycle*

Date	Feast	Station	Type
6–13 January	Epiphany	(various)	commemoration
11 January	Peter and Abisolom		commemoration
17 January	Antony	Anastasis	commemoration
19 January	Theodosius	Anastasis	
14 February	40th after Nativity	Martyrium	commemoration
9 March	40 Martyrs	St Stephen	commemoration
18 March	Cyril of Jerusalem		commemoration
29 March	John II of Jerusalem		commemoration
	Lent–Easter Week	(various)	
1 May	Prophet Jeremiah	Anatoth	commemoration
7 May	Apparition of the Cross	Golgotha	
9–18 May	Holy Innocents	Bethlehem	
22 May	Constantine	Martyrium	commemoration
10 June	Prophet Zachariah		*depositio*
14 June	Prophet Elisha		
2 July	Ark of Covenant	Kiriathiaram	
6 July	Prophet Isaiah		*depositio*
1 August	Maccabees		
15 August	Mary *Theotokos*	3rd mile from Bethlehem	
23/24 August	Apostle Thomas	Bethphage	
29 August	John the Baptist		
13/14 September	Encaenia	Anastasis	
14 September	Cross		
15 November	Apostle Philip		
30 November	Apostle Andrew		
25 December	James and David	Sion	
27 December	Stephen		
28 December	Peter and Paul		
29 December	Apostles James and Evangelist John[51]		

51 Adapted from Walter Ray, 'August 15 and the Jerusalem Calendar' (PhD dissertation, University of Notre Dame 2000), p. 3.

certainly after the time of both Cyril of Jerusalem's and his successor John's episcopate there, since both of these bishops are included. In addition to these bishops and the monk Antony on 17 January, of significance also is that here we see the 15 August feast of Mary *Theotokos*, a commemoration of the emperors Constantine and Theodosius I, the 14 September feast of the Cross in connection with the anniversary of the dedication of the Church of the Holy Sepulchre, the listing of Old Testament figures (which will become common in the East but not the West), and, not least, the clustering of Stephen the Protomartyr and the apostles James and John together in late December, *prior* it should be noted to the acceptance of the 25 December date for Christmas. That is, if the feast of the Holy Innocents is related conceptually and chronologically to Christmas, those of Stephen and John are not.

Second, a similar cycle of feasts is present in Cappadocia in roughly the same time period (see Table 19.4). While no calendar actually exists for Cappadocia, Jill Burnett Comings' study of the homilies of the Cappado-

Table 19.4: Cappadocian sanctoral cycle

3 January	Gordius (martyr)
1 February (or 21 September or 22 July)	Phocas
9 March	40 Martyrs of Sebaste
26 March	Peter of Sebaste
2 May	Athanasius
8 June	Theodore
3 July (?)	Orestes (martyr)
	Euphemia (or 16 September, 16 May or 11 July)
15 July	Julitta
2 September (?)	Mamas (martyr)
7 September	Eupsychius (martyr)
29 September	Holy Martyrs
2 or 4 October	Cyprian (of Antioch?)
26 December	Stephen
27 December	James and John
28 December	Peter and Paul

cian Fathers (Basil of Caesarea, Gregory of Nyssa and Gregory of Nazianzus)[52] together with other documents, most notably the Syriac Martyrology of 411[53] and the later so-called Hieronymian Martyrology,[54] reveals that at least the feasts listed were celebrated there already in the late fourth century. In many cases, however, for Cappadocia specifically, the dates for the feasts must remain tentative. Nevertheless, we see some parallels with Jerusalem above, including the same clustering of the apostles in late December, and already Athanasius of Alexandria has an anniversary on 2 May, where he is still commemorated today both in East and West.

Finally, although this goes somewhat beyond our time period, a calendar (see Table 19.5, page 194), based on the Chronograph of 354 and the so-called Hieronymian Martyrology, was reconstructed many years ago by Walter Frere[55] in an attempt to provide a picture of the *sanctorale* in the West towards the end of the patristic period.[56] While this should not be taken as exhaustive, it does still function as a helpful summary of the early development of what we have seen above, namely, a calendar of commemorations dominated by the martyrs but gradually expanding to include other 'saints' in the process, an expansion that will continue unabated at Rome until the attempts at calendar reform by Pope Gregory VII in the eleventh century.

The liturgical and popular celebration of feasts in early Christianity was, in large part, the celebration of the feasts of the saints. As we have seen, the roots of these celebrations were as ancient as the celebration of Easter in most communities and the celebration of their local heroes generally appealed much more strongly to Christian congregations than some of the newer feasts that ecclesiastical authorities later attempted to introduce. In a very real sense, therefore, saints' days rather than festivals of Christ tended to form the heart of the annual calendar for most ordinary worshippers and to excite their devotion and attendance at church and related events.

---

52 Jill Burnett Comings, *Aspects of the Liturgical Year in Cappadocia (325–430)*, Patristic Studies 7 (New York: Lang 2005).

53 Bonaventura Mariani (ed.), *Breviarium Syriacum*, Rerum Ecclesiasticarum Documenta, Series minor, Subsidia studiorum 3 (Rome: Herder 1956), pp. 27–56.

54 H. Quentin (ed.), *Les Martyrologes historiques du moyen âge* (Aalen: Scientia Verlag 1969).

55 W. H. Frere, *Studies in Early Roman Liturgy: I The Kalendar*, ACC 28 (London: SPCK 1930).

56 The list itself in this form was constructed from Frere's work by Michael Perham, *The Communion of Saints*, ACC 62 (London: SPCK 1980), pp. 18–19.

Table 19.5: Walter Frere's reconstructed Roman *sanctorale*

Date	Name	Date	Description	Place	Notes
14 Jan.	Felix	*c.* 260	no evidence of martyrdom	Nola	
16	Marcellus	*c.* 309	pope, not martyr	Rome	D
20	Fabian	250	pope and martyr	Rome	T
	Sebastian	?	martyr	Rome	T
21, 28	Agnes	*c.* 304	martyr	Rome	CT
5 Feb.	Agatha	3rd cent.	martyr	Sicily	CDT
14	Valentine	?	martyr	?	
14 April	Tiburtius, Valerian and Maximus	?	martyrs	Rome	
28	Vitalis	?	martyr	Rome	D
1 May	Philip and James	1st cent.	apostles and martyrs	(biblical)	CT
12	Nereus and Achilleus	?	martyrs	Rome	T
	Pancras	304?	martyr	Rome	T
2 June	Peter and Marcellinus	*c.* 304	martyrs	Rome	CDT
18	Mark and Marcellian	?	martyrs	Rome	
19	Gervasius and Protasius	?	martyrs	Milan	D
23, 24	John the Baptist	1st cent.	martyr	(biblical)	CT
26	John and Paul	?	martyrs	?	CD
28, 29, 30, 6 July	Peter and Paul	1st cent.	apostles and martyrs	(biblical)	CDT
10	The Seven Brothers	?	martyrs	Rome	C
21	Praxedis	?	?	?	D
30	Abdon and Sennen	?	martyrs	Rome	
2 August	Stephen	1st cent.	protomartyr	(biblical)	CDT
	Stephen	255	pope and martyr	Rome	
6	Sixtus, Felicissimus and Agapitus	258	martyrs	Rome	DT
8	Cyriacus	?	martyr	Rome	D

Date	Name	Date	Description	Place	Notes
9, 10, 17	Lawrence	258	martyr	Rome	CDT
11	Tiburtius	?	martyr	Rome	
	Susanna	?	martyr	Rome	D
13	Hippolytus	*c.* 235	martyr	Rome	C
18	Agapitus	?	martyr	Palestrina	
28	Hermes	?	martyr	Rome	
14 Sept.	Cornelius and	*c.* 258	pope and martyr	Rome	CT
	Cyprian		martyr	Carthage	
16	Euphemia, Lucy and Geminian	?	martyrs	Chalcedon	
29	Michael		Archangel		CT
7 Oct.	Mark	336	pope, not martyr	Rome	D
14	Callistus	*c.* 222	pope and martyr	Rome	T
1 Nov.	Caesarius	?	martyr	Terracina	
8	The Four Crowned Ones	306?	martyrs	Rome	D
21	Cecilia	?	martyr	Rome	CDT
23	Clement	1st cent.	pope and martyr	Rome	CT
	Felicitas	?	martyr	Rome	C[57]
24	Chrysogonus	304?	martyr	Aquileia	CD
29	Saturninus	?	martyr	Rome	
29, 30	Andrew	1st cent.	apostle and martyr	(biblical)	CT
13 Dec.	Lucy	304?	martyr	Syracuse	CT
27	John	1st cent.	apostle	(biblical)	CDT
28	The Holy Innocents	1st cent.	martyrs	(biblical)	T

C: named in the Roman canon
D: patron saint of one of the earliest Roman churches
T: still named in the Roman calendar today, though not necessarily on the same date

---

57 Although Frere did not list this Felicitas as part of the Roman Canon, it is probably this martyr and not the Felicity usually associated with Perpetua who is actually intended. On this, see V. L. Kennedy, *The Saints of the Canon of the Mass*, 2nd edn, Studi di Antichità Cristiana 14 (Vatican City: Pontificio Istituto di Archeologia Cristiana 1963), pp. 98–100.

Chapter 20

Mary: devotion and feasts

Conspicuously absent from the preceding chapter was reference to feasts of or devotion to the Virgin Mary, with the single exception of noting the 15 August listing of 'Mary *Theotokos*' in the fifth-century Armenian Lectionary. It is important to note, however, that as with the cult of the martyrs, some form of devotion to and veneration of Mary also appears to have existed quite early in Christian history.[1] For this we need to take into account the shaping of early Christian Marian devotional piety by the mid-second- to early-third-century *Protoevangelium of James*, that apocryphal Syrian work which, as Robert Eno notes, is 'unusual in that it showed some interest in and development on Mary for her own sake'.[2] This Gospel, termed doctrinally 'orthodox' by George Tavard,[3]

- gives us the names of Mary's parents, Joachim and Anna;
- defends Mary's *virginitas in partu* and even *post partum* in rather graphic detail;

---

1 See the helpful comments on this by Ignazio M. Calabuig, 'The Liturgical Cult of Mary in the East and West' in Anscar Chupungco (ed.), *Handbook for Liturgical Studies* 5 (Collegeville: The Liturgical Press 2000), p. 228.
2 Robert Eno, 'Mary and Her Role in Patristic Theology' in H. George Anderson *et al.* (eds), *The One Mediator, the Saints, and Mary*, Lutherans and Catholics in Dialogue 8 (Minneapolis: Augsburg 1992), p. 164. ET of the *Protoevangelium of James* in Wilhelm Schneemelcher (ed.), *New Testament Apocrypha* 1 (2nd edn, Cambridge: James Clarke & Co/Louisville: Westminster John Knox Press 1991–2), pp. 370–88.
3 George Tavard, *The Thousand Faces of the Virgin Mary* (Collegeville: The Liturgical Press 1996), p. 19. On the influence of the Apocryphal Gospels on Marian piety and iconography, see Ioannis Karavidopoulos, 'On the Information Concerning the Virgin Mary Contained in the Apocryphal Gospels' in Maria Vassilaki (ed.), *Mother of God; Representations of the Virgin in Byzantine Art* (Milan: Skira editore 2000), pp. 67–89.

- provides us with the narrative contents of what will become two Marian feasts later in the Christian East and West, that is, her Nativity on 8 September, and, when she was three years old, her Presentation in the Temple on 21 November;[4]
- associates her closely with the Jerusalem Temple, and describes her as a 'weaver' of the purple and scarlet for the Temple veil, both images that, according to Nicholas Constas, will have a great influence on the Marian theology of Proclus of Constantinople in the fifth-century controversy with Nestorius[5] (indeed, the Virgin Mary as the 'Ark' or 'Tabernacle' in which the Logos made flesh dwells will be well attested in later Greek patristic literature[6]).

All of this is already in place – at least in this text – by the end of the second or beginning of the third century! That this narrative somehow remained dormant for two or three centuries and then, all of a sudden, is 'discovered' and starts suggesting Marian feasts, imagery and theology seems to us rather unlikely.

Within this context early Christian catacomb art should also be reconsidered. In the Roman catacombs of St Priscilla and the Cimitero Maggiore one sees two famous images of a woman and young child, which tour guides today regularly designate as early (second-century) representations of the Virgin and Christ Child. Art historian André Grabar, however, writes:

> But who can provide any final solution to the puzzling scene in the catacomb of Priscilla, where one person seems to point to a star in the presence of a woman and child? And who can identify with any certainty, in the catacombs of the Cimitero Maggiore, the mother and child who appear with a monogram of Christ on either side and are flanked by two donors? Is this really the Virgin Mary, or is this some Christian woman with her child?[7]

But, of course, whatever early hermeneutical key might have been available to interpret such iconographic depictions of a 'Christian

---

4 See below, pp. 211–12.
5 Nicholas Constas, 'Weaving the Body of God: Proclus of Constantinople, the Theotokos, and the Loom of the Flesh', *JECS* 3 (1995), pp. 169–94.
6 See Gary Anderson, 'Mary in the Old Testament', *Pro Ecclesia* 16 (2007), pp. 33–55.
7 André Grabar, *Christian Iconography: A Study of Its Origins* (Princeton: Princeton University Press 1968), p. 9. Our thanks to John Klentos of the Patriarch Athenagoras Institute, Berkeley, CA, for directing us to this reference.

woman with her child' would have long been replaced by the interpreta-
tive lens or key provided by the Virgin and Child. And, given the overall
context that appears to have been developing with regard to Marian
symbols and theology, it would be surprising if, at least, the possibly
third-century St Priscilla image did not come quickly to be interpreted
as the prophet Balaam or Isaiah pointing to the star of Jacob and the
woman with her child as the Virgin and Christ Child.[8]

Further, even the term *Theotokos* seems now to have been used earlier
and rather more widely than many have assumed previously. Some
modern biblical scholars, in fact, would push the evidence for the idea,
if not the title, back into the New Testament infancy narratives, where,
at least, Elizabeth's designation of Mary as 'Mother of my Lord' (Luke
1.43) may well mean 'Mother of Yahweh'![9] Similarly, Ignatius of
Antioch, in his letter to the Ephesians, says 'our *God*, Jesus the Christ,
was conceived by Mary by the dispensation of God'.[10] And by the
beginning of the third century the word Μήτηρ in reference to Mary
was starting to appear in an abbreviated form (MP) as a *nomen sacrum*
in New Testament papyri.[11] At the end of the third and beginning of the
fourth century the word may have appeared in a lost treatise of Pierius
(d. 309) called Περὶ τῆς θεοτόκου[12] and in a fragment attributed to
Peter I of Alexandria.[13]

If not earlier already, the term *Theotokos* appears to have been used
by the mid third century in Egypt. The Byzantine historian Socrates
provides the following information about Origen of Alexandria:

> Origen . . . in the first volume of his *Commentaries* on the apostle's
> epistle to the Romans, gives an ample exposition of the sense in
> which the term *Theotokos* is used. It is therefore obvious that
> Nestorius had very little acquaintance with the treatises of the
> ancients, and for that reason . . . objected to the word only; for that

---

8 See Sandro Carletti, *Guide to the Catacombs of Priscilla* (Vatican City: Pontifical Com-
mission for Sacred Architecture 1982), pp. 21–3; also Averil Cameron, 'The Early Cult
of the Virgin' in Vassilaki, *Mother of God*, p. 5.
9 See C. Kavin Rowe, 'Luke and the Trinity: An Essay in Ecclesial Biblical Theology',
Scottish Journal of Theology 56 (2003), pp. 1–26.
10 Ignatius, *Ephesians* 18 (emphasis added). See also *Ephesians* 7; 19.
11 A. H. R. E. Paap, *Nomina Sacra in the Greek Papyri of the First Five Centuries* (Leiden:
Brill 1959), p. 15.
12 See J. Quasten, *Patrology* 2 (Westminster: Newman Press 1953), p. 112.
13 Fragment 7 (*PG* 18:517B).

he does not assert Christ to be a mere man, as Photinus did or Paul of
Samosata, his own published homilies fully demonstrate.[14]

Unfortunately, the Greek text of Origen's *Commentary on Romans* is lost
and Rufinus' Latin translation omits any reference to the term in the
section of chapter 1 where it may once have been present. In her recent
critical edition of this commentary, however, Caroline P. Hammond
Bammel does indicate in the notes where the term may have occurred in
the Greek text, as part of Origen's comments on the description by Paul
in 1.3–4 of Christ being both the Son of God and Son of David in the
flesh.[15]

Apart from Socrates' statement, there are other references to
Theotokos in at least two fragments of Origen's writings, which do tend
to be considered authentic. According to a search of Origen's writings
on the *Thesaurus Linguae Graecae*, there are three occurrences of the
term in *Fragmenta in Lucam* (not surprisingly, all in the context of Luke
2) and one appearance in *Selecta in Deuteronomium*. In other words,
there are, including Socrates' text, as many as *five* possible references to
the *Theotokos* in Origen's writings. And, as Marek Starowieyski notes,
while theologians often contest this 'evidence', patristic scholars
generally accept it![16]

It is also in the same third-century context of Origen, and Egyptian
Christianity in general, where scholars have often dated the famous and
earliest short Marian prayer, usually called by its Latin title, *Sub tuum
praesidium*, and translated as:

To your protection we flee, holy Mother of God (*Theotokos*):
do not despise our prayers in [our] needs,
but deliver us from all dangers,
glorious and blessed Virgin.[17]

---

14 Socrates, *Historia ecclesiastica* 7.32; ET from *NPNF*, 2nd Series 2, p. 171.
15 Caroline P. Hammond Bammel, *Der Römerbriefkommentar des Origenes: Kritische
Ausgabe der Übersetzung Rufins, Buch 1–3* (Freiburg: Herder 1990), p. 56.
16 Marek Starowieyski, 'Le titre Θεοτόκος avant le concile d'Ephèse', *SP* 19 (1989), pp.
236–42, here at p. 237: 'Ce témoignage contesté souvent par le théologiens, est générale-
ment accepté par les patrologues.'
17 ET from the Latin by Kilian McDonnell, 'The Marian Liturgical Tradition' in
Maxwell E. Johnson (ed.), *Between Memory and Hope: Readings on the Liturgical Year*
(Collegeville: The Liturgical Press 2000), pp. 385–400, here at p. 387.

Used liturgically in the Coptic, Greek and Ambrosian Rites (for which the evidence is no earlier than the fifth and sixth century), and in the Roman Rite (for which evidence is no earlier than the seventh), the somewhat corrupted Greek version of this text in the manuscript published by C. H. Roberts in 1938 has been viewed as third century or even earlier.[18] But even if the text of the *Sub tuum praesidium* is no older than the early *fourth* century, it remains the earliest Marian prayer in existence – unless the greetings to Mary of the angel and Elizabeth (Luke 1) are already Christian hymn texts themselves – and testifies at least to some kind of Marian devotional piety well before Ephesus. Indeed, it was already in the middle of the fourth century that Emperor Julian the Apostate in his *Against the Galileans* criticized 'the superstition of Christians for invoking the Theotokos'![19]

At the same time, there is nothing in this prayer of supplication to the *Theotokos* that would be inconsistent with Origen's own advocating of prayer to the saints, as we saw in the previous chapter,[20] nor with his quite possible use of the title *Theotokos* in the third century. There is also nothing really inconsistent here between this *Sub tuum praesidium* prayer and the reference to the saints in the Strasbourg Papyrus we also noted in the previous chapter. But whatever one might conclude about Marian devotional piety in the first three centuries, certainly by the middle of the fourth century prayers, hymns and other texts illustrate that such devotion, and not only the title *Theotokos*, was becoming rather widespread.

In the time period of the mid to late fourth century the term *Theotokos* was generally being used in this sense of a widespread title, without necessarily implying a *particular* Christological or doctrinal position. Such, at least, is the conclusion of Marek Starowieyski, who provides an impressive list of fourth-century and early (pre-Ephesine) fifth-century authors where the title appears.[21] Since this list includes Orthodox, Arian, Arianizing, Apollinarist and anti-Apollinarist authors, Starowieyski rightly concludes:

18 Text in C. H. Roberts, *Catalogue of the Greek and Latin papyri in the John Rylands Library 3* (Manchester 1938), nr. 470. See also McDonnell, 'The Marian Liturgical Tradition'; P. Feuillen Mercenier, 'La plus ancienne prière à la Sainte Vierge: le *Sub tuum praesidium*', *Questions liturgiques et paroissiales* 25 (1940), pp. 33–6.
19 As quoted in Jaroslav Pelikan, *Mary through the Centuries; Her Place in the History of Culture* (New Haven: Yale University Press 1996), p. 56.
20 See above, p. 181.
21 Starowieyski, 'Le titre Θεοτόκος avant le concile d'Ephèse'.

[L]e terme est employé, même s'il ne s'accorde pas avec leur christologie respective. Ce titre n'a donc pas de repercussions sur leur théologie ni leur théologie sur le titre . . . Les texts proviennent d'Egypte – certainement le plus grand nombre, de Palestine, du Syrie, de Mésopotamie, d'Arabie, d'Asie Mineure. Leur emploi est donc général dans toute la region de la Mediterranée. En prenant en considération le contexte, on constate que le titre Θεοτόκος n'est employé que comme une simple appellation, à l'exception des textes de la fin du IVe s.[22]

In the first quarter of the fourth century, therefore, that is, about one hundred years *before* the Council of Ephesus itself, the term *Theotokos* had already become – or was becoming – a common title for the Virgin Mary.

Sebastian Brock has drawn attention to the presence of the title 'Mother of God' in East Syrian liturgical texts and to the rich poetic imagery regarding Mary in the authentic hymns of Ephrem.[23] Two examples of this, clearly reflecting the ancient patristic Eve–Mary typology, follow:

The virgin earth of old gave birth to the Adam who is lord of the earth,
But today another virgin has given birth to the Adam who is Lord of
    heaven. (*Homily on the Nativity* I, 16).

Adam brought forth travail upon the woman who sprang from him,
But today she (Mary), who bore him a Saviour, has redeemed that
    travail.
A man (Adam) who himself knew no birth, bore Eve the mother:
How much more should Eve's daughter (Mary) be believed to have
    given birth without the aid of a man (*Homily on the Nativity* I,
    14–15).[24]

---

22 'The term is employed, it seems, with no accord to their respective Christologies. This title has no repercussions on their theology, nor their theologies on the title. The texts come from Egypt (certainly the greater number), from Palestine, Syria, Mesopotamia, Arabia and Asia Minor. Its use is thus general in the Mediterranean region. In taking the context into consideration, it is certain that the title is only employed as a simple appellation, with the exception of texts from the end of the fourth century.' Starowieyski, 'Le titre Θεοτόκος avant le concile d'Ephèse', p. 238.
23 Sebastian Brock, 'Mary in Syriac Tradition' in A. Stacpoole (ed.), *Mary's Place in Christian Dialogue* (Wilton: Morehouse-Barlow 1982), pp. 182–91.
24 Brock, 'Mary in Syriac Tradition', pp. 186–7.

Of special interest as well, Ephrem relates the baptismal womb of the Jordan to the womb of Mary in giving birth to Christ and even views the Incarnation of Christ as Mary's own baptism:

> O Christ, you have given birth to your own mother
> In the second birth that comes from water . . .
> The Son of the Most High came and dwelt in me,
> And I became his mother. As I gave birth to him,
> – His second birth – so too he gave birth to me
> A second time. He put on his mother's robe
> – His body; I put on his glory. (*Homily on the Nativity* XVI, 9, 11)

> Fire and Spirit are in the womb of her who bore you,
> Fire and Spirit are in the river in which you were baptized,
> Fire and Spirit are in our baptism,
> And in the Bread and Cup is Fire and Holy Spirit.
> (*Homily on Faith* X, 17)[25]

It is on the basis of such Marian imagery, clearly reflecting an incarnational-sacramental-liturgical context, that Brock can conclude:

> [I]n actual fact, the Christological differences that separate the Syrian Orthodox, Greek Orthodox (Chalcedonian) Churches and the Church of the East do not appear to have had much effect on their attitudes to Mary . . . Thus those who are familiar with the Byzantine tradition will find much of what Syriac writers say on the subject of Mary not unfamiliar.[26]

If some kind of poetic devotion is present in mid-fourth-century Syria in Ephrem, developing Marian devotion and theology certainly also have a place at the same time in Cappadocia. Gregory of Nazianzus has no qualms about declaring that 'if anyone does not agree that Holy Mary is the Mother of God, he is at odds with the Godhead[27].' It is also Nazianzen who, in a story about Cyprian of Antioch and the virgin Justina, refers to a prayer of intercession offered by Justina to 'the Virgin

---

25 Brock, 'Mary in Syriac Tradition', p. 190.
26 Brock, 'Mary in Syriac Tradition', p. 183.
27 *Letter to Cledonius the Priest, Against Apollinaris*; ET from W. A. Jurgens, *The Faith of the Early Fathers* 2 (Collegeville: The Liturgical Press 1979), pp. 40–1.

Mary, imploring her to help a virgin in danger'.[28] Similarly, Gregory of Nyssa in his treatise on virginity writes that death

> found at last in virginity a barrier beyond which he could not pass. Just as in the time of Mary, the Mother of God, the Death who had reigned from Adam until then found, when he came to her and dashed his forces against the fruit of her virginity as against a rock, that he was himself shattered against her . . .[29]

And, of special interest in a devotional context, it is in his *Vita Gregorii thaumaturgi* where Nyssa refers to an apparition of both Mary ('the mother of the Lord') and the apostle John to Gregory the Wonder-worker, thereby providing the first reference to a Marian apparition in the history of the Church.[30] If, of course, neither of the above references to a prayer of intercession (Nazianzen) or to an apparition of Mary (Nyssa) tells us anything about the third-century context, they do 'tell us . . . about the situation in the time of the writers'.[31] For developing Marian devotional piety, that is what is significant.

That 'there was a popular veneration for the Virgin Mother which threatened to run extravagant lengths'[32] in the fourth century is attested by the *Panarion* of Epiphanius of Salamis (315–403). According to his witness, not only was there in existence an anti-Marian group called the Antidicomarianites, who denied Mary's perpetual virginity,[33] but also an extreme pro-Marian group, known as the Collyridians (from κολλυρίδας, 'cakes'), a group comprising mostly women who worshipped Mary as a 'goddess', offered to her and then consumed small cakes, and had a female priesthood. Epiphanius' critique of the Collyridians, while certainly warning against excessive Marian piety, tends

---

28 Gregory of Nazianzus, *Oratio* 24; ET from Hilda Graef, *Mary: A History of Doctrine and Devotion* 1 (New York: Sheed and Ward 1963), p. 64.

29 ET from Jurgens, *The Faith of the Early Fathers* 2, p. 44.

30 See *PG* 46:912. Such would explain why the *Thesaurus Linguae Graecae* provides some nine references to a homily on the Incarnation by Gregory the Wonderworker. This attribution, however, is not regarded as correct. See M. Jugié, 'Les Homélies Mariales attribuées à Saint Grégoire le Thamaturge', *Analecta Bollandiana* 43 (1925), pp. 86–95. At the same time, Jugié believed the vision itself to be authentic.

31 Eno, 'Mary and Her Role in Patristic Theology', p. 166.

32 Herbert Thurston, 'Devotion to the Blessed Virgin Mary down to the Council of Nicaea', *The Catholic Encyclopedia* 15 (New York: Robert Appleton 1913), pp. 459–60.

33 *Panarion* 79. Augustine himself (*De haeresibus* 56), based on Epiphanius, also refers to this group but *not* to the Collyridians.

to be more about the subordinate role he believed that women should aspire to in the Church in imitation of the passivity of Mary. Nevertheless, if he is a credible witness here, we do not only see some developing Marian popular piety in the time period of the fourth century but we see that it was even prevalent enough to become problematic and heretical. As such, already in the fourth century we have some corroborating evidence for the statement of E. Ann Matter that 'the practice of the pious often takes its own course',[34] a maxim that will be demonstrated over and over again especially in the later history of Marian doctrine and devotion even to our own day.

Perhaps, however, the best example of a popular Marian piety comes in early-fifth-century Constantinople on the very eve of the controversy with Nestorius and the resulting Council of Ephesus. In his studies of the theology of Proclus of Constantinople, Nicholas Constas refers us to the following event, which took place shortly after Nestorius had become Patriarch of Constantinople:

> Nestorius was scandalized by the devotion to the Virgin which he encountered upon his arrival in Constantinople. Nestorius was further outraged to learn that during the reign of his predecessor the empress Pulcheria [whose spiritual advisor, in fact, had become Proclus] had been permitted to receive communion within the sanctuary of the Great Church. According to one source, Nestorius, barring the empress from the chancel screen, insisted that 'Only priests may walk here,' to which she replied, 'Why, have I not given birth to God?' 'You?' he retorted, 'have given birth to Satan,' and proceeded to drive Pulcheria from the sanctuary. Not long after this confrontation, Nestorius publicly challenged the dignity of the Virgin Mary and began to preach against the propriety of calling her the Theotokos – the Birth-giver of God . . . The people of Constantinople, who are said to have been passionately devoted to theological discussion, were greatly offended at this. Besides, the term had been generally accepted by the bishops of the capital from at least the time of Gregory the Theologian. Unlike the term 'homoousious' . . . the title 'Theotokos' was a powerfully evocative word which belonged to the language of liturgy and devotion. As a result, local resistance to

---

34 As quoted in Elizabeth Johnson, *Truly Our Sister: A Theology of Mary in the Communion of Saints* (New York/London: Continuum 2003), p. 119.

Nestorius formed quickly and was actively supported, and to a certain extent orchestrated by Proclus and Pulcheria.[35]

As this event certainly demonstrates, the ultimate dogmatic decision at Ephesus of Mary as *Theotokos* was not simply rooted in the theology of the unitive personhood of Christ but was also, undoubtedly, the product both of the *lex orandi* and popular piety and devotion. As far back as 1940, P. F. Mercenier had argued that

> in defending himself against Nestorius with a relentlessness, one might say, St. Cyril does not battle only with an opinion or a scholarly word, but with an expression and a belief consecrated for a long time by liturgical usage . . . This would be a new application of the adage: *Legem credendi statuat lex supplicandi.*[36]

Indeed, consistent with the Marian theology of Nestorius' predecessor, Atticus of Constantinople (d. 425), who had instructed Pulcheria and her sisters, Arcadia and Marina, that if they imitated the virginity and chastity of Mary, they would give birth to God mystically in their souls,[37] Pulcheria's Marian self-identification ('Have I not given birth to God?') indicates that such personal or popular devotion to the *Theotokos* could even become a kind of Marian mysticism.

The historical context of Proclus and Nestorius is also important for the history of Marian feasts since the first two words of Proclus' famous homily delivered at the Great Church of Constantinople in the presence of Nestorius, probably in the year 430, make reference to 'the Virgin's festival' being celebrated that day.[38] While it is a matter of debate which Marian feast is intended by Proclus' reference (Annunciation, the Sunday before, and the Sunday after Christmas have all been suggested), current scholarship has argued that the feast in question was probably the day after Christmas, 26 December, 'a day on which the Byzantine Church continued to celebrate a "synaxis" in honor of the Theotokos'.[39] In two places in his writings Athanasius refers to the necessity of keeping a

---

35 Constas, 'Weaving the Body of God', pp. 173–5. See also Nicholas Constas, *Proclus of Constantinople and the Cult of the Virgin in Late Antiquity: Homilies 1–5*, Supplements to Vigiliae Christianae 66 (Leiden/Boston: Brill 2003).

36 Mercenier, 'La plus ancienne prière à la Sainte Vierge', p. 36.

37 See Constas, 'Weaving the Body of God', pp. 171–2.

38 Constas, *Proclus of Constantinople and the Cult of the Virgin in Late Antiquity*, p. 136.

39 Constas, *Proclus of Constantinople and the Cult of the Virgin in Late Antiquity*, p. 58.

'memory' or 'commemoration' (μνήμη) of Mary.[40] Because of this, Jaroslav Pelikan, in line with the much earlier work of Martin Jugié[41] and Hilda Graef,[42] who both underscored the pre-Ephesine existence of a Marian 'feast' on the Sunday either before or after Christmas in the East, has suggested 'that evidence and his language seem to make it plausible that such a commemoration of Mary was being kept already during his time and that his argument was based on it'.[43] Such would make this Marian feast already associated with Christmas a mid-fourth-century reality at Alexandria. Of course, it cannot be ruled out that Athanasius may simply be referring to the memory of Mary or, perhaps, even to the type of commemoration of Mary in the eucharistic prayer. That the Virgin Mary ultimately should come to be commemorated liturgically in relationship to the feast of Christmas in both East and West is surely no surprise. But apart from Athanasius' use of μνήμη there is simply no clear evidence of such a feast prior to Proclus' homily, and it is quite possible that this feast had been instituted at Constantinople no earlier than Atticus himself or Sisinnius (426–7).[44] But that a feast associated so closely with Christmas should already be known by Athanasius does not seem likely. Indeed, our first reference to Christmas itself being celebrated in the East is usually dated *c.* 381.

This does not mean, however, that there was not a Marian feast or commemoration in existence prior to the fifth century or that Athanasius himself could not have known of its existence and celebration at Alexandria. Indeed, the oldest Marian feast in existence is usually identified as the 15 August celebration of Mary *Theotokos*, having its origins in Jerusalem and first documented in the fifth-century Armenian Lectionary, one of our major guides to liturgical life in late-fourth-century Jerusalem. The entry reads:

40 *Letter to Epictetus* 4; *Letter to Maximus the Philosopher* 3.
41 Martin Jugié, 'La Première Fête mariale en Orient et en Occident, l'Avent primitif', *Echos d'Orient* 26 (1923), pp. 129–52.
42 Graef, *Mary: A History of Doctrine and Devotion* 1, p. 133.
43 Pelikan, *Mary through the Centuries*, p. 61.
44 See Constas, *Proclus of Constantinople and the Cult of the Virgin in Late Antiquity*, p. 58; also Margot Fassler, 'The First Marian Feast in Constantinople and Jerusalem: Chant Texts, Readings, and Homiletic Literature' in Peter Jeffery (ed.), *The Study of Medieval Chant: Paths and Bridges, East and West: In Honor of Kenneth Levy* (Woodbridge: Boydell Press 2001), pp. 29–42.

Com. MARY THEOTOKOS, at *Second Mile from Bethlehem*,
   15 August
PS + ANT: 132 (a8)
O.T. LESSON: Isa. 7—10
APOSTLE: Gal. 3.29—4.7
ALL/PS: 110.1
GOSPEL: Luke 2.1–7.[45]

Pierre Jounel summarizes the standard theory about this feast succinctly:

> The liturgical cult of Mary originated in Jerusalem, with the feast of
> August 15 as its foundation. Initially celebrated at the Kathisma or
> place where according to tradition Mary paused to rest before going
> on to Bethlehem, the feast was transferred, toward the end of the
> fifth century, to Gethsemane and the basilica where people venerated
> the tomb of the Virgin. The feast of Mary Theotokos thus became
> the feast of the Dormition of the Mother of God. At the end of the
> sixth century, Emperor Maurice ruled that this feast was to be cele
> brated throughout the empire.[46]

With regard to the 15 August date, however, various explanations have
been offered, including seeing 15 August as but the date of the
Kathisma's dedication, or of Jerusalem deliberately distancing itself
from Constantinople's Christmas-related Marian feast since, as we have
seen, it held out longer before succumbing to the new 25 December
date for the celebration of Christ's beginnings. But no one has been able
to offer conclusive arguments beyond speculation as to why 15 August
in particular became the date of this feast.

In his study of the date and contents of the feast, Walter Ray notes
that a core structure present still in the liturgical calendar of the
Armenian Lectionary displays what he calls a parallel 'narrative
framework' to a calendrical structure also found 'in the pre-Christian,
Essene, or proto-Essene *Book of Jubilees*', which centred on the story of
Isaac. According to Ray, in the calendar and narrative world of *Jubilees*

---

45 ET from John Wilkinson, *Egeria's Travels* (3rd edn, Warminster: Aris & Phillips
1999), p. 191.
46 Pierre Jounel, 'The Year' in A. G. Martimort *et al.* (eds), *The Church at Prayer* 4 (Collegeville: The Liturgical Press 1986), p. 131.

the festival of Pentecost on 3/15 (= 15 May), always a Sunday, was *simultaneously* the celebration of the birth of Isaac, who was conceived by Sarah nine months earlier on 6/15 (= 15 August!). And, significantly, it is the Isaac–Jesus typology emerging from this tradition that occupies the principal theological attention of St Paul, especially in his Galatian correspondence (see Gal. 4.21–31). Ray writes:

> The Feast of Weeks, understood as the 15th of the third month, had particular meaning for the Jubilees calendar as the completion of the fifty days, the time of the ultimate fulfillment of covenant renewal which was both promised and foreshadowed in the birth of Isaac. In its Christian form the final day of the feast would have been remembered as the time of divine adoption of the community and the giving of the Spirit (Acts 2, Gal. 4.5–6), but also the time of particular revelation of the divine sonship of Jesus in the power of the Spirit, first in light of the resurrection/ascension (cf. Rom. 1.3, Acts 2.33) but also in light of his special birth (Luke 1.35) . . . We should perhaps add Christ's baptism to the list, where we again find the themes of divine sonship and the coming of the Spirit . . . [I]n Luke-Acts both the birth and baptism of Jesus manifest the same narrative pattern as Pentecost.[47]

Interestingly enough, then, Jesus' own *beginnings*, according to Ray, whether at his conception, his birth in Bethlehem, or at what might be called his 'spiritual birth' in the Jordan, have clear Pentecost connotations, quite possibly stemming from an early Jerusalem Christian adaptation of this ancient Qumran–*Jubilees* calendrical and narrative tradition. And, together with all of this, a compelling reason has been given for how the date of 15 August fits in with such emphases.

In developing this approach, Ray also takes into account the fact that one of the apparent anomalies of the Armenian Lectionary's calendar of feasts is the presence of the Feast of the Infants or 'Holy Innocents' on 18 May in some manuscripts. Based on this feast in May, Botte had suggested many years earlier that the Jerusalem liturgy may have once had some sort of commemoration of Christ's nativity in May as well.[48] Ray summarizes:

---

47 Walter Ray, 'August 15 and the Development of the Jerusalem Calendar' (PhD dissertation, University of Notre Dame 2000), p. 262.

48 Bernard Botte, *Les Origines de la Noël et de l'Épiphanie*, Textes et Études liturgiques 1 (Louvain: Abbaye de Mont César 1932), pp. 9ff.

The feast of the Infants in May is the remnant of the beginning of a course reading of the epistle to the Hebrews and the gospel of Matthew and of a feast of Christ's nativity coinciding with Pentecost, dated according to the fixed-date *Jubilees* calendar to May 15. This commemoration of Christ's nativity, along with the feast of Mary on August 15, understood as a commemoration of Christ's conception, and the commemoration of Christ's crucifixion at Passover, evidences a Christ cycle that mirrors an Isaac cycle in the calendar of *Jubilees*. There we read that 'in the middle of the sixth month the Lord visited Sarah and did for her as he had said. And she conceived and bore a son in the third month, in the middle of the month . . . on the feast of the firstfruits of the harvest' [*Jubilees* 16:12–13]. *Jubilees* is unique in pre-Christian literature in dating the sacrifice of Isaac to the time of Passover.[49]

Ray has made here a solid contribution not only to the study of the early liturgical year at Jerusalem but also to that of developing early Christian Mariology. In addition to establishing a compelling reason as to why 15 August should emerge as a date for a commemoration or celebration centred on the Incarnation of Christ in Mary, Ray, in so doing, has also pushed the possibility of a type of Marian commemoration or focus to a very early period as well. In fact, as he himself notes, even the earlier station for the feast, two or three miles from Bethlehem, is already part of the narrative of Christ's birth in the *Protoevangelium of James*.[50] Such, of course, would be consistent with what we have already seen, and it may be that if Athanasius has any feast in mind by his use of the word μνήμη, it is this one. Although Egeria never refers to the existence of this feast in her diary, it must be noted that she generally makes no references to feasts in the sanctoral cycle at all.

At the same time, if Ray is correct in his analysis of the origins and development of this feast, it is the case then that the earliest so-called Marian feast, which will ultimately become her Dormition and/or Assumption, began as an early Jerusalem commemoration of the Incarnation or annunciation, nine months before a primitive celebration of Christ's nativity. In other words, the origins of even *this* Marian feast, as

---

49 Walter Ray, 'Toward a Narrative-Critical Approach to the Study of Early Liturgy' in M. E. Johnson and L. E. Phillips (eds), *Studia Liturgica Diversa: Essays in Honor of Paul F. Bradshaw* (Portland: The Pastoral Press 2004), pp. 3–30, here at p. 9.
50 See Ray, 'August 15 and the Development of the Jerusalem Calendar', pp. 56ff.

with the 26 December feast in Constantinople or the much later 1 January feast of the *Theotokos* in Rome, appear to be closely tied both Christologically and calendrically with some type of nativity cycle.

The feast of Mary *Theotokos* on 15 August, of course, is not the only Marian feast in early Christianity. As noted above, there was in Constantinople by the early fifth century some kind of Marian feast on 26 December, a day which the Syrian churches also continue to celebrate as a feast of congratulations to the Mother of God. We noted above that both Jugié and Graef referred also to the existence of a Marian 'feast' on the Sunday before Christmas in the East.[51] And, as we saw in our chapter on Advent, such is noted in the West as well, with the Sunday before Christmas becoming associated with the annunciation or Incarnation, including the reading of the Annunciation Gospel (Luke 1.26–38) either on that Sunday or a week before Christmas, in various Western liturgical traditions (e.g., Ravenna, Milan and Spain).[52] The precise origins of the 25 March feast of the Annunciation of Our Lord, however, remain a mystery. Although 25 March is important in the Computation hypothesis for determining the 25 December date of Christmas, there is no evidence for this date being a commemoration specifically of the annunciation until the middle of the sixth century in the Christian East and only later in the West.[53] Constantinople itself has been credited with the origins of the feast in 550, according to a letter of the Emperor Justinian, as well as hymns for the feast composed by Romanus the Melodist in the same year.[54] At the same time, the Armenian Church, which, as we have seen, never accepted the 25 Dec-

---

51 See above, p. 206. Stéphane Verhelst has argued, alternatively, that 15 August was originally a celebration of the nativity, held at the third milestone between Jerusalem and Bethlehem, where Mary had not only rested but given birth to Jesus, according to the *Protoevangelium of James* and other later Jewish-Christian writings. A church eventually built on this spot, he argues, enshrined the place associated with the birth of Christ among Jewish Christians at Jerusalem. He sees the 15 August celebration as part of a Jewish-Christian response to the commemoration of the destruction of the Temple on the 9 of Av. See Stéphane Verhelst, 'Le 15 Août, Le 9 Av e le Kathisme', *QL* 82 (2001), pp. 161–91. We do not find Verhelst's conclusions compelling, especially because, as with his theory on Lent (see above p. 96, n. 15), he is too dependent upon an alleged liturgical commemoration of the destruction of the Temple among the Jerusalem church, which, in turn, served to shape the Jerusalem calendar in general. This may have been the case, but there is no hard evidence that it was so.

52 See above, pp. 159, 164.

53 See Adolph Adam, *The Liturgical Year: Its History and Meaning after the Reform of the Liturgy* (New York: Pueblo 1981), p. 152.

54 See Calabuig, 'The Liturgical Cult of Mary in the East and West', p. 256.

ember date for the nativity, celebrates the annunciation on 6 April, and so it becomes difficult to know if this is not, in fact, the earlier tradition in the East.

Other Marian feasts in early Christianity, or feasts that, like the Annunciation, have Marian connotations, are the Presentation of the Lord in the Temple on 2 February and the Nativity of the Virgin Mary on 8 September. The Feast of the Presentation, called the *Hypapante* (Meeting) of Christ with Simeon and Anna, and later in the West Candlemas and the Purification of the Blessed Virgin Mary, is known already in late-fourth-century Jerusalem, as documented by Egeria:

> Note that the Fortieth Day after Epiphany is observed here with special magnificence. On this day they assemble in the Anastasis. Everyone gathers, and things are done with the same solemnity as the feast of Easter. All the presbyters preach first, then the bishop, and they interpret the passage from the Gospel about Joseph and Mary taking the Lord to the Temple, and about Simeon and the prophetess Anna, daughter of Phanuel, seeing the Lord, and what they said to him, and about the sacrifice offered by his parents. When all the rest has been done in the usual way, they celebrate the sacrament and have their dismissal.[55]

Forty days after Epiphany (6 January) places this feast on 13 February in Egeria's time, which would have been transferred to 2 February when both the 25 December date for Christmas and this feast itself were accepted and received by other churches.[56] But, again, consistent with the early Jerusalem festal structure, the Armenian Church continues to celebrate this feast on 13 February.

The 8 September feast of the Nativity of Mary appears to owe its origins in Jerusalem to the dedication of a church to Holy Mary next to the pool of Bethesda and near to the house of Anne, in which Mary was presumably born. This church may have been dedicated on 8 September 543, and the annual anniversary of this dedication may be the

55 Egeria, *Itinerarium* 26; ET from Wilkinson, *Egeria's Travels*, pp. 147–8.
56 For studies of the origins and theology of the Feast of the Presentation, see K. W. Stevenson, 'The Origins and Development of Candlemas: A Struggle for Identity and Coherence?', *Ephemerides Liturgicae* 102 (1988), pp. 316–46; Martin F. Connell, *Eternity Today: On the Liturgical Year* 1 (New York/London: Continuum 2006), pp. 211–39; Nicholas Russo, 'The Origins of Lent' (PhD dissertation, University of Notre Dame 2009), pp. 109–25.

origins of the feast, the thematic contents of which were supplied by the *Protoevangelium of James*.[57] While this explanation is probable, the mere fact that the church was built on this site may suggest, alternatively, that there was already a commemoration of Mary's birth on 8 September in Jerusalem at this site that gave rise both to the feast and to the dedication of the church on this date, rather than the other way around.

These four Marian feasts, all having their origins in the Christian East, will be accepted at Rome by the seventh century, during which time Pope Sergius I (687–701), ordered public processions to be held in conjunction with them from the Church of St Hadrian in the Roman Forum to the Basilica of St Mary Major, the basilica itself having been dedicated to Mary shortly after the Council of Ephesus (431) by Pope Sixtus III (432–40) and associated, owing to its possession of Christ's crib, as the Roman Church of the Nativity. Together with these four feasts, however, Rome also had its own indigenous feast of Mary under the title of the *Theotokos* on 1 January, the octave of Christmas, but there is no evidence for this feast before the seventh century. While other local Marian feasts would develop throughout the Christian world (e.g., a mid-January feast of Mary in sixth-century Gaul, the Dormition of Mary celebrated on 16 January in Egypt, and the feast of Mary's Presentation in the Temple on 21 November, in relationship to yet another church in Jerusalem, the Nea or New Church, dedicated on 21 November 543), these five Marian feasts will remain the only Mary-related feasts in the general Roman calendar until the fourteenth century.[58]

Devotion to and liturgical celebration of Mary *Theotokos* did not spring up out of thin air or somehow fall out of heaven in a tin box in the context or aftermath of the Council of Ephesus. Nor did it begin to spread only after that council. Rather, such devotion is rooted in developing piety and devotion from at least the third century. As we have seen in this chapter:

- the title *Theotokos*, while, of course, Christological in a broad sense, appears as a more general honorific title for Mary among diverse fourth-century authors with diverse Christological positions! In

---

57 See Calabuig, 'The Liturgical Cult of Mary in the East and West', p. 254.

58 For the above, see Jounel, 'The Year', pp. 134–6. For further development of Marian feasts in both East and West, see also McDonnell, 'The Marian Liturgical Tradition'; Calabuig, 'The Liturgical Cult of Mary in the East and West', esp. pp. 257–97; Neil J. Roy, 'Mary and the Liturgical Year' in Mark Miravalle (ed.), *Mariology* (Goleta, CA: Queenship Publishing, Seat of Wisdom Books 2007), esp. pp. 642–65.

other words, *Theotokos* as a title for Mary does not appear to be tied originally to a particular Christological position as a banner of orthodoxy as it will come to be at and after the Council of Ephesus – prior to that it is simply one honorific way in which to refer to Mary;

- the use of the title itself, as well as our earliest Marian prayer, the *Sub tuum praesidium*, may well be mid-third-century Alexandrian in origin, and Origen himself, as testified to by Socrates, may well have been the first to have used this title in theological discourse;
- such use of the title and devotion to the *Theotokos*, including liturgical use noted immediately above, appears to be consistent with the growing development of prayer and supplication to the saints, as attested in general by the cult of the martyrs and by Origen in particular;
- already by the beginning of the third century the *Protoevangelium of James* reflects an interest in Mary herself and provides several Marian elements which will develop further and become, ultimately, the content of theological reflection, liturgical feasts (e.g., her Nativity and Presentation in the Temple), and popular devotion to her in the life of the Church;
- the earliest Marian feast on 15 August in Jerusalem, quite possibly a commemoration of Jesus' conception nine months before an earlier 15 May Jerusalem commemoration of his birth, rooted in the sectarian Jewish *Jubilees* tradition, would seem to place the origins of this feast back to within the earliest days of Christianity itself; and
- even the doctrinal controversy with Nestorius of Constantinople is not merely about doctrine, but rather, in the context of the late fourth and early fifth centuries, where Marian devotion is witnessed to not only in Egypt but in Cappadocia (Gregory of Nyssa and Gregory of Nazianzus) and Syria (Ephrem) as well, the controversy is also devotional, as certainly indicated by what might be called the 'Marian mysticism' of Atticus, Pulcheria and Proclus.

Such elements suggest strongly that, as with the developing cult of the martyrs in antiquity, we need to view what happened historically in the increase of both liturgical and popular Marian piety and devotion, especially in the East, where the Christological focus of *Theotokos* has always remained stronger than in the West, as an *evolution* in piety and devotion and not as a *revolution*. Such an evolution, we would suggest, is consistent with what came before and was not something radically new or brought about simply by an elevated Christology. Again, as with devotion to the martyrs and saints, the building blocks of a later popular and liturgical Marian piety appear quite early.

Index of modern authors

Index of ancient authors and subjects